Paris Inside Out

An Insider's Guide for Residents, Students, &
Discriminating Visitors

on Living in the French Capital!

David Applefield

◆

The American University of Paris

 Frank
BOOKS

B.P. 29
94301 VINCENNES Cedex
France

45 Newbury Street
Suite 305
Boston, MA 02116
USA

Design:
Deborah Applefield, A-L Books.
Layout/Production:
Cory McCloud
Editorial Assistance :
Ross Pruden, Sarah Walsworth, Julia Alvarez-Grosser, Tanya Leslie,
Suzanne Quittner, Betty Abu'Gheida, John Strand
Front and back cover image:
Timbres Série Liberté, "Panarama de Paris, 1989," PH.
© Musée de la Poste, Paris

*Achevé d'imprimer en avril 1992
sur les presses de l'imprimerie Fricotel
Epinal-Paris
Dépôt Légal No 2504 avril 1992*
Special thanks to Claude Briot
Flashage: Compo Rive Gauche (Tel: 43.25.33.43)

Paris Inside Out is published by Frank Books, S.A.R.L.

CONTENTS

WELCOME to Paris—and the new, updated and expanded edition of *Paris Inside Out!*

There is no better way of becoming aware of the amount of changes that a city goes through in two years than by updating a guide book. In this process what have we changed? Structurally, we've streamlined the internal organization of this new edition; we've strengthened the book's graphic presentation. As for the contents, the sections concerning the visual arts, galleries, museums, cinema, wine, and education, have been greatly expanded with commentary from experts in these fields. The only other significant changes are the multitude of facts: new addresses, telephone and fax numbers, names, times, and prices that have been added and up-dated. The rest is the same. The key to *Paris Inside Out,* we feel, continues to be the guide's intimate tone and its up-to-the minute cultural reporting.

Gloriously, your life will never be the same! Living outside your country, culture and language—not just traveling or visiting, but living—will set into motion a whole new way of seeing the world. And there are few places on the globe better suited for this than Paris. It's for good reason that Paris cannot shake the myths that engulf it, that the romanticize image of Paris as Celestial city of beauty, grace, and bohemian self-discovery lives on in the imaginations of those who choose to spend time here. Even in the rapidly changing Nineties, the most exhausted clichés miraculously still apply.

But *Paris Inside Out* is about the reality of Parisian life today.

Admittedly, there are scores of guides on Paris, perhaps too many. Millions of tourists visit Paris each year, all groping for information, help, leads, and tips. What sets *Paris Inside Out* apart is its attention to the needs of residents, students, and long-term visitors. It is not a tourist guide! It digs beneath the surface, offers larger cultural observations, and anticipates the problems and confusions and questions of its readers. Successfully living away from home requires you to sort out the fiction from the reality. The information assembled here, both objective and subjective, is based on experience, and experience is the key to knowing a place—*inside out!*

Everything in this book you eventually would have learned anyway. But *Paris Inside Out* should help you save many hours and lots of francs. It will facilitate your integration into French life, and hopefully reduce the frustration of finding yourself alone, dependent, tongue-tied, and handicapped by a totally new setting that you're going to think of at first as "foreign." Remember, everything around you is native; it's you that's foreign—whether you come from New York City; Winnipeg; Cairo; Dubai; Bombay; Madrid; or Helsinki. Paris is capable of confusing and exhilarating you. Living outside a familiar cultural and social setting always takes adjustment and acclimation. There will be strange little moments when you crave blueberry pancakes or the Sunday edition of your city's newspaper, and then others, when you simply desire the sound of your own language, when you don't want to have to struggle to be understood. This is all normal. *Paris Inside Out* should be a first step in helping you hurdle early traumas while becoming more Parisian yourself.

Most guidebooks don't approach the feelings inherent in living in a new city; *Paris Inside Out* attempts to provide insight into the interior, as well as material, experience of living and/or studying overseas. Although these pages should be helpful over and over, one can't expect to understand Parisian life and culture intimately by reading a guide book. Learning how a new country and culture functions is a gradual and evolutionary process. It takes time and patience, and a willingness to experience both the exciting and lonely sensation of being isolated and anonymous in a far-off place. There will be a new-found freedom and sense of awareness that accompanies the uncertainty of being away from what you know.

Despite the overwhelming popularity of Paris, and its hoards of summer tourists, you shouldn't feel less unique. Most of those individuals arrive and depart—taste the food and wine, glaze past the sites, wait in lines, hear the sounds of a tongue they cannot join in with, formulate a handful of sketchy observations and comparisons (some totally erroneous) about the land, people, and culture, and hurry back home with a mixed bag of stories, a variety of souvenirs, and a few rolls of color slide film or recorded video cassettes—all the richer for the experience.

The experience of the tourist has nothing to do with you. You are not a tourist! You live here— or are about to. You have a greater emotional investment in the life of the city. You want to learn; you want to know what it's like living in France. Paris is your city, and the more you come to believe this the deeper the relationship you will forge with "the City of Lights," as Paris is romantically called in many of those guide books.

Paris Inside Out has been designed to benefit all English-speaking residents in Paris. It has been conceived to provide practical information, answer a wide variety of key questions pertinent to student and residential life, and present in an easy and comfortable format essential facts and details necessary for you to meet daily academic, social, and administrative requirements. The guide does tend to be rather American in its orientation and cultural and linguistic references; this was unavoidable in that the book, while aspiring to address all English-speaking students and residents, had to be created with its largest readership in mind. Every attempt has been made, however, to resist ethnocentricity and provincialism.

With that said, be reminded that although facts and information are useful and necessary, alone they cannot guarantee you an understanding of French manners, ways of being, attitudes, traditions, tendencies, institutions, and what is commonly called in French, "*la mentalité.*" In giving you the facts, verified and updated for this edition, we've tried to comment on as often as possible the small but significant details that make France culturally distinct. You'll see. Living in another country is a process of losing your innocence all over again. This glorious path, with its share of awkward moments, should create a profusion of pleasurable and thought-provoking experiences. —D.A.

L IVING in a place requires at least a basic knowledge of a few key facts. Here are a few facts, statistics and background info that will help you situate yourself in France.

Capital: Paris

Official Language: French

Regional Languages: Basque, Breton, Catalan, Corsican *(corse)*, Provençal

Surface Area: 551,965 square km

Gross National Product: $8850 U.S. per inhabitant.

Population

France: 58,452,500
Paris: 2,188,918
Marseille: 878,689
Lyon: 418,476
Toulouse: 354,289
Nice: 338,486

Strasbourg: 252,338
Bordeaux: 211,197
Nantes: 247,227
Lille: 174,039
Grenoble: 159,503
Dijon: 145,569

CONVERSIONS

Weights
1 kilo = 2.2 pounds
Demi-kilo = 1 livre = 1.1 pounds

Lengths
1 centimeter = .394 inches
1 meter = 3.28 feet
1000 meter = 1 kilometer = 0.62 mile
(to calculate miles multiply kilometers by .6)

Measurements
1 litre = 0.265 U.S.gallon
1 gram = .033 ounce

Temperatures
Converting Fahrenheit to Celsius:
Multiply Celsius temperature by two
and add 32 for approximate conversion.

Conversions for Cooking

1 ounce = 30 grammes
3.5 ounces = 100 grammes
1 lb = 454 grammes
1 tbsp = 15 grammes
1 cup = nearly 1/4 litre
4 1/3 cups = 1 litre
3/4 cup minus 1 tbsp = 100 grammes
1 pint = 0,473 litre
1 quart = 0,946 litre
1 gallon = 3,785 litres

Fahrenheit		Celsius
0		-17.8
32	(freezing)	0
50		10
68	(room temperature)	20
77		25
86		30
98.6	(normal body temp.)	37
100.4		38
104		40

Clothing Sizes

Women's dresses

France	36	38	40	42	44	46	48
U.S.	6	8	10	12	14	16	18

Men's pants

France	42	44	46	48	50
U.S.	32	34	36	38	40

Shoes

France	37	38	39	40	41	42	43
U.S.	6	7	7.5	8	9	10	10.5

Men's shirts

France	37	38	39	40	41	42	43
U.S.	14.5	15	15.5	15.75	16	15.5	17

Dates: In France, 1/3/92 is *not* January 3, 1992, but March 1, 1992.

Time of Day: Is generally expressed by the 24-hour clock. Thus, 8 a.m.= 8h, or 8h00, and 8 p.m. = 20h or 20h00. Midnight = 24h, 24h00, or *minuit,* Noon =12h, 12h00, or *midi.* 12:30 a.m.= 0h30; 5 p.m. = 17h or 17h00.

Numbers: Commas are used where Anglo-Saxons use periods, and vice versa. For instance, 1.025,60 in France =.1,025.60 in North America and elsewhere.

Currency: The French franc (FF) is divided into 100 *centimes.* Coins consist of five, ten, twenty, fifty centimes, and one franc, five franc, and ten franc pieces. In 1991, the old clunky ten franc piece was taken out of circulation and only the new two-tone, smaller piece is used today. Bank notes come in twenty, fifty, one hundred, two hundred and five hundred franc denominations.

Districts: Called *arrondissements,* the twenty districts that make up Paris can be found at the end of a postal code. For example, 75005=Paris' 5th district, 75020=Paris' 20th district. See map for a breakdown of Paris by *arrondissement.*

Electric Current: France's system is 220 volt, 50 cycles. To use standard American 110 volt, 60 cycle, British 250 volt, 60 cycle, or other appliances you will need a plug adapter and a transformer that is appropriate for the wattage of the appliance. Some 220 volt appliances have a combination 50/60 cycle motor that allows them to operate in France without any problems. Lamps from the U.S. will work without a transformer with 220 volt bulbs. Clock radios work but the clock part is not always reliable. Plug adaptors and transformers can be found in the basement of the BHV (*Bazaar de l'Hotel de Ville*) on the rue de Rivoli, which has a special section for adapting foreign telephones, answering machines, fax/computer equipment and other appliances.

Floor Numbers: The floor in which you enter a building is not the first floor, but the *rez-de-chausée* (RC). In France the street level is not officially an *étage* (floor). Thus, the *première étage* (first floor) is actually the the second level of the building, one floor up from the *rez-de-chausée.*

Religions

Catholic: (90%); 1 out of 5 French claims to be "practicing"
Muslim: 1.7 million
Protestant: 1 million
Jewish: .7 million

ETHNIC MIX (Population in 1982 Census)

Algerian 8,050,000
Portuguese 7,570,000
Moroccan 4,410,000
Italian 3,400,000
Spanish 3,270,000
Tunisian 1,900,000
Turkish 1,220,000
Polish 640,000
Yugoslavian 620,000
Belgians 530,000
Germans 440,000
Cambodian 380,000
British 340,000
Vietnamese 340,000
Senegalese 320,000
Malian 240,000
Americans (USA) 190,000
Cameroonian 150,000

HOLIDAYS

Holidays in France bring out two typically French traits: the respect for ceremony and ritual and the joy of not having to work. The French long weekend *(faire le pont)*—actually an extended weekend created when a holiday falls on a Thursday or Tuesday—is an occasion for most Parisians to exit to the country. The month of May is particularly affected. Beware of heavy traffic on the autoroutes, the *périphérique*, and at the main *portes* (gateways to the city). This is good news for those who stay because the pace of Paris slows down remarkably, leaving the tourist and others to enjoy the absence of traffic and noise. Being aware of holidays helps you stay in touch with the rhythms of French life (see Annual Events). Plan your activities around these dates since many shops, restaurants and museums close on public holidays.

The French are rather conscious of the Christian calendar as far as each day is assigned to a different saint. Best known is *La Sainte-Catherine* on November 25, the day that all 25 year old, single women are presented with funny hats and dances are held in their honor. New Year's Eve is called St. Sylvestre.

The French also celebrate April Fools Day with jokes and pranks, namely hanging paper fish on the backs of friends and strangers.

Vacation Time

French law guarantees everyone who works *(salarié)* five weeks of paid vacation. *Les vacances (congés payés)*, a cherished institution among the French, is a right, not a privilege. What you plan to do on vacation, or what you've just finished doing, is usually the subject of casual conversation for about four months of the year. In general, it's safe to say that the French are willing to trade higher wages for security and benefits, in other words, a higher quality of daily life.

Aside from the five week vacation, which most people divide between summer and winter (three to four weeks in summer, one to two in winter), here is a list of holidays and their respective customs. Note that traditionally Paris empties out in August, with July being the second heaviest vacation month. Avoid traveling on July 1, July 30, August 1 and August 30. Or else be prepared to leave in the pre-dawn hours. The 15th of each summer month are difficult traveling days as well. School vacations *(vacances scolaires)* are nationally coordinated with all schools within each of the three zones of France sharing the same dates. Similarly, train and domestic flight schedules are divided into blue, red, and white days on the calendar with blue days being the cheapest to travel. Check these with a travel agent.

January 1   *Jour de l'An* (New Year's Day)*
This day is generally devoted to visiting parents and older relatives and exchanging gifts (instead of on Christmas Day). Concierges expect to be tipped at this time. Postmen, firemen, street cleaners, etc. solicit their New Year's gifts as early as November, offering dingy and tacky calendars in exchange for year-end tokens of appreciation (cash).

Late March/April   *Pâques* (Easter)
First Sunday following the full moon of the equinox of spring, at the end of March or early April.

Monday after Easter   *Lundi de Pâques* (Easter Monday)*

May 1   *Fête du Travail* (Labor Day)*
May 1st was designated a International Labor Day in 1889 and is observed in France as a legal holiday (celebrated everywhere in the world except the US). Labor groups generally parade in different sections of Paris. A custom in France on this day is to present *muguets* (lilies of the valley) to friends and loved ones to bring them happiness and *porte bonheur* (good luck). Everyone is entitled to pick wild *muguet*, found in the forests surrounding Paris. May 1st is the only day of the year that anyone can sell *muguet* or other flowers without a license. If you find yourself at the Elysées Palace, you might see *Les Forts des Halles* (porters of the Paris market), dressed in the traditional porters outfits, presenting *muguet* to the President of France.

May 8   *Victoire* 1945 (V.E. Day)*
Défilés (parades) take place throughout the city, the largest and most impressive on the Champs-Elysées.

Sixth Thursday after Easter   *Ascension* (Ascension Day)*

Last Sunday in May   *Fête des Mères* (Mother's Day)

Second Monday after Ascension   *Pentecôte* (Pentecost)*

2 or 3 weeks after Mother's Day   *Fête des Pères* (Father's Day)

July 14   *Fête nationale/14 juillet* (Bastille Day)*
Celebrations begin on the 13th and include fireworks and street dances. Admission is free to performances in all National Theaters on this day.

August 15   *Fête de l'Assomption* (Feast of the Assumption)*
Christian holiday commemorating the assumption of the Virgin Mary. Celebrations such as harvest festivals and the blessing of the sea happen on this day.*

November 1 *Toussaint* (All Saints' Day)*
Halloween, the North American celebration related to this Christian holiday, is not acknowledged in France.

November 2 *Jour des Morts* (All Souls Day)*
It is the custom in France to visit the graves of relatives on the day before the *Jour des Morts* or on the day itself. Flowers (usually chrysanthemums) are placed on the graves. Chrysanthemums were the seasonal flowers before greenhouses existed, and are the traditional flowers used on this day. Thus don't even consider offering chrysanthemums when invited for dinner, etc.

November 11 *Fête de l'Armistice* (Veteran's Day)*

December 25 *Noël* (Christmas)*
It is the time to eat the holiday foods at the traditional Christmas dinner *(le réveillon)*: *boudin blanc* (white sausage), *fois gras*, pheasants, *saumon fumé*, *huîtres*, and *bûches de Noël* (yule log-shaped cake).

*National public holidays are denoted with * (Most schools and businesses are closed).*

ANNUAL EVENTS

A new offering from the *Office du Tourisme et des Congrès de Paris* is a comprehensive card called *Carte Paris Sélection*. The cost is 260 FF for an annual membership. Card holders receive monthly mailings of every publication published by the *Office du Tourisme et des Congrès*, including a calendar of the month's *manifestations* (cultural events), *spectacles*, conventions, information on hotels and restaurants, maps and a calendar of major annual events. Discounts are also offered at many museums, monuments and conferences (guided tours of historic sites, art exhibitions and public seminars).

**Office du Tourisme
et des Congrès de Paris**
127, ave des Champs-Elysées
75008 PARIS
Tel: 47.23.03.02

Annual Events

January

Fashion shows (summer collection).

February

Bread and Pastry Exposition.

March

Palm Sunday, *Prix du Président de la République*, at Auteuil race track, Bois de Boulogne.

April

April-May: Paris Fair (commercial exhibition) at Parc des Expositions.

Early April-early October: *Son et Lumière* at les Invalides.

May

May-September: Illuminated Fountains at Versailles.

Mid-May: Paris Marathon (foot race around Paris).

Mid-May-late June: Versailles Music and Drama Festival.

Late May-early June: French Open Tennis Championships, Roland Garros Courts.

June

Early June: Paris Air Show (odd years only), Le Bourget Airport.

Early June-mid-July: Marais Festival (music, drama, exhibitions).

June: a festival of music, drama, and dance at Saint-Denis.

Mid-June: *Grand Steeplechase de Paris* at Auteuil race course, Bois de Boulogne.

Mid-June: *Fête du Pont-Neuf* (booths and street performers on the bridge and in the Place Dauphine).

June 21: *Fête de la Musique*—music groups and free open air concerts throughout the city.

June 24: *Feux de la Saint-Jean* (fireworks) at Sacré Cœur.

End of June: *Grand Prix de Paris*, Longchamp race track, Bois de Boulogne.

July

Early July: Festival de Saint Denis, Tel: 42.43.77.72. Classical music festival with concerts throughout Paris.

July 14: *Fête nationale* (celebrations throughout the city and military display in the Champs-Elysées).

Mid-July: finish of the *Tour de France* cycle race on the Champs-Elysées.

Throughout July:

Fashion shows (winter collection).

Festival International d'Opéra, Tel: 42.68.23.32. Numerous events held for two weeks at Versailles.

Mid-July-mid-September: Festival Estival de Paris, Tel: 48.04.98.01. Classical music, concerts, and recitals throughout the city.

September

Festival de Montmartre

Late September-early December: *Festival d'Automne*, Tel: 42.96.12.27. Music, drama, ballet, exhibitions.

October

First Sunday: *Prix de l'Arc de Triomphe* at Longchamp race track, Bois de Boulogne.

Early October: Montmartre wine festival, Paris Motor Show at the Parc des Expositions (even years only).

Beaujolais Festival: when *"le beaujolais nouveau est arrivé,"* the party starts at midnight as the first bottle of the new harvest is allowed to be opened. People generally stop whatever they are doing and go for a glass at the nearest café or bar.

Late October-early November: *Festival de Jazz de Paris*, Tel: 47.83.84.06. Two-week festival which includes lots of big name jazz artists.

October-November: *Festival d'Art Sacré*, Tel: 42.77.92.26. Concerts and exhibitions held in churches throughout the city.

November

November 11: Armistice Day ceremony at Arc de Triomphe.

December

Christmas Eve: midnight mass at Notre-Dame.

For further details call the *Office du Tourisme de Paris*, Tel: 47.23.61.72

CLIMATE

The word for weather as in "what's it doing out," is *le temps*, not to be confused with "time." Otherwise, the weather report is the *Météo*.

Although the weather in Paris is seldom extremely hot or extremely cold, it is variable since the city lies at the junction of marine and continental climates which have opposite

characteristics. Autumn in Paris is absolutely lovely, mild and somewhat sunny with a tinge of melancholy in the air. The foliage is nice but not always noticeable in the center of the city. Sweaters and light coats are needed. In the spring and autumn, temperatures average about 11° C. (52° Fahrenheit) with warm days and cool nights.

During the winter, the average temperature is about 3° Celsius (37° Farenheit) and there are rarely more than 20 very cold days a year. The winters are wet, and warm rain gear and an umbrella are indispensable. The winters have tended to be milder and milder over the last few years. There is rarely any snow, other than a few flakes in February and perhaps a strange and short barrage of hail once or twice a year. Nonetheless, winter coats or down jackets can be necessary in that the cold is damp and penetrating and often annoying. Ski jackets aren't usually worn in town, but students can get away with anything.

Spring comes late or winter seems to linger and fuses with summer. The blooming of the nubby, cut-back magnolia and horse chestnut trees along some of the boulevards is a pleasant sight and the leaves give off a sweet but strange fragrance that only seems to be found in Paris. April in Paris is often cold and rainy and the chestnuts do not blossom until the last week of the month. It is often a subject of conversation as it is so fugacious. It's a good idea to have an umbrella handy during the months of December through June.

Summers in Paris can be rather hot and uncomfortable.

AVERAGE TEMPERATURES RANGE					
CITY	ALT.	JAN.	JULY	RAIN	# DAYS RAIN
	(m)	(Temp. in C°)		(mm)	
Lille	44	3.1	15.9	596	185
Lyon	200	4.2	19.7	973	186
Strasbourg	150	0.6	17.9	585	184
Brest	98	7.1	15.1	1,030	204
Paris	75	4.9	18.6	631	193
Bordeaux	47	6.6	19.6	801	184
Marseille	4	8.4	23.4	498	79
Nice	5	9.3	22.3	576	59
Ajaccio	4	10.4	20.9	433	185

The pollution gets thick and the air heavy. The tourists start arriving on Easter weekend, but the Parisians don't start leaving until July (see Vacations). Temperatures in the summer average about 18° Celsius (65° Fahrenheit) with some very warm days, especially in July and August.

A FEW WEATHER EXPRESSIONS

il fait beau	it's nice out
il ne fait pas beau	it's not very nice out
il fait mauvais	the weather is bad
ça caille	it's freezing (slang)
il pleut	it's raining
il fait froid	it's cold
il fait chaud	it's hot
il neige	it's snowing
il fait moche	it's ugly out

T RAVELING to and from Paris is relatively easy from all corners of Europe and the rest of the world. If you are coming from the United States or Canada there are a number of reduced-rate travel possibilities available to students. Reduced rates are also possible for those under 30. The Council on International Educational Exchange (C.I.E.E.) issues international student and youth cards which allow substantial discounts on flights. Otherwise, you should consult your travel agent for the most recent rates on scheduled airlines serving Paris.

Council on International Educational Exchange (C.I.E.E.)
Centre Franco-Américain Odéon
1, Pl. de l'Odéon
75006 PARIS
Tel: 43.59.23.69 or 46.34.16.10
Director: Mme Andrea MASON

Council on International Educational Exchange (C.I.E.E.)
205 E. 42nd Street
New York, NY 10017
(212) 661-1450

Other Locations (C.I.E.E./Council Travel)

ARIZONA
• Tempe
120 E. University Drive
Suite E
Tempe, AZ 85281
Tel: (603) 966-3544

CALIFORNIA
• Berkeley
2511 Channing Way
Berkeley, CA 94704
Tel: (415) 848-8604
• La Jolla
UCSD Price Center
Q-076 9500 Gilman Drive
La Jolla, CA 92093
Tel: (619) 452-0630

• Long Beach
1818 Palo Verde Avenue
Suite E
Long Beach, CA 90815
Tel: (213) 598-3338
    (714) 527-7950
• Los Angeles
1093 Broxton Ave Suite 220
Los Angeles, CA 90024
Tel: (213) 208-3551
• San Diego
953 Garnet Avenue
San Diego, CA 92109
Tel: (619) 270-6401
• San Francisco
312 Sutter Street, Suite 407
San Francisco, CA 94108
Tel: (415) 421-3473

• San Francisco
919 Irving Street
Suite 102
San Francisco, CA 94122
Tel: (415) 566-6222
• Sherman Oaks
14515 Ventura Blvd.
Suite 250
Sherman Oaks, CA 91403
Tel: (818) 905-5777

COLORADO
1138 13th St.
Boulder, CO 80302
Tel: (303) 447-8101

CONNECTICUT
• New Haven
Yale Co-op E., 77 Broadway
New Haven, CT 06520
Tel: (203) 562-5335

DISTRICT OF COLUMBIA
• Washington
3300 M Street
Washington, D.C. 20007
Tel: (202) 337-6464

GEORGIA
• Atlanta
12 Park Place South
Atlanta, GA 30303
Tel: (404) 577-1678

ILLINOIS
• Chicago
1153 N. Dearborn St.
Chicago, IL 60610
Tel: (312) 951-0585
• Evanston
831 Foster Street
Evanston, IL 60201
Tel: (312) 475-5070

LOUISIANA
• New Orleans
Danna Student Center
6363 St. Charles Av.
New Orleans, LA 70118
Tel: (504) 866-1767

MASSACHUSETTS
• Amherst
79 South Pleasant Street
(2nd floor rear)
Amherst, MA 01002
Tel: (413) 256-1261
• Boston
729 Boylston Street
Suite 201
Boston, MA 02116
Tel: (617) 266-1926
• Boston
156 Ell Student Center
Northeastern Univ.
306 Huntington Ave.
Boston, MA 02115
Tel: (617) 424-6665
• Cambridge
1384 Massachusetts Ave
Suite 206
Cambridge, MA 02138
Tel: (617) 497-1497
• Cambridge
Stratton Student Center
M.I.T., W20-024
84 Massachusetts Ave
Cambridge, MA 02139
Tel: (617) 225-2555

MICHIGAN
1220 S. University Ave., Room 208
Ann Arbor, MI 48104
Tel: (313) 998-0200

MINNESOTA
• Minneapolis
1501 University Ave, SE
Room 300
Minneapolis, MN 55414
Tel: (612) 379-2323

NEW YORK
• New York
356 West 34th Street
New York, NY 10001
Tel: (212) 661-1450
• New York
35 West 8th Street
New York, NY 10011
Tel: (212) 254-2525

NORTH CAROLINA
•Durham
703 9th Street, Suite B
Durham, NC 27705
Tel: (919) 286-4664

OREGON
• Portland
715 S.W. Morrison, Suite 600
Portland, OR 97205
Tel: (503) 228-1900

PENNSYLVANIA
•Philadelphia
3606A Chestnut St.
Philadelphia, PA 19104
Tel: (215) 382-0343

RHODE ISLAND
• Providence
171 Angell Street, Suite 212
Providence RI 02906
Tel: (402) 331-5810

TEXAS
• Austin
1904 Guadalupe Street, Suite 6
Austin, TX 78705
Tel: (512) 472-4931

• Dallas
6923 Snider Plaza, Suite B
Dallas, TX 75205
Tel: (214) 350-6166

WASHINGTON
• Seattle
1314 NE 43rd Street, Suite 210
Seattle, WA 98105
(206) 632-2448
• Seattle
219 Broadway Avenue East
Alley Building, Suite 17
Seattle, WA 98102
Tel: (206) 329-4567

WISCONSIN
• Milwaukee
2615 N. Hackett Ave.
Milwaukee, WI 53211
(414) 332-4740

ELSEWHERE
• France
49, rue Pierre Charron
75008 PARIS
Tel: (33) (1) 45.63.19.87
• England
28A Poland Street
LondonW1V3D
Tel: (44) (71) 437-7767
• Germany
18,Graf Adolf Strasse
4000 DÜSSELDORF 1
Tel: (49) (211) 32.90.88
• Japan
Sanno Grand Building
Room 102
2-14-2 Nagata-cho
Chiyoda-ku
Tokyo 100
Tel: (81) 581-7581

The national student associations of most European countries participate in an international network of student flights under the aegis of the Student Air Travel Association. Connections between Paris and cities in Europe, Africa, the Far East and Australia do currently exist. The fares on SATA flights are normally 40% below commercial fares. More information is available from the national student association of your country of residence. These same offices can supply informawtion on special student train and ship fares. For example, the Deutsche Bundesbahn offers a reduction to students traveling from Germany to Paris. The reduction applies only to the portion of the trip made in Germany. Applications, which must be certified by the University Registrar, are available in any German train station.

If you live in Europe and intend to return home by train several times during the year, you should be aware of two reduced-fare plans offered by the French National Railways (SNCF). The first is a 50% reduction card *(une carte demi-tarif)* which, when purchased at a flat rate for a given distance and period of validity, entitles the bearer to a 50% reduction on each trip made between his or her home and Paris. For international travel, this reduction applies only to the part of the trip made in France. A second reduction-plan possibility is a subscription card *(abonnement ordinaire)* which allows you to take an unlimited number of free trips and is purchased for a fixed period of time. Whether the *carte demi-tarif* or the subscription plan is more economical will depend on the number of trips taken in a given period. Information on these reductions is contained in a brochure, *cartes demi-tarif et cartes d'abonnement ordinaire,* available from any major French train station. Similar reductions are offered by other national railways in Europe.

Most likely you'll be getting to Paris by plane. The two main international airports are Charles-de-Gaulle (also known as Roissy because it's located in the northern suburb by that name) and Orly, the older of the two, located twenty kilometers south of Paris. Both are very well served by taxis, public buses, and commuter subway lines called the RER (see Transportation). Those first moments in a foreign airport are always filled with a rush of impressions—you'll immediately notice the racial and ethnic mix indigenous to France. The culture's sense of style and aesthetics are present in the design and advertising. The cars and signs are new.

If you're flying into Paris from North America on a regular scheduled flight, you'll most likely be arriving at Roissy in the early morning. The sounds of Roissy announcements and the strong wafts of *express* coffee are details that you will pleasantly recognize upon each return. After passing through immigrations, nabbing one of the numerous and free baggage carts, and claiming your baggage, you are faced with the choice of whether or not to make a customs declaration. The two exits are side by side.

Most likely, as a student, you will have nothing to declare and will be able to pass freely without stopping through the exit marked in green RIEN A DECLARER. North Americans are rarely bothered, but should you be carrying many large packages or computers or electronics in their original cartons you could be asked to open them and be assessed a duty (see Customs Regulations).

If you need to change money right away, proceed to the Société Générale, one of France's largest and most popular banks located on the arrival level near the exit (for detailed discussion of currency exchange and French banking practices, see Banking).

If you're not overloaded and are trying to keep down the expenses, the best options for getting into Paris are the public buses which take you to Porte Maillot (Bus 350) in the 16th *arrondissement* (see map) or Nation (Bus 351) in the 12th *arrondissement,* or the well-equipped and comfortable Air France buses which take you to the *aérogare* at Les Invalides, the Gare de Montparnasse or the Porte Maillot. These can be picked up at the curb outside all terminals and are well-marked. Once in central Paris, it will be cheaper to take a taxi to your place of residence.

Additionally, there is the RER (Direction St. Rémy-les-Chevreuse), which can be easily accessed by a free airport shuttle bus which circles around all terminals. This train makes stops in Paris at the Gare de Nord in the 10th *arrondissement,* Châtelet (the transportation hub for the RER and Métro lines in central Paris), St. Michel (Notre Dame-Latin Quarter-Left Bank), Luxembourg Gardens, Port-Royal, Denfert-Rochereau, and Cité

Universitaire (international student residences). The price of a one way ticket to any of these Paris stations is 31 FF and includes the shuttle bus from your terminal to the RER station at the airport. The buses from Orly take you to Denfert-Rochereau or the Air France terminal at Les Invalides and cost 21 FF. The RER line from Orly serves the Gare d'Austerlitz, St. Michel, Invalides/Orsay, Pont de l'Alma (get off here for the American University of Paris), or the Champ de Mars (Eiffel Tower). The price for any

of these Paris stations is: 24 FF. Save your ticket; you'll need it to get out at your desired station (see map for all these options) or to prove you've paid if you are "controlled."

If you are loaded down with luggage, you'll probably want to take a taxi into Paris. First, you must wait your turn in the clearly marked Taxi Stand line. This is a strict rule and taxi drivers will almost never break it. A normal drive into central Paris without heavy traffic should cost between 130-160 FF from Charles-de-Gaulle and 80-130 FF from Orly. From Charles-de-Gaulle, allow 200 FF if you have lots of baggage. If traffic is very heavy, count on an additional 30%. Baggage, pets, skis, bicycles each cost 5 FF extra. You may tip a bit, but don't overdue it. A ten franc tip from the airport is fine. In the city, a few francs is all that is really expected. No need to calculate 15%. Taxis in Paris always operate with set meters.

Arriving by Train

If you're arriving by train the sensation is very different. If you've never been to Europe before, pulling in under the metal hooded roof of the Gare du Nord can be exciting. The smell, the pigeons, the cold echo all ruminate with a Europe that hasn't changed in a half a century. There are few baggage carts along the long *quais* (platforms), so luggage hauling can be painful. Some porters with large carts can sometimes be hired at the general rate of 5 FF a bag. All Paris train stations have currency exchange points and information stands. Additionally, all stations are served by at least two subway lines (see Métro Map). For a list of Paris train stations and the general directions they serve, along with reservation and ticket information, see Public Transport on the following page.

Upon arriving, again you have the choice of RER, Métro, or taxi. Note that taxi lines at Gare du Nord around rush hour (6 p.m., or 18h)—French rush hour is about one hour later than its North American equivalent—can be very long and frustrating.

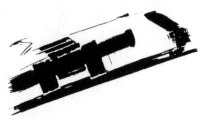

No vaccinations are required to enter France from any country. As for customs, if you are 17 years or older, you have the right to bring in 300 cigarettes or 75 cigars if arriving from an EEC country, or 200 cigarettes or 50 cigars—or 150 *cigarettos*—from any other country. As for spirits, from EEC countries you can bring in one and one-half liters of over 44 proof alcohol, or three liters of sparkling wine, and five liters of non-sparkling wine. From other countries, the limit is one liter of alcohol over 44 proof, two liters each of sparkling and non-sparkling wine. A few no-nos: no more than two kilograms of fish, 250 grams of caviar, and no meat products from Africa. New goods or provisions originating outside the EEC for personal use are limited to 300 FF per person. Goods originating in EEC countries can value up to 4200 FF per adult, 2800 FF for children 15–18 years of age, and 700 FF for those under 15.

Leaving Paris or meeting someone's plane, at either Charles-de-Gaulle or Orly, make sure you are clear as to which airport and which terminal you're supposed to be at. General airport information and message services can be obtained by calling:
Aéroport Charles-de-Gaulle
Tel: 48.62.22.80
Aéroport Orly
Tel: 49.75.15.15

Minitel service is also available for flight information/departure and arrival times by dialing on your telephone: 3615, and HORAV on your Minitel unit. (See Minitel under Communications). A recent addition to

Terminal One of Charles de Gaulle Airport is Cocoon, on the Boutiquaire level, offering 60 "cabins" to sleep, rest, shower or work in during extended visits to this airport.
Tel: 48.62.06.16.

Major Airlines Serving Paris

Aer Lingus
47, ave de l'Opéra
75002 PARIS
res: 47.42.12.50

Air Outre-Mer
Strategic Orly
1315 rue du Pont des Halles
94526 Rungis Cedex
Tel: 49.79.12.34

Air Canada
31, rue Falguière
75015 PARIS
res: 43.20.12.00
FAX: 43.21.30.80

Air Europe
45, rue de Richelieu
75001 PARIS
res: 49.27.91.00

Air France
119, ave des Champs-Elysées
75008 PARIS
res: 45.35.61.61
FAX: 42.99.24.09
Minitel: 3615 AF or 3616 AF

Air Inter
17, rue de Provigny
94 Cachan
Tel: 45.46.90.90

American Airlines
109, rue Fbg. St.-Honoré
75008 Paris
res: 42.89.05.22
FAX: 45.63.37.08

Biman Bangladesh Airlines
90 ave des Champs-Elysées
75008 PARIS
res: 42.89.11.47
FAX: 45.62.67.04

British Airways
Ticket Office
12, rue Casteglione
75001 PARIS
res: 47.78.14.14
FAX à Lyon: (16) 72.35.11.11

Continental Airlines International
24, ave Hoche
75008 PARIS
res: 49.53.07.07
FAX: 49.53.04.81

Continental Airlines
92, ave des Champs-Elysés
75008 PARIS
res: 42.25.31.81
FAX: 42.25.31.89

Dan Air
31, rue du Pont
Neuilly sur Seine
92520
Tel: 47.47.44.44

Delta Airlines
Immeuble Lavoisier
4, Pl. de Vosges
92052 PARIS Cedex 74
res: 43.35.40.80
FAX: 47.68.52.82

Hautes-Alpes
4, av de l'Opéra
75001 PARIS
Tel: 42.96.05.08

Northwest Airlines
16, rue Chauveau Lagarde
75008 PARIS
res: 42.66.90.00
FAX: 42.66.94.66

Qantas Airways Limited
7, rue Scribe
75009 PARIS
res: 42.66.53.05
FAX: 42.66.90.03

Republic Airlines
6, rue Chaussée d'Antin
75009 PARIS
Tel: 48.24.32.24

Tower Air
11, Bd Montmatre
75002 PARIS
Tel: 40.13.80.80

Trans World Airlines (TWA)
101, ave des Champs-Elysées
75008 Paris
res: 47.20.62.11
FAX: 40.70.05.76

United Airlines
40, rue Jean Jaurès
93170 BAGNOLET
res: 49.72.14.14
FAX: 47.72.80.25

US Air
23 bis, rue d'Anjou
92100 BOULOGNE
Tel: 49.10.29.00
toll free: 05.00.30.00

UTA
3, Bd Malesherbes
75008 PARIS
res: 40.17.44.44
FAX: 40.17.45.27

**Other Airlines
(Res. & Info.)**

Aeroflot
Tel: 42.25.43.81
Aerolineas Argentinas
res: 42.56.31.16
Aéromexico
res: 47.42.40.50
Air Afrique
res: 44.21.32.32
Air Algérie
res: 42.60.31.00
Air Gabon
res: 43.59.20.63
Air India
res: 42.66.13.72
Air Lanka
res: 42.97.43.44
Air Madagascar
Tel: 42.60.30.51
Air Malta
Tel: 48.74.39.56
Air Mauritus
Tel: 47.42.75.02
Alitalia
res: 40.15.00.21
Austrian Airlines
res: 42.66.34.66
Cameroon Airlines
res: 47.42.78.17
Cathay Pacific Airways
res: 40.68.61.00
Ceskoslovenske Aerolinie
res: 47.42.45.26
China Airlines
Tel: 42.25.63.60
Dan Air
Tel: 47.47.44.44
Egypt Air
res: 42.66.55.59
El Al
res: 47.42.41.29

Ethiopian Airline
Tel: 42.66.16.26
Finnair
Tel: 47.42.33.33
Gulf Air
res: 47.23.70.70
Iberia
res: 47.23.01.23
Icelandair
Tel: 47.42.52.26
Iran Air
Tel: 43.59.01.20
Iraqi Airways
Tel: 45.62.62.25
Japan Air Lines
res: 42.25.85.05
Kenya Airways
Tel: 49.24.00.42
K.L.M. (Dutch Airlines)
res: 47.42.54.40
Korean Airlines
res: 42.61.51.74
Kuwait Airways
Tel: 42.60.30.60
Libyan Arab Airlines
Tel: 45.62.33.00

L.O.T. Polish Airlines
Tel: 47.42.05.60
Lufthansa
res: 42.65.37.35
Olympic Airways
res: 42.65.92.42
Pakistan International Airlines
Tel: 45.62.92.41
Royal Jordanian
Tel: 42.60.46.91
Sabena
res: 47.42.47.47
Scandinavian Airlines (SAS)
res: 47.42.06.14
Singapore Airlines
Tel: 45.53.90.90
Swissair
Tel: 45.81.11.01
TAP (Portugal)
Tel: 42.96.16.09
Thai Airways
res: 47.20.70.15
Varig
Tel: 47.20.03.33

Train Travel

The French rail system, the SNCF, is, on the whole, extremely extensive and efficient. You may have heard of the TGV, *train à grande vitesse,* or high speed train that has cut the traveling time in half between Paris and, for example, Marseille, 800 kilo-meters away, to a little over four hours instead of eight. The TGV currently serves the Paris, Lyon, Marseille line to the south and the Bordeaux line to the southwest. Additionally, the TGV goes to Geneva and Lausanne, and a new ultra high speed western line to the Atlantic has recently been inaugurated. High speed train travel is expanding rapidly in Europe with a network being prepared to tie in with London (via the Eurotunnel) and several German cities within the next two years. The TGV requires reservations, which can be made in most travel agencies, all train stations, and at home with the Minitel (see Communications). Seat reservations for regular trains are also recommended during busy periods.

Paris has six main rail stations, all of them on Métro lines. All offer a wide range of services: bars and restaurants, refreshment stands, newsstands and information booths (sporadically staffed).

SNCF Train Info.
Information: 45.82.50.50
Reservations: 45.65.60.60
Open daily from 8h-20h

Paris Train Stations and the Directions They Serve

Gare du Nord: Serves the north, including the Channel ports, where trains connect with ferries and hovercrafts from Britain; also services Belgium, Holland and the Scandinavian countries.

Gare de l'Est: Serves the east, Nancy and Strasbourg, and Germany and East Europe, including Moscow.

Gare d'Austerlitz: Serves the southwest; Bordeaux, Toulouse, and Spain and Portugal via Orleans, Tours, Poitiers and Angouleme.

Gare St. Lazare: Serves Normandy and boat trains to/from Dieppe.

Gare Montparnasse: Serves western France, especially Bretagne.

Gare de Lyon: Serves southwestern France, Switzerland, and Italy, Yugoslavia and Greece.

When leaving Paris by train, make sure you know from which station your train leaves. Before boarding your train make sure you punch (*composter*) your ticket and reservation stub in one of the automatic cancellation machines located at the head of each platform. Failure to do so may result in a stiff fine—train travel within France is essentially based on the honor system. In most cases a conductor will check your tickets anyway.

Persons under 26 are eligible for discounts of up to 50% on train travel in Europe. These special tickets—often called BIGE—can be purchased at the following agencies:

Usit Voyages
12, rue Vivienne
75002 PARIS
Tel: 42.96.15.88
FAX 47.03.39.14

Transalpino
16, rue Lafayette
75009 PARIS
Tel: 48.24.29.29
FAX: 42.46. 81.04

Frantour
Gare St. Lazare
75008 PARIS
Tel: 43.87.61.89
FAX: 43.87. 33.87

Tours 33
85 bd St Michel
75005 PARIS
Tel: 43.29.69.50
FAX: 43.25.29.85

The most advantageous and inexpensive way to travel extensively in Europe is with the INTER RAIL card. This offers students (under age 26) unlimited train travel in second class during one month from the date of the first part of the journey for the fixed sum of 1793 FF. The Inter Rail Card is valid in all of western Europe, Yugoslavia, Greece, Hungary, Romania, and Morocco. It gives a 50% reduction in the country of purchase.

There is also the Liberté scheme, which is a way of traveling by rail and stopping off around the country for as little as $364 a week. The package includes a rail pass and seven nights of bed and breakfast in any of a dozen hotels.

Other reductions are possible at certain times of the year for destinations more than 1000 kilometers from Paris. Information can be obtained from:

SNCF
127 av des Champs-Elysées
75008 PARIS
Tel: 47.23.54.02

For train information on other national railroads for other countries:
British Rail
57 rue St Roch
75001 PARIS
Tel: 42.60.36.92
German Railroad
13 rue Alsace
75010 PARIS
Tel: 46.07.13.40
Spanish Railroad
3 ave Marceau
75016 PARIS
Tel: 47.23.52.01
Amtrak Railways
c/o Wingate
19 bis, rue du Mt. Thabor
75001 PARIS
Tel: 42.60.39.85
Canadian National Railway
1, rue Scribe
75009 PARIS
Tel: 47.42.76.50
Venise Simplon Orient Express
4, rue Sansbouef
75008 PARIS
Tel: 42.93.81.82

A few notes on long distance train travel. Aside from the ultra-modern TGV, the SNCF uses primarily two models of train cars. The older ones are divided into compartments of six moderately uncomfortable seats, while the newer ones are merely organized into rows of comfortably reclining seats. Trains are always divided into Second Class and First Class, Smoking and Non-Smoking. Most trains offer snacks and drinks and many are equipped with dining cars. Having your dinner on a train, elegantly seated at a table with linen tablecloth and real silverwear can be a lot of fun, but be prepared to spend close to 150 FF per person for the meal. Otherwise, bring along your own provisions, especially a bottle of water.

The overnight trains to Amsterdam, Copenhagen, Frankfurt, Venice, Athens, Rome, Madrid, etc. can make for highly memorable experiences. The least expensive sleeping arrangement on a night train is the *couchette* or six-bunk compartment. Depending who you get in your compart-ment, you may be able to sleep well or not at all. Be warned: theft does exist in trains, even on first class. Though rare, the most remarkable thefts happen on trains going to or coming from Southern France and Italy, where entire cars have been gassed and robbed! We can offer no advice for these Mediterranean journeys, unless you wish to take a gas mask with you.

Each bunk comes with a blanket, pillow, and sleeping-bag shaped sheet which comes sealed in a plastic wrapper to insure hygiene. When crossing international borders at night, the train conductor will keep your passport until morning to be able to show to the border police and customs inspectors. This is totally normal. Don't be

Bus/Coach Travel

There are some very cheap bus excursions from Paris to London, Amsterdam, and other European cities. In the days prior to the Islamic Revolution in Iran, there were weekly buses originating in London and passing through Paris on their way across Europe to Istanbul, Tehran, Kabul, and finally India.

For $30 a rugged individual could get from Paris to Bombay. The route changed in the Seventies, passing through Pakistan instead of Afghanistan on its way to India. There are still bus excursions, but few foreigners risk going through Iran anymore. Bus information can be obtained from:

Eurolines (buses)
3, ave Porte de la Villette
75019 PARIS
Tel: 40.38.93.93
Nouvelles Frontiers (bus trips)
90, bd Montparnasse
75014 PARIS
Tel: 43.35.40.91
Trans-Channel (buses to England)
24, rue Saint Quentin
75010 PARIS
Tel: 40.34.71.50

Fédération Nationale
des Transports Routiers
6, rue Paul-Valéry
75016 PARIS
Tel: 45.53.92.88
Usit Voyages
12, rue Vivienne
75002 PARIS
Tel: 42.96.15.88
FAX: 47.03.39.14

Boats/Ferries

Brittany Ferries
9, rue du 4 Septembre
75002 PARIS
Tel: 42.86.03.03

Irish Ferries
8, rue Auber
75009 PARIS
Tel: 42.66.90.90

Hoverspeed
135, rue Lafayette
75010 PARIS
Tel: 42.85.44.55

Sealink Ferries
21, rue Louis le Grand
75002 PARIS
Tel: 47.42.86.87/47.42.00.26

P. & O. Lines
9, Pl. de la Madeleine
75008 PARIS
Tel: 42.66.40.17

Hitchhiking

It's rare to see people *faire du stop* (hitchhike) in Paris itself, but you may see hitchhikers (with signs), called *autostoppeurs*, at the entrance ramps to the beltway around Paris called the *périphérique*, especially at the Porte d'Orléans and Porte d'Italie, where the *Autoroute du Sud* feeds in. Hitchhiking is illegal on the autoroute ramps themselves. This is essentially the only route to Lyon, Orleans, and the rest of central France (Midi) and the south of France. Hitchhiking is not ill-advised but it tends to be slow in that Europeans are rather cautious and slightly distrustful about letting strangers into their cars, or houses for that matter.

A much better solution exists in most European countries: an organized hitchhiking agency that dispatches riders with drivers for a small fee. For 65 FF Allô-Stop will find you a seat in a car leaving for most destinations at around the same time you want to leave. Participation in the expenses for gas and tolls depends on the driver but tends to be standard. Weekend bus trips one-way to Amsterdam for 230 FF (210 FF for those under 26) and London for 360 FF (300 FF for those under 26) are also organized by Allô-Stop. Round trip price for Amsterdam and London are respectively 360 FF/330 FF (under 26) and 510 FF/450 FF (under 26).

Allô-Stop
84, Passage Brady
75010 PARIS
Tel: 42.46.00.66

Student Excursions

The following student organizations have planned domestic and international excursions at reasonable rates. Write or call for their programs and schedules. Traveling with French students can be an excellent way to meet new friends, improve your French and see new parts of the world.

L'Autobus
4bis, rue St. Sauveur
75002 PARIS
Tel: 42.33.86.72

Bureau des Voyages de Jeunesse
20, rue Jean-Jacques Rousseau
75001 PARIS
Tel: 42.33.55.00
FAX: 42.33.40.53
(Italy, Austria, Yugoslavia)

Centre de Coopération Culturelle et Sociale
7, rue Notre-Dame-des-Victoires
75002 PARIS
Tel: 42.61.53.84
FAX: 42.60.24.74
(England, Sweden, Germany, Israel, Austria, Russia, Greece, Denmark)

Centre Touristique des Etudiants et de la Jeunesse
20, rue des Carmes
75005 PARIS
Tel: 43.25.00.76
FAX: 43.54.48.97
(charter flights)

Fédération Unie des Auberges de la Jeunesse
27, rue Pajol
75018 PARIS
Tel: 46.07.00.01
(issues student hostel cards for all of Europe)

Office du Tourisme Universitaire (OTU)
39 ave Bernanos
75005 PARIS
Tel: 43.29.12.88
(cheap charters, good bulletin board. International Student Card required)

Usit Voyages
12, rue Vivienne
75002 PARIS
Tel: 42.96.15.88
FAX: 47.03.39.14
(international travel and student IDs—English speaking staff)

Distances from Paris

Amsterdam: 504 km	Marseille: 776 km
Athens: 2918 km	Mexico City: 9194 km
Berlin: 1054 km	Milan: 826 km
Boston: 5531 km	Miami: 7361 km
Brussels: 308 km	Montreal: 5525 km
Budapest: 1257 km	Moscow: 2851 km
Cairo: 3210 km	Munich: 832 km
Chicago: 6664 km	New York: 5837 km
Dublin: 854 km	Oslo: 1337 km
Edinburgh: 867 km	Prague: 1035 km
Florence: 878 km	Rio de Janeiro: 9166 km
Frankfurt: 465 km	Rome: 1388 km
Geneva: 402 km	San Francisco: 8971 km
Helsinki: 1894 km	Stockholm: 1549 km
Hong Kong: 9982 km	Tel Aviv: 3289 km
Istanbul: 2243 km	Tokyo: 9998 km
Koweit: 4403 km	Toronto: 6015 km
Lisbon: 1817 km	Venice: 838 km
London: 414 km	Vienna: 1227 km
Los Angeles: 9107 km	Warsaw: 1044 km
Lyon: 460 km	Washington, D.C: 6164 km
Madrid: 1316 km	

F RANCE'S international reputation represented by those three great words: *Liberté, Egalité, Fraternité* tell only a part of the story. Anyone who has lived in France for at least a year will be able to confirm the same thing: French bureaucracy can be enough to provoke fits of rage. You have to learn to flow with the tide, to figure out the inner logic and, when applicable, use it to the ends that you're after. Don't panic. Everything administrative in France takes time, and most things, you will learn, are *en cours* (in process). There are, nonetheless, a number of practical pointers that can ease you through the administrative labyrinth.

The fact that you're not just visiting France, you're no longer a passing visitor, means your legal and administrative status in France takes on new proportions. As a tourist, one is allowed to remain in France for a maximum of three months—and is forbidden to work, of course. As a student, you'll need a student visa before entering France if you stay more than three months. This will be your first step towards obtaining the infamous *carte de séjour* (extended visitors card).

French administration is famous for its own sense of logic, the long lines, the eternal delays, the mammoth frustrations. So be prepared. Aside from your battery of papers, documents, certificates, photocopies, letters, receipts, statements, etc. always be equipped on your person with stamped envelopes, pictures of yourself, bank statements, electric and gas bills (EDF-GDF—the only reliable and widely accepted proof of address in France), a stack of one, two, five, and ten franc coins for photocopies, instant photos, envelopes, etc. (Make sure you keep copies of *all* bills and receipts.) And remember, in France it's the written document that matters. Everything must have an official stamp on it (*tampon*) so the more *tampons* the better your documents will be received. The document carries more weight in France than the spoken word. And, don't forget, as well prepared as you think you are for your administrative procedures you will have to come back at least once. "*C'est comme ça*," and it's like that for everyone. In some cases, your university may have established regular inside contacts, *pistons*, as they're called in French, with the local authorities and will proceed to procure your papers for you. The system or practice of having a *piston* is inherent in the centralized bureaucracy. Don't get moralistic about this; if you have a good contact and are really in need of help call your *piston*, but don't waste a favor on a small and banal matter. In other cases, you'll be on your own. And you'll complain. But that's okay; the French complain all the time; it's built into the national charm.

Some contend that living legally in France is not as difficult as most foreigners tend to think. The key is learning the ropes fast. Problems only arise when people decide to remain in France after having entered as a visitor or tourist. The French are taking illegal immigration with increasing seriousness, although most cases of severe legal action being taken usually have been directed toward North Africans, black Africans, and Asians. North Americans and Europeans are usually dealt with more leniently. But nonetheless French employees of the State, *fonctionnaires* (Federal employees—a term you will hear a lot), don't appreciate broken laws and the public at large has grown less tolerant of illegal foreigners.in France.

To repeat, all foreigners residing in France for more than three months must have either a visa allowing them to do so, or a *carte de séjour*. Until the age of 18 minors may reside in France without a *carte de séjour* but they must still enter the country legally. Many foreigners who want to stay in France for more than three months, but do not want to start the administrative process in motion for regularizing their long term status, simply take the train to Brussels or Geneva or London at the end of each three-month period to have their passports stamped and thus reinitiate another three-month period. This is feasible but somewhat impractical and of course not a real solution for those who think they might want to stay longer or hope to study or work legally in France. And, local border authorities have in the last few years been on alert for people trying to use this technicality to subvert the law. However, if you don't need to work and you're sure you're only staying 6-12 months, this may be your best option.

A student falls into a slightly

REPUBLIQUE FRANÇAISE

CARTE DE RESIDENT

Préfecture

Validité territoriale   N

Nom

Prénoms:

Né(e) ie: 29 AVRIL 1956   Sexe M

à: USA ELISABETH NEW JERSEY

Nationalité: AMERICAINE

Date d'expiration: 24 SEPTEMBRE 2001

Signature du titulaire   Signature de l'autorité

different category than a foreigner coming to work or reside in France. Students can be in France on either short or long term basis, and the visa they solicit reflects the length of their stay. Students who are nationals of EEC (European Economic Community) countries (with the exception of Spain and Portugal) do not require student visas, but must still follow French requirements to obtain the temporary resident permit or *carte de séjour* through the year 1992. After that—we'll see. Nationals from Andorra and Switzerland fall under the requirements for EEC nationals. Spanish and Portuguese students must first solicit a student visa in their home countries and then the *carte de séjour*. If you hold non-EEC passports but you have parents or grand-parents who were born in an EEC country, you might qualify for a passport from that country. Cases of this are known concerning Ireland, Italy, and Portugal.

Student Visa Procedures and Residence Permits

Most students who are planning to pursue university-level studies in France are required to obtain a student visa (*not* a tourist visa) **before leaving their country of residence**. Visas are a strict requirement of French law and may be issued to you only in your country of residence. The French police refuse to "normalize" students who enter France without visas. Once you have arrived in Paris, your university may assist you in completing the necessary formalities which allow you to reside legally in France.

Who Must Obtain a Visa?

All students who intend to enroll at an American university program in France, and of course the French university system, must obtain a visa **except:** those already holding a valid *carte de séjour* and citizens of Andorra, Belgium, Denmark, Germany, Greece, Ireland, Italy, Luxembourg, Netherlands, Switzerland, the U.K. and French nationals. **It is not possible to obtain a visa after arriving in France.** If you do not already have one, you will be told to return to your home country for a visa.

What Type of Visa is Necessary?

The type of visa you request depends on two factors: your nationality and the amount of time you plan to spend at a university in France.

• If you will be attending a university program for just one semester, a *"visa d'étudiant pour six mois avec plusieurs entrées"* should be requested. This releases you from *"carte de séjour"* or temporary residence permit formalities as the visa is, in itself, your temporary permit. Please note that this visa is not granted to all nationalities. Consult your local French consulate for further information.

• If you are applying for at least one year, a *"visa de long séjour pour études"* should be requested.

How is the Application Made?

The French consulate nearest you will require the following:

• A certificate of admission from the university in Paris that has accepted you. Most consulates will not issue a visa without a certificate of admission or some proof of official contact. The visa is valid if you matriculate as a full-time student.

• A financial guarantee as specified by your consulate. In most countries, this will be a letter from your parents or your bank, signed in the presence of a notary public. It will certify that you will have an income of at least 1,800 FF per month for the duration of your stay in France. This figure is subject to change.

• A statement proving that your health insurance covers you in France. This is also required to apply for a residence permit and to register at the university you've selected. (See Health).

• Authorization by a parent or guardian if you are under 18 years of age.

• Several photographs as

specified by the consulate.
• Your valid passport (should not expire before the visa does).

In order to avoid unnecessary delays, it is recommended that you write or telephone the consulate, requesting exact details concerning the documents required. Since different procedures are in effect for students seeking admission to French universities, if you're attending an American program you must clearly request visa information for study in France *outside the French university system.* Since the time required to issue a visa will vary from consulate to consulate and from country to country, you are urged to apply for your student visa as far in advance of your departure date as possible.

Since September 1989, students intending to study in France for only six months have been issued a six month or 180 day student visa which enables them to stay in France without having to complete *carte de séjour* procedures. However, it must say this (*"le titulaire de ce visa est dispensé de solliciter une carte de séjour,"* or *"le présent visa vaut autorisation de séjour").* If these magical words are not found somewhere on the visa, you have to follow the *carte de séjour* routine like everybody else.

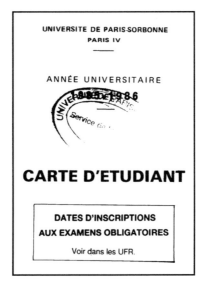

UNIVERSITE DE PARIS-SORBONNE
PARIS IV

ANNÉE UNIVERSITAIRE 1985-1986

CARTE D'ETUDIANT

DATES D'INSCRIPTIONS
AUX EXAMENS OBLIGATOIRES
Voir dans les UFR.

FRENCH CONSULATES IN THE U.S.

In order to find out where to apply for your student visa, consult the columns that follow. The number which follows your state of residence indicates the reference number of the consulate you should contact.

Alabama	7	Montana	9
Alaska	9	Nebraska	2
Arizona	5	Nevada (c)	5
Arkansas	7	Nevada (d)	9
California (a)	5	New Hampshire	1
California (b)	9	New Jersey	6
Colorado	5	New Mexico	5
Connecticut	6	North Carolina	10
Delaware	10	New York	6
Washington, D.C.	10	North Dakota	2
Florida	11	Ohio	3
Georgia	12	Oklahoma	4
Hawaii	9	Oregon	9
Idaho	9	Pennsylvania	6
Illinois	2	Puerto Rico (e)	8
Indiana	2	Rhode Island	1
Iowa	2	South Carolina	10
Kansas	2	South Dakota	2
Kentucky	2	Tennessee	7
Louisiana	7	Texas	4
Maine	1	Utah	9
Maryland	10	Vermont	1
Massachussetts	1	Virginia	10
Michigan	3	Washington	9
Minnesota	2	West Virginia	3
Mississippi	7	Wisconsin	2
Missouri	2	Wyoming	9

1)Boston
3 Commonwealth Avenue
Boston, MA 02116
(617) 266-9413

2)Chicago
737 No. Michigan Avenue
Olympic Center, Suite 2020
Chicago, IL 60611
(312) 787-5359

3)Honolulu
2 Waterfront Plaza, Suite 300
500 Ala Moana Boulevard
Honolulu, HI 96813
(808) 599-4458

4)Houston
2727 Allen Parkway
Suite 976
Houston, TX 77019
(713) 528-2181

5)Los Angeles
The Oppenheimer Tower
10990 Wilshire Blvd., Suite 300
Los Angeles, CA 90024
(213) 479-4426-3120

6)New York
934 Fifth Avenue
New York, NY 10021
(212) 606-3688

7)New Orleans
Suite 2105
Lykes Building
300 Poydras Street
New Orleans, LA 70130
504) 523-5772

8)San Juan
Mercantil Plaza Blvd.Suite 720
Avenida Ponce de Leon
Stop 27-1/2, Hato Rey
San Juan, PR 00918
(809) 753-1700

9)San Francisco
540 Bush Street
San Francisco, CA 94115
(415) 397-4330

10)Washington, DC
4101 Reservoir Road NW
10 Washington, DC 20007
(202) 944-6000

11)Miami
One Biscayne Tower
2 S Biscayne Blvd
Miami, FL 33131
(305) 372-9798

12)Atlanta
Marquis Two Tower
285 Peachtree, Center Avenue
Suite 2410
Atlanta, GA 30303
Tel: (404) 522-4226/4423

a: Counties of Imperial, Inyo, Kern, Kings, Mono, Orange, Riverside, San Bernardino, San Diego, San Louis Obispo, Santa Barbara, Ventura
b: All counties *excluding* those listed in (a)
c: Counties of Clark, Lincoln, Nye, Esmeralda, Mineral only
d: All counties *excluding* those listed in (c)
e: Also: Viegues, Virgin Islands (US), Turks and Caicos Islands, Montserrat, Virgin Islands (UK), Cayman Islands, Antigua, Barbuda, Redonda, Dominica, St. Christopher, Nevis, Anguilla, St. Lucia, St. Vincent.

For student visas and more information, contact the French consulate nearest you. Here is a list:

• **Austria**
Technikerstrasse 2
A-1040 Wien
Tel: (43-222) 65.47.47

• **Bahrain**
Diplomatic Area 319
Road 1901
P.O. Box 26134
Manama
Tel: (973) 29.17.34

• **Belgium**
4, Avenue des Arts
1040 Brussels
Tel: (31.21) 210.12.72

• **Denmark**
Ny östergade 3
1101 Copenhagen K
Tel: (45.1) 15.51.22

• **Egypt**
2, place Ahmed Orabi
P.O. Box 474
Alexandria
Tel: (20.3) 800.207 to 800.488

• **Finland**
Itaïnen Puistotie 13
00140 Helsinki 14
Tel: (358.0) 171.1521

• **Germany**
Kappellenweg 1 A.
5300 Bonn 2
Tel: (49.228) 36.20.31 or 36.20.35

Cecilienallee 10
4000 Düsseldorf 30
Tel: (49.221) 49.90.77/78

Bettinastrasse 62
6000 Frankfurt-am-Main
Tel: (49.69) 74.01.37 to 39

Pöseldorferweg 32
2 Hamburg 13
Tel: (49.40) 44.14.00

Möhlstrasse 5
8000 München 80
Tel: (49.89) 47.50.16/17

• **Greece**
36, Blvd. Amalias
Athens 10558
Tel: (30.1) 322.71.63

• **Netherlands**
Vijzelgracht 2
P.O. Box 20018
1000 HA Amsterdam
Tel: (31.20) 22.58.11 to 13

• **Israel**
Immeuble "Migdalor"
1-3, rue Ben Yehouda
63801 Tel-Aviv
Tel: (972.3) 65.15.25 to 27

• **Italy**
Via Giulia 251
00186 Roma
Tel: (39.6) 656.52.41

1, Piazza Ognissanti
50123 Firenze
Tel: (39.55) 21.35.09 or 21.83.80

Via del Vecchio
Politecnico 3
20121 Milano
Tel: (39.2) 79.43.41/42

95, Corso Vittorio Emanuele—11
10128 Torino
Tel: (39.11) 51.74.86 to 88

• **Japan**
Obhayashi Building 24th floor
37 Kyobashi 3 Chome Higashi-ku
Osaka 540
Tel: (81.78) 946.6181/82

• **Jordan**
Djebel Amman, rue Mutanabi
P.O. Box 374
Amman
Tel: (962.6) 41.273/74

• **Kuwait**
Bloc N° 12
Lot N° 156/158
Jabriya-Kuwait
P.O. Box 1037 Safat
Tel: (965) 531.98.50 to 53

• **Lebanon**
Mar-Takla
Bairut
Tel: (961) 450.580/451.611

• **Mexico**
Havre N°15
06600 Mexico 6 D.F.
Tel: (52.5) 533.1360 to 64

• **Monaco**
Immeuble Monte-Carlo Sun
74, Bd d'Italie
P.O. Box 345
Monte Carlo
Tel: (16) 93.50.51.67

• **Morocco**
Rue du Prince Moulay Abdallah
B.A. 15810 Casablanca Principal
Tel: (212.9) 27.14.18 & 27.99.81

49, Avenue Allal Ben Abdallah
P.O. Box 139, Rabat
Tel: (212.7) 248.24 or 309.36

• **Norway**
Drammensweien, 69
0271 Oslo 2
Tel: (47.2) 44.18.20

• **Portugal**
123, Calçada
Marquês de Abrantes
Lisboa 1200
Tel: (351.1) 60.81.31 to 33

• **Saudi Arabia**
Immeuble Saoud Al Fayan
Quartier Olaya
Riyadh
Tel: (966.2) 642.12.33

Cheikh Mohammed Bin Abdul
Wahab Street, Sharafiah
P.O. Box 145
Jeddah
Tel: (966.2) 642.12.33

• **Spain**
Paseo de la Castellana N°79
Edificio U.A.P.
Madrid
Tel: (34.1) 455.54.50

28, rue Madrid
11, Paseo de Gracia
08007 Barcelona
Tel: (34.3) 317.81.50 or 317.82.08

• **Sweden**
Linnégatan 78
115-23 Stockholm
Tel: (46.8) 630.270

• **Switzerland**
11, rue Imbert-Galloix
P.O. Box 1205 Geneva
Tel: (41.22) 29.62.11 to 15

Muhlebachstrasse 7
P.O. Box A 112
CH 8008 Zurich
Tel: (41.1) 251.85.44

• **Turkey**
8, Istiklâl Caddesi (Taksim)
Istanbul
Tel: (90.1) 143.1852/53

• **United Arab Emirates**
Street Cheikh Khalifa
P.O. Box 4014
Abou Dhabi
Tel: (971) 33.11.00

• **United Kingdom**
24 Rutland Gate
London SW7
Tel: (44.1) 581.52.92 to 99

• **Venezuela**
Edificio Los Frailes (5th floor)
Calle la Guairita
Chuao
A.C. 60385 Caracas 1060
Tel: (58.2) 910.333 & 910.634

Types of cartes de séjour

The French authorities issue two types of *cartes* to foreigners, depending on their status: a *carte de séjour temporaire* and a *carte de résident.*

Cartes de séjours are issued to individuals of 18 years of age and above. Parents of children below the age of 18 should obtain a *visa de long séjour* for their children before coming to France.

Most foreigners coming to France for more than three months are issued a *carte temporaire.* This card is valid for up to one year, and it may be renewed. There is no fee for the initial *carte.* If the prefectoral authorities decline to renew a *carte de séjour temporaire*, the bearer must leave France before his/her initial *carte* expires.

The *carte de résident* is for foreigners who come to France with the intention of taking up residence. It is valid for ten years and renewable if the holder can show proof that he/she either is exercising a profession in France or has sufficient means to maintain him/herself without being employed in France. A medical examination is usually required. In order to qualify for a ten-year card, the foreigner must show proof that he/she has lived in France for at least three consecutive years. Spouses of French citizens and parents of French-born children, however, are automatically entitled to the ten-year card, although the process may take a year or longer to complete.

How to Get the carte de séjour

Students entering certain programs in Paris, like The American University of Paris', benefit from a group procedure which makes obtaining a *carte de séjour* a simple routine. This is obviously the easiest for you. The only thing demanded of the student is that he or she: a) comply with the basic physical examination required by the French Government for the first card (not required for EEC nationals) and b) pick up the card on the required date and submit a copy to the indicated office.

If you're a returning student living in Paris you may submit requests for renewals at the same office in your university.

Legally enrolling at a university in France entails showing proof that the student has entered France legally and has completed, or is in the process of completing, *carte de séjour* formalities. So, don't take these instructions too lightly. Listed below are the basic documents required by the *Préfecture de police* when soliciting a *carte de séjour*. This list is in no way definitive as *Préfecture* requirements can undergo modifications and can vary from *Département* to *Département.*

Those arriving in France with the appropriate long-stay visa and planning to live in Paris should, within eight days of arrival, present themselves with their visa-stamped passport to the appropriate police center (*centre d'accueil des étrangers*) for their *arrondissement.* These centers are open from 8:45 a.m. to 4:30 p.m. daily except Saturdays, Sundays and French holidays.

• **Centre de Réception des Etrangers du 14e**
114-116, av du Maine
75014 PARIS — Métro Montparnasse for 1st, 2nd, 3rd, 4th, 5th, (6th, 7th, 13th,14th and 15th *arrondissements)*
• **Centre de Réception des Etrangers du 12e**
163, rue de Charenton
75012 PARIS—Métro La Fourche (for 11th, 12th, and 20th *arrondissements)*
• **Centre de Réception des Etrangers du 17e**
19-21, rue Truffaut
75017 PARIS—Métro Crimée (for 8th, 9th, 10th, 16th and 17th *arrondissements)*

For **all** students residing in Paris:
**Centre de Réception
des Etrangers du 19e**
218, rue d'Aubervilliers (first floor)
75019 PARIS—Métro Cambronne
or Parmentier

At the police center, the visitor takes the initial step of filling out a questionnaire and providing a local address. The applicant will immediately be given a convocation to the *Préfecture de Police* for a date fixed two to twelve weeks later, depending on the number of pending applications. The convocation will cite the date, time and location of the office at which the applicant should appear.

Location of the Préfecture de Police

The main *Préfecture de Police* for Paris is centrally located at:

Services des Etrangers
1, rue de Lutèce
(Place Louis Lépine)
75195 PARIS RP (4e)—Métro Cité
Tel: 42.77.11.00 or 42.60.33.22 or 43.29.12.44 Ext. 4873
Hours: Monday through Thursday: 8:35 a.m.-5:00 p.m.
Friday: 8:45 a.m.-4:30 p.m.

Those who will wish to live outside of Paris should inquire at their local police station or at the *Mairie* (town hall) about procedures for obtaining a *carte de séjour*. In some *départements*, the *préfectures* have delegated the authority to process such applications to local officials. In others, the individual may have to apply at the *Direction de la Réglementation* of the *Préfecture* or the nearest *Sous-Préfecture*.

In Paris, all students applying for the *carte de séjour* must present themselves at the *Préfecture de Police*. Students have been uniformly siphoned off to the *Préfecture de Police* in the 19th *arrondissement*, at 218 rue d'Aubervilliers, which has cut down but not eliminated the waiting time. At certain times of the year, September and October, for example, lines can be four to five hours long. Arriving early, curiously enough, is not always the best strategy, because everyone else will have had the same idea. Some prefer going later in the afternoon (the *carte de séjour* service closes at 16h). There is no best bet. Bring a good book and a picnic, however, because even with the best strategies, lines are inevitable. All others go to their local *préfecture* (each *arrondissement* has its own).

It is always useful to request a complete list of all necessary documents before making your *demande* (request) for the *carte de séjour.* This will minimize the amount of trips to the *préfecture*, the time spent in lines, the frustrations, etc. Sometimes it's hard getting your questions answered. State employees handling these requests can be impatient, short-tempered, and seemingly spiteful. They are as stuck in the system as you. Remember to be as organized and efficient and as polite and pleasant as possible, even when you really want to scream and punch. You might not get very far by charming the clerk, but you certainly will slow down the procedure if you create an adversary relationship. Nothing at all administrative can be done over the phone so don't even give it a thought. And don't ask for the clerk's name or to see the supervisor. French employees never give out their names, will rarely call over a supervisor, and will only be vexed by your attempt to overpower them. Don't get huffy; just learn how to manœuvre.

Required Documents at the Préfecture

To apply for a *carte de séjour*, the following basic documents must be submitted (others may be required in individual cases):
•Valid passport with a long-stay visa (with photocopy of passport title page and French visa page);
•Three black and white passport-type photographs (3.5cm x 4.5cm);
•Proof of financial resources (applicable in all cases); the most acceptable proof of financial resources is a statement from the applicant's French bank showing account number and amount, or a letter from the French bank certifying that the applicant's account is regularly credited with a specified amount from an external source. In subsequent years, you should keep receipts of bank transactions or bank statements from your French bank to prove that you have been receiving funds regularly from abroad to support you.
•Medical Insurance/Medical Certificate issued by a doctor approved by the French consulate; full translation of a foreign medical insurance; or results of medical visit from the OMI (*Office des Migrations Internationales*). This you will get once you have done the exam at the date requested by the *Préfecture*. It is taken with you when you go to pick up your card, and thus it is extremely important that you do not miss this.
•Proof of domicile in France (ie: electric and gas bill—EDF/

GDF—in your name or your rent contract, or a letter from the person who is housing you, a copy of their electric and gas bill and a copy of their *carte d'identité française* or *carte de séjour*;

•For students: pre-registration form (*Certificat de scolarité*) or letter of admission to a school; the *Préfecture de Police* will require evidence that the student is a full-time student. Before issuing a student's *carte de séjour temporaire*, for example, the *Préfecture* expects to see a pre-registration form that clearly indicates the schedule of classes and the number of hours of study. The *Préfecture* reports that 20 hours is the minimum weekly requirement for French-language studies; prefectoral authorities are, therefore, not likely to automatically waive the 20-hour requirement, especially if the student has already been in France for some time. Students who attend only evening classes or who are enrolled as only auditors ("*auditeurs libres*") do not qualify for student status.

•For students: proof of adequate insurance coverage in France with specific mention of medical repatriation. This should be in French, and clearly state the exact coverage for which the student is insured.

•For an *au pair*: contract approved by French Ministry of Labor, 80, rue de la Croix Nivert, 75015 PARIS, and pre-registration form or letter of admission to a school.

•For a worker: contract with an employer;

•One self-addressed and stamped envelope (2,50 FF stamp).

•Some *préfectures* require birth certificates, while others request originals as well as copies of all documents listed above.

Temporary Residence Document

If it is not possible to issue the *carte de séjour* immediately, the applicant will be given a temporary authorization "*récipissé de demande de carte de séjour*" which is evidence that an application has been made for a residence permit. The applicant should carry it until he/she receives his/her *carte de séjour*. This could take several months.

Residence Permits (*cartes de séjour*)

An individual not claiming citizenship of France or any of the other ECC countries, intending to stay in France for more than three months, whether to study, to work or to reside without being gainfully employed, must have the appropriate long-stay visa (*visa de long séjour* or *visa de plus de trois mois*) in his/her passport on arrival in France in order to be able to apply for a *carte de séjour*. The visa must be obtained from the French consulate having jurisdiction over the non-French citizen's place of residence in their country. U.S. citizens may consult the U.S. Embassy's information sheet: "Visa Requirements for France"). Applications for long-term validity French visas cannot be made by individuals in third countries, e.g., England or Belgium, unless the individual is a local resident of that country for one or more years.

It is not possible to come to France without a long-term visa and then apply within France for a residence permit. The French authorities will require such persons to return to their country of residence to apply for the appropriate visa.

It should be noted that the U.S. Embassy is *not* in a position to intervene on behalf of American citizens who, knowingly or unknowingly, enter France without any visa or without the appropriate visa, or who change their plans after their arrival in France. Such Americans will have to comply with the French Government visa requirement before they can apply for a *carte de séjour*.

If the holder of a residence permit moves, he/she must inform the police commissariat having jurisdiction over his/her new place of residence in France. This is especially important if the resident is in the process of renewing his/her *carte de séjour* as the *Préfecture de Police* will not approve the application unless the change of address has been recorded by the local police in the appropriate space on the card.

Renewal of the carte de séjour

In the years that follow your first student *carte de séjour*, you no longer need to solicit a new student visa. The card must never expire in order to avoid having to repeat all the above steps. Renewals are simple, but you should be aware that you have to justify your student status of the past year. You have to take the same documents listed above with the exception of the medical results. In addition, you need a *certificat d'assiduité* (letter from school or university you attended stating that you attended classes and passed your exams) and a copy and the original of the *carte de séjour*.

Renewal of the *carte de séjour* costs 224 FF (160 FF for students) payable by *timbre fiscal* (government tax stamp) that can be purchased at a Tax Office or, easier, in any *tabac* (tobacco shop). Sometimes they're out of stock, so you'll have to hunt down another. For renewal of a student *carte de séjour*, in addition to the documents listed under "Required Documents at the *Préfecture*," the student will have to produce proof of the amounts of money received from their own country during the previous year.

The first student *carte de séjour* is free; the medical exam costs 270 FF (1990 prices, anticipate small annual increases).

To renew a *carte de séjour*, the holder again contacts one of the five police centers to obtain an appointment at the *Préfecture de Police*. This initial step should be taken one month before the expiration date of a *carte de séjour temporaire* (two months for *cartes de résident*). If the *Préfecture* is satisfied with the explanation given by the applicant, the renewal of the *carte de séjour temporaire* is granted upon payment of the fiscal stamp.

For renewal of a *carte de séjour 'salarié'* and *'visiteur,'* the bearer must have proof that he/she has declared and paid (if appropriate) taxes *(les impôts)*. The documents must either be originals or copies certified by the tax authorities.

Carte de Résident

The *carte de résident*, created in 1984, permits its holders to live and work in France. It is valid for 10 years and is automatically renewed, and it replaces a former system of *carte de séjour* and *carte de travail*, both of which were valid for periods of one, three or ten years. According to the *Office National d'Immigration*, you can request the ten-year *carte de résident* if you have a *carte de séjour temporaire* and have been present in France for at least three years. Additionally, you need to prove that you have regular and sufficient revenue to support yourself and your dependents. This proof takes the form of a work contract or promise of contract. Foreign students are considered to be a valuable asset to their country of origin and for this reason the French government tends to discourage the awarding of the ten-year card to students who want to remain in France.

There are other legal means of working in France for both short and long-term periods. Aside from the short-term possibilities, it is advised that you consult a lawyer. The first step is to obtain a *visa de long séjour* (one year) from a French consulate in your home country. This will give you access to your first *carte de séjour*. Once in France and having obtained the card you can proceed to request status as a *travailleur indépendant*, or self-employed person. This cannot be done as a student. The initial visa requires your ability to prove a minimum of $1000 per month for the year in France on deposit in your home country. And with *travailleur indépendant* status you'll be obliged to pay monthly sums to the URSSAF, the Social Security administration for self-employed individuals located in Montreuil. Although this may seem like an expensive option in the beginning, it gives you the ability to work legally and benefit from the social advantages offered in France. Also, as a *travailleur indépendant* you'll increase your employment chances in that employers are not obliged to pay the high social charges for employing you. This is a particularly useful option for individuals whose professional activities lend themselves to free-lance work. For further discussion, see Carol Pineau and Maureen Kelly's *Working in France.*

(based on: *The Economists
Guide to Paris*)

30,000-15,000 B.C.: Cro-Magnon man, whose cave paintings still exist in the southwest, peoples a France laid bare by the Ice Age.

600 B.C.: Greek traders found Massilia, later to be called Marseille.

59-50 B.C.: Julius Caesar conquers France.

AD 987: Hugh Capet, first of the Capetian monarchs, elected king of France.

1207-29: King Philip Augustus brutally suppresses the Cathar (Albigensian) heresy.

1226-70: Louis IX (St Louis), greatest of the the Capetian kings, founds Sorbonne (1253) and wages 7th and 8th Crusades.

1309-77: The papacy establishes itself in Avignon.

1337-1453: The Hundred Years' War (against England).

1515-47: Reign of François I; Renaissance flourishes in Europe.

1562-98: The Wars of Religion between Catholics and Protestants (Huguenots), ending with the Edict of Nantes under which Protestantism is officially recognized.

1643-1715: Reign of Louis XIV, whose revocation of the Edict of Nantes (1685) leads to mass Huguenot exodus.

1715-74: Reign of Louis XV (who was heavily influenced by his mistress, Madame de Pompadour).

1789: The attack on the Bastille starts the French Revolution, leading to the execution of Louis XVI (1793) and then of the revolutionary leaders themselves, notably Robespierre (1794).

1799: Napoleon Bonaparte appointed first consul and then crowned emperor (1804).

1812: Napoleon's empire reaches its zenith with the capture of Moscow, but he is then forced into a humiliating retreat from Russia.

1814-15: Napoleon is forced to abdicate and is exiled to the island of Elba. He escapes, raises a new army, but is defeated at Waterloo. He dies in exile on St Helena (1821).

1814-30: Bourbon monarchy restored, under Louis XVIII, then Charles X.

1830: Revolution in Paris: Charles X replaced by Louis-Philippe.

1830-48: Conquest of Algeria.

1848: Another Paris revolution. Napoleon's nephew Louis-Napoleon elected president, then becomes emperor (Second Empire, 1852-70).

1870-71: The Franco-Prussian War: France is defeated at Sedan, then cedes Alsace and Lorraine to the victors.

1871: In Paris, the revolutionary government of the "Commune" is bloodily suppressed.

1875-87: French vineyards ravaged by phylloxera epidemic.

1894-99: The Dreyfus affair: Jewish officer falsely convicted of treason.

1909: Louis Bleriot is first to fly a non-balloon aircraft across the Channel.

1914-18: World War I, leading to Treaty of Versailles (1919) and the return of Alsace and Lorraine to France.

1936: *"Front Popular"* left-wing government under socialist Leon Blum. The railways, some factories and the Banque de France nationalized.

1939: Outbreak of World War II, leading to German invasion and fall of Paris (1940): a collaborationist government is set up at Vichy, in the unoccupied zone, under Marshal Pétain.

1944: Allies liberate France and de Gaulle forms a provisional government. Sweeping nationalizations begin.

1946: Fourth Republic formed.

1954: Fall of Dien Bien Phu leads to French exodus from Indo-China.

1957: Treaty of Rome is signed, setting up European Community.

1958: De Gaulle returns to power: Fifth Republic is created.

1962: France grants independence to Algeria, after an eight-year war.

1968: Student uprising and general strike. De Gaulle resigns (1969).

1974-81: Presidency of Valéry Giscard d'Estaing.

1981-86: Socialist-led government, with François Mitterrand as President. Continued nationalizations.

1986: Chirac government elected and a period of "cohabitation" begins.

1988: Socialists regain power and Mitterrand names Michel Rocard as *premier ministre.*

1991: Mitterrand replaces Rocard with Edith Cresson as *premier ministre*

1992: Pierre Bérégovoy replaces Cresson following Socialists' loss in regional elections

1993: Plans for implementing European reforms following Maastricht agreement

Political Geography

Départements

The division of France into 95 *départements* is a result of the Revolution and was accomplished in 1790. The three following principles were decisive in its formation: the size of each *département* was to be approximately 6,100 kilometers; the seat was to be located strategically so that it could be reached in the period of one day on horseback from any point in the *département*; and the name

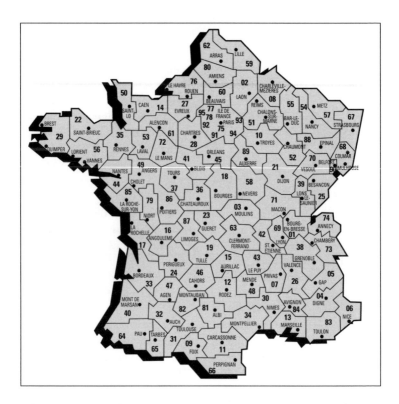

of each was to refer to its provincial history and character.

France is also divided into 22 regions, which are less important for administrative purposes but should not be confused with the *département* names. The present organization of the regions dates from only 1960, and is the result of economical considerations.

Principal cities and département

The numbers found after the name represent the postal codes for the *département*. These codes are used in the postal codes, on license plates, and other standardized nationwide forms. People tend to refer to certain *départements* by their numbers:

Paris 75
    Seine et Marne 77
    Yvelines 78
    Essonne 91   (Ile de France)
    Seine St. Denis 93
    Val de Marne 94
Bordeaux (Gironde) 33
Toulouse (Haute-Garonne) 31
Grenoble (Isère) 38
Montpellier (Hérault) 34
Tours (Indre-et-Loire) 37
Lille (Nord) 59
Strasbourg (Bas-Rhin) 67
Dijon (Côte d'Or) 21
Lyon (Rhône) 69
Aix-en-Provence
(Bouches-du-Rhône) 13
Nice (Alpes-Maritimes) 6

No matter where you are in France, you're never very far away from a café, a restaurant or politics. The French, as you may have noticed, have opinions on most everything and don't hesitate to voice them. This is particularly true in politics, where one is either on the Left or on the Right, and never, but never the twain shall meet.

Back in the early days of the French Revolution, the first National Assembly met with the radical revolutionaries seated to the left of the Speaker, the cautious conservatives to the right. The division has been maintained ever since. Today, even the Right bows to the ideals of the Revolution—if not its methods—which founded the modern republic. There are still a few die-hard monarchists left around, gathering cobwebs in the wealthier quartiers (the Count of Paris, an elderly gentlemen, is the living descendant of the last deposed King, and remains ever ready to sit upon the throne again, should the need arise, but his phone isn't exactly ringing off the hook).

In the waning years of the 20th century, France's Socialist Party, led by President François Mitterrand, emerged as the dominant political party. These are hardly the radical politicians of the early 80s when they first won the presidency and a majority in the *Assemblée Nationale*. Their early policies of nationalizing industry and intervening in the economy have been abandoned in favor of a lighter hand. Today, their policies are less radically Left, more attuned to *"la France profonde"* (something akin to "the silent majority" in America). One thing they do have in common with their conservative predecessors, though, is a large and strong central government, with a massive bureaucracy: the power of the State in France is supreme.

François Mitterrand has been a prominent leader of the Socialist Party since the Sixties. His reelection to a second seven-year term as President assured him of being the longest serving president in French political history. He has a reputation as a clever and patient politician—his nickname is "The Sphinx." He has managed to stay relatively aloof and above the fray of everyday politics, which has strengthened his popularity. The French like their presidents with a bit of haughtiness that reminds one of the attitude of royalty, a quality that Charles-de-Gaulle, another successful

French leader of the Right, had in abundance. They also want to see visible signs of intelligence. Mitterrand, for instance, is the author of several books and has been known to surprise reporters with his wide knowledge of literature and the arts. The idea of a populist, "just one of the boys" president à la former U.S. president Ronald Reagan is unthinkable in France.

The big question of the early 90s is who will be Mitterrand's successor as Socialist Party leader and presidential candidate. The battle a few years back had raged between Michel Rocard, the dapper and articulate former Prime Minister, his predecessor, the brash but sharp-witted Laurent Fabius, and long time party boss Pierre Mauroy, also a former Prime Minister. Following the short mandate of Edith Cresson, France's first woman Prime Minister, who tumbled dramatically with the Socialist's defeat in the regional and *cantonal* elections of 1992, the political scramble for a legitimate Left Wing leader persists. Some feel that the French president of the EEC in Brussels, Roland Dumas, is likely to ascend in national politics. Current caretaker Prime Minister, Pierre Bérégovoy, hopes to re-secure confidence in

the party before the next presidential elections, but for the moment political instability characterizes the climate.

The leading figure of the French Right has been Jacques Chirac, the mayor of Paris, who lost the last presidential election to Mitterrand but is so firmly entrenched in the Hotel de Ville he may hold the job of mayor well into the next century. The Right, however, is suffering from internal arguments between the two major parties, Chirac's RPR and the more centralist UDF.

There are always extremes in French politics, too, which at least keeps things interesting. On the extreme Right is the *Front National*, the nationalistic, xenophobic party led by Jean-Marie Le Pen, a somewhat loutish and loud politician who has been charged with being racist and anti-semitic. Although not previously seen as a serious force on the national scene, Le Pen and his party have managed to continue to win significant percentages of the local and regional vote in various areas across the country, totalling over 18% in several regions in 1992 and winning outright in Right Wing pockets. The most successful political cards they play deal with crime and violence and fear of immigrants, especially Africans and Arabs. Le Pen's 50 Measures to deal with the foreigners in France was enough to send chills down many backs.

On the other extreme is the French Communist Party, the PCF, led for years by the aging party boss Georges Marchais. From the 1950s through the 70s, the French Communists were a significant force in national and local politics. During the years of the Nazi occupation of France (1940-1944), the Communists were especially active members of the French Resistence, and much of their popularity is founded on their exploits during this period. They have also been, historically, the party of the worker and the immigrant, and have always been good at grass roots political organization. In recent years, though, the PCF has lost a large percentage of its electorate, and the party has been seriously weakened, not least because under Marchais, the French Communists have closely, even slavishly followed the Moscow party line, and have thus been branded as "Stalinist," a different position in today's politically volatile world.

Labor unions in France have been strong since the end of the Second World War. It is rare to go more than six months without strikes at one or another of the public services, such as transportation, postal or civil service, and rarer still to go through the Spring without at least one major march through the streets of Paris by one or several of the major unions, the CGT (the Communist-led union), the CFDT (Left, more Socialist-oriented) or the FO (relatively independent). The right to strike is fundamental to the French conception of the relationship between workers and management in a democracy, and there is surprisingly little serious grumbling by the general public when the Métro or railways are shut down because of strike. General strikes are always announced, so if you live on a major avenue where the *grévistes* ('strikers') will be marching, you would be wise to not be at home that day.

French Press

The newspapers in France follow the general political divisions. The best and most respected is *Le Monde*, which is slightly Left of center, and the closest one can come to the unattainable goal of objectivity in the French press. Its tone is authoritative, intelligent and serious, and it has sometimes been called the best newspaper in the world. Further to the Left is the younger and more irreverent daily, *Libération*, which features some remarkable good cultural coverage and the occasional investigative piece. The two big newspapers of the Right are the morning daily *Le Figaro*, and its evening sister, *France Soir*, both owned by the same newspaper magnate, Robert Hersant. *Le Figaro* has softened its aggressive political tone in recent years, and has been hoping to gain more readers among the younger, upwardly mobile set. Its classified ads are the best and most complete. *Le Parisien* is a relatively neutral daily newspaper, politically, and looks something like *USA Today*, with its color photos.

A new addition to the French press scene is *Courrier International*, a weekly composite of articles, commentary, and car-toons from the world press, translated into French.

The Spoken Word

Speaking the language is absolutely essential and clearly one of the most significant prerequisites for participating in the life of the society that surrounds you. And in France this is particularly true. So much of French culture and so many French attitudes are present in the language—the verbal and facial gestures, the syntax, the vocabulary, the role of dialogue. You may find it difficult at first, especially when you realize that what you say and what you mean may not be the same thing. You may feel a sense of loss in that expressing yourself in another language means losing the comfort of the personality through which you have learned to define yourself. But making the effort will pay off in ways that are incalculably enriching—learning French will open your eyes to a different way of thinking and living in the world, and enable you to share the concerns and feelings of the French.

The French in general like to talk, and the language in all its richness gains much of its melodic quality from the long and circular phrases needed to express what could be said in a word or two in English or German. This love of words and dialogue, though, is reserved for specific places and contexts...the café, the dinner table, the *table ronde*, the conference. You might notice that people don't talk very loudly in subways, buses, streets or public places. This comes from the French distinction between public and private life. Personal life is private and is handled discretely. The French will not openly talk about or be overheard discussing family matters, emotions, or money. With this silent backdrop it's not surprising that tourists seem remarkably loud and obnoxious.

On the other hand, the French can be highly vocal and overt when in the public mode—partaking in a *débat* (debate), *manifestation* (demonstration), or *grève* (strike), for example—and these are regular institutions in Parisian life. French intellectual life, which often carries over into the popular culture, tends to be characterized by obsessive analysis and verbal gymnastics. This is a phenomenon that applies mostly to political, social, and social issues as opposed to personal or emotional ones. Very often, films shown on television are preceded and followed by a panel discussion or debate. Such was even the case recently with the popular Spielberg film, *ET.*

The Written Word

The French attention to form is primordial. When it comes to written French there are no short cuts; you must abide by the set forms for addressing someone or some problem, even in the most banal circumstances. Salutations and forms of *politesse* (politeness) may strike you as long-winded and even hypocritical but their absence may very well be read as an insult. The best bet here is to memorize one of the following and use it to close all your letters of official or administrative nature. Otherwise, purchase a small and inexpensive book called *La correspondance pratique* by Jean-Yves Dournon (Livre de Poche) which, although a bit dated, provides models for all necessary forms of correspon-dence. If you violate these rules, be prepared to be judged poorly.

For formal letters addressed to someone you don't know well, here are three polite but neutral ways to close, roughly equivalent to the English sincerely yours; yours very truly, or yours truly. Remember that *Monsieur* can be changed to *Madame*. When you're not sure, it's best to write *Madame, Monsieur,* instead of the more traditional *Messieurs,* which is now not highly appreciated by some women.

—*Je vous prie de recevoir, Monsieur, l'assurance de mes sentiments distingués.*
—*Veuillez croire, Monsieur, en l'expression de mes sentiments les meilleurs.*
In writing to a "superior" (i.e. cover letters to possible employers, etc):
—*Veuillez agréer, Monsieur, l'expression de ma respectueuse considération.*
For friends and parents:
N'oublie pas d'embrasser Jeanine pour moi.
Meilleurs/Affectueux souvenirs
Amicalement
Bien cordialement à vous/toi
Grosses bises!
Salut!

Note: The French have a high regard for the handwritten letter. In France you are judged by your handwriting (See graphology chapter in Working in France). Telephone skills tend to be less than proficient, spotty at best, but the way the hand constructs words on a page in even the individual with the most basic level of education is taken seriously. And the skills are surprisingly high. The handwriting you may find difficult to decipher at first, but this is no fault of the writer (See Handwriting). Even the occasional clochard (beggar) or down and out street person in the subway station or along the street often takes the trouble to write out his or her story in chalk on the sidewalk or on a piece of cardboard. "I am 56 years old, unemployed, recently released from the hospital. Can't you help me?" Or the more direct and classic: *"J'ai faim. S.V.P."* When applying for a job or responding to a classified ad, it is always appropriate to reply with a handwritten letter, neatly formulated, beginning with your name and address, the city you're writing from and the date. All documents and contracts require that you close with *"Lu et approuvé"* in your handwriting, followed by the date and your signature.

Handwriting is often analyzed professionally as an indicator of character and stability. Often the most inoffensive and slightest error will provoke the average French person to start all over. Don't send messy letters.

The letter plays an important role in France for a number of historic reasons. Whereas Americans often prefer the quickness and effectiveness of a telephone call, the French opt for the *courrier* (correspondence) especially in business, financial, and official matters. A letter creates a trace or proof of the exchange and everything done in France must be backed up by a signed piece of paper, as you will soon learn (if you haven't already). The French are *méfiant* (distrustful) of the spoken word, banking everything on the signed contract,

Sample of French Handwriting

63

whereas the English sense of honor relies deeply on the spoken word and the handshake; the Gentleman's Agreement. So don't be overly casual when leaving a note for even the gas company, let alone your banker or the owner of the apartment you are renting. And, yes, penmanship counts a lot.

The typewriter kind of got skipped over in the history of French communications. The French jumped from the handwritten page and carbon paper to the computer. Many young people in Paris own personal computers, whereas the typewriter has been a far rarer item in the French household. Not surprisingly, most French students cannot type and those who study at North American universities or business schools complain bitterly when required to type academic papers. French university professors never require that papers be typed.

"ça va"

Even if it was only French 100 or some light-weight course in rudimentary *français* at night or summer school, chances have it that you probably know at least that one great French catch-all: *"Comment allez-vous?"* or its familiar counterpart *"Comment ça va?* (How goes it?) simplified as *ça va?* (It goes?). But, did anyone tell you that you can't just prance down the *pâté de maisons* (block) and sputter to complete strangers, *ça va?* You just can't ask any random person how he or she is doing, the way you'd toss into the air a friendly or mechanical "Hi!" "Howdy!" "What's up?" "What's happening?" or "How ya doin?" Make eye contact and ask a passerby how he or she is doing and in most cases the person will look behind him to see if you're addressing someone else, ignore you totally, or stop in his tracks with a perplexed glaze on his face, lower lip pursed, and inquire: *On se connaît?* Have we met? Do we know each other?

The textbooks back home often forget in their first lessons on "Greetings" to discuss language as a function of culture. And face it, understanding a culture foreign to your own is precisely what's needed to assure a rewarding and meaningful *séjour* (stay) in your new, albeit temporary, country. The more you absorb about the social relations and interactions of the French and the cultural underpinnings of French society the more you will not only enjoy being part of Parisian life but begin to comprehend better your own culture and language. The world doesn't grow, but your conception of it does. So, if you're ignored on Day One or you let yourself be influenced by the derogatory comments of cursory travelers who lambast the French for alleged rudeness, arrogance, or chilliness, you're missing the much larger point and only widening cultural barriers.

A good rule of thumb is to suspend all judgments for at least a month! Admittedly, there is a certain formality and pace of interchange deeply engrained in French culture (as witnessed in both verbal and written expression) that is at first going to separate the friendly and direct North American from his new environs. This is par for the course. It shouldn't be distressing; it's interesting! As North American or non-French students or newly-arrived residents in Paris, an openness to your surroundings in a French—not North American—context will be your passport to an enriching and pleasurable time.

The two of the main exchanges with the familiar *ça va* reveal several important attitudes.
–*Ça va?* the question, literally meaning How goes it?, is often answered with itself, *Ça va!* meaning "It goes."

This makes for easy language learning, but what in fact does it mean? Everything lies in the intonation of the response. *Ça*

va could reflect a great enthusiasm for life, a pang of desperate depression, or a plain moment of daily mediocrity. The nuances abound. So learn to listen for them and use them yourself. These are rich words.
–*Ça va?* or the formal *Comment allez-vous?* are often answered directly with the question *Et vous?* (And you?)

The first few times you get involved in this interchange you are liable to get annoyed. Don't ignore me, that's not an answer, you'll want to complain. The repetition of the answer for the question simply demonstrates the French love of form. It's the asking of the question that counts, not the answer. There is nothing I can do if you aren't doing well; the best I can do is to ask you how you're doing. Soon, you'll see that this little tidbit of dialogue is really very adorable and convenient.

Figuring out how French society works and how its people interact will undoubtedly take a fair amount of time. Think about your understanding of the society you live in—all those cumulative years spent learning to participate in a system with its multitude of layers of unspoken rules, codes and underlying assumptions. With an open mind you will broaden your knowledge of both French society and your own; you'll get sharper in knowing what people are saying when they're not talking.

Greetings - *Les Bises*
When greeting someone you know, the French shake hands and/or give a quick succession of impersonal kisses on alternating cheeks called *les bises*. There are lots of nuances here that only experience can sort out, but here are a few. Some people give two kisses, some three, and others four. If there are six people in the room and you give four bises each, that calls for a lot of kissing. Remember this is just a form of saying *bonjour*. What's interesting to note here is that the French are used to and comfortable with close personal contact. They are not bothered by human proximity or touching. They don't require the same distance Anglo-saxons insist upon when talking. So get used to *les bises*. Even French people have cute little moments when two people are unsure if it'll be two, three, or four bises. Two is the most common, four is more classical; three is for those who want to be a bit different without abandoning tradition. People from the south of France and the younger generation tend to kiss more. *Les bises* are usually for men and women or women and women, but good male friends *font les bises* also. Start on the left cheek and don't really kiss, just touch cheeks and steer your lips inwards.

Handshakes are required particularly when men greet each other equally for the first time or the zillionth time. When you arrive at work, for example, you shake your co-workers' hand and say *bonjour*. It may seem highly repetitious, but it's a very pleasant way for people to acknowledge each other. Similarly, the handshake and *les bises* are repeated when leaving.

Going Out

The French almost always organize their social lives around a meal. This is true also for a lot of professional and commercial activities. So count on a long and languorous dinner if you get asked out by a French person. If you're doing the asking, you should probably count on a meal too, although your guest might be interested in or impressed by a meal indigenous to your culture. It's very common to meet someone at a café at 20h or 20h30, have an *apéritif* (a kir or a glass of wine) and then proceed to dinner somewhere. Learn by heart the names of a few cafés that you like and that are convenient, so you'll be able to suggest a meeting point. Remember that usually, even among young people, the person who does the inviting also pays for the dinner. For the French this is highly normal. Going "Dutch" is foreign. Often the guest will offer to pay the next time. *Je t'invite la prochaine fois.* You will almost never see French people dividing up a bill at the table. Sometimes they'll fight over who will pay, each wanting to pay, but the idea of determining who ordered what and the "did you have wine?" kind of thing is alien, and even distasteful. So be forewarned. Money still has a vulgar connotation.

The French also go to the cinema a lot (see Cinema).

If you're invited to someone's house in the evening, it's almost always going to be for dinner, unless it has been clearly stated otherwise. It's always appropriate to bring something, usually a good bottle of wine— never a *vin de table* (table wine) or inexpensive unknown wine (see Wine). A well-wrapped bouquet of flowers, not the plain ones sold in the Métro, is always appreciated. But don't show up empty-handed. Dress slightly better than you think is appropriate. The French, even young people and students, tend to dress well when going out socially. Only in the last five years or so have people dared to go out in the streets in sweatpants and sweatshirts, even for food shopping, etc.

Sexuality

It's always very difficult and dangerous to generalize about how people think and act. In the area of sex this is particularly so, but a few comments might be useful. Young French women, although not prudish, can often be highly sentimental. The men, although not extremely macho, tend to embrace a fair amount of Latin attitudes. The French concept of flirting—with the intention of "picking up" someone, is called *draguer* (to drag). This is actually closer to "chatting up" than "picking up." It has a million variations and nuances and can be either flattering or annoying. Paris is the northern edge of the Latin spirit. Male attitudes in general aren't as obviously macho as in Spain or Italy, but there are still attitudes here that might seem sexist to you. (73% of French married men, a recent survey found, have mistresses or extra-marital affairs, whereas 38% of married women have extra-marital lovers.)

On the whole, it is fair to say, in any case, that the French are less inhibited or up-tight and have less hang-ups about sex, nudity and human functions than Anglo-saxons, for instance. Some French men, though, have pre-conceived notions about North American women, especially Californians, in terms of accessibility, "openness," "wildness." These can be reenforced unknowingly by the fact that North Americans do tend to be publicly more expressive and open.

The French don't judge public officials by their private lives, and view sex scandals (like the one which ruined Gary Hart's political career) as silly and typically American in their Puritan values.

The movement for safe sex in France didn't get much further at first than the sensuous television ads for the use of condoms. The French approach was not to scare the public with AIDS (SIDA) but to convey the positive message that sex with condoms is beautiful and exciting, and thus an advantage. The AIDS situation in France is much like in any western country today. Free public health centers provide confidential *depistages* (AIDS tests) and accurate information. (See Health). Generally, there are less stigmas regarding health, sexuality, and illness in France than in Anglo-saxon culture, but on the whole the situation isn't all that different.

The gay and lesbian communities in Paris, although more open and public now than ten years ago, are still somewhat discreet. On the rue Vielle du Temple in the Marais a number of busy, gay night spots and bookstores can be found. The gay community has a Paris magazine called *Gai Pied Hebdo*, 45 rue Sedaine, 75011 PARIS, Tel: 43.57.52.05 (which also has an *SOS Ecoute Gai* phone line,

Tel: 48.06.19.11). There are also several Minitel services catering to the gay community.

On the whole, you will see a general lack of puritanical attitudes. The French are quite comfortable with nudity and all that concerns the human body. The same ad in a London subway station with a clothed woman would show her topless in Paris. Topless advertising is not considered sexist by either women or men. *C'est beau* or *c'est normal*. Toplessness isn't even really considered nudity. In some boutiques, you may see women try on blouses without stepping into a changing room or change from their swimsuit into street clothes on the beach.

The rue Saint Denis traditionally has been the main prostitution street in Paris. Women stand out by their doors openly and, for the most part, unharassed day and night. Around 16h it's interesting to observe the undisturbed mixture of prostitutes coming out to work and school kids returning from school. This is indicative of a larger tolerance. Other areas of dense prostitution have traditionally included the Bois de Boulogne, where prostitutes and dazzling Brasilian transvestites line the roadways peddling their wares to passing motorists, as well as all the major boulevards near the *portes de Paris*. Due to the AIDS situation, the Bois has now been shut down to vehicular traffic at night. Prostitution is not considered an illegal activity but soliciting business in an aggressive manner is, so you won't see pimps doing this for the girls. The area around Métros Blanche and Clichy are also filled with prostitutes and pornography, with the rue Fontaine being noted for its transvestites.

Drinking

The legal drinking age is 16 years of age. But there is essentially no enforcement of this law. You'll never get "carded" or turned away in a café, bar or liquor store. You can buy whiskey along with your daily groceries in supermarkets, local shops, and even gas stations. As a positive consequence, public drunkenness by rowdy youths is not very prevalent. It has been estimated that the average French person over 20 years old consumes an average of 53 grams (1.87 ounces) of pure alcohol per day, making him a participant in an impressive percentage: the French remain the world's heaviest consumers of alcohol per capita after the Luxembourgeois. Wine is still served with both lunch and dinner in many families, but the meal is no longer considered incomplete without it. (see Wine). Alcoholism in France is responsible for 17,000 deaths a year, caused more by cheap red wine than hard alcohol, and it is a phenomenon which is vastly more common in rural and slum areas.

Smoking

A very large portion of French society smokes cigarettes. Consciousness is changing but very slowly. Restaurants still readily accept smoking at all tables, although this is scheduled to charge soon with new legislation regulating all public places. Whether the public abides and managers enforce the new laws remain to be seen. For the moment, only McDonald's and a select few have created Non-Smoking sections. So, if you're intolerant of smokers, be warned. Similarly, for those of you who smoke, you'll not experience the ostracism that occurs to smokers in North America. If you ask others to put out their cigarettes or to re-direct the smoke elsewhere, be prepared for some looks and gestures of displeasure.

Cigarettes can only be purchased in a *tabac*. They are not available in drug stores, gas stations or department stores. Some cafés sell cigarettes as a service to their customers. They will cost about 15 FF a pack in the cafés, 5 to 8 francs more than at the *tabacs*.

Although smoking habits are beginning to change in Paris and new laws limiting public smoking and tabacco advertising are being enacted, the pace belongs to an *escargot*. If you are a non-smoker, as many of you undoubtedly are, be prepared for a lot of smoke and an overall indifference to the rights of non-smokers. If the smoke has a pungent, unfamiliar odor this is because in France hard-core smokers consume the classic, blue packed and filterless Gauloises or Gitanes, made of *blonde*, untoasted tobacco. Also, a number of people roll their own cigarettes. It's cheaper.

Drugs

Drug possession is a serious offense in France, and laws are particularly hard on foreigners. Drug use isn't nearly as much of a social problem, though, as it is in the United States, England, Germany, or Holland. Nor has it resulted in deperate and wide spread urban violence as is true elsewhere. Until recently, there was a cinema in Paris where it was understood that marijuana smokers would not be bothered. And late at night in the Métro as well as in certain bars and clubs a whiff or two of the popular hash and tobacco mixture may come your way. But attention! If you want to remain in France without problems, think twice before breaking the law. It is strictly ill-advised to buy drugs from anyone on the street, especially near Beaubourg or the Gare Montparnasse as the police, who are often undercover and have the right to frisk anyone at any time, are omnipresent. Crossing international borders is of course particularly unwise, especially traveling from any island of southern latitude or returning from Amsterdam, where charter buses are often searched with the aid of police dogs.

Even at parties, smoking hash—marijuana is nearly impossible to find—can be met with disapproval. Cocaine use is not nearly as wide-spread as in North America.and in general, French youths seem to feel less pressured to spend time, energy and money on socially rebellious activities and habits.

Parties

Even among young people parties are rarely given without a specific occasion to celebrate. A party can be called a *fête, une soirée* or *une boum*. A *fête* is usually a celebration like a birthday or graduation. A *soirée* is a civilized evening party with not necessarily a lot of people. *Une boum* tends to be larger and louder, and usually reserved for the high school crowd. Every city, however, has its limits for noise and rowdiness: for week-nights, Parisian law requires that all noise stop after 22h (1h for weekends), but once or twice a year, weekend festivities are allowed to go all night—as long as you inform the local police station and the neighbors as far in advance as possible. On weekdays, the police will come banging on the door if you exceed the 22h code. A surefire strategy to avoid problems with the neighbors is to start the party in the early afternoon, and have it wind down of course before 22h. Not very practical, admittedly. In any case, be very sensitive about loud noises, blasting stereos, etc. in public places in Paris; rowdy partying is not part of the French version of decadence and hedonism. They have their own which you'll have to discover on your own.

A n i m a l s   &   S o c i e t y
The French are highly indulgent with animals, children and senior citizens. However, they clearly have a love affair with dogs. Paris alone counts 500,000 dogs, or 4760 dogs per square kilometer, which by far outnumbers the number of children. The colloquial French equivalent of "pooch" is *toutou*, and *minou* for "kitty." The most popular dog name in France is Rex. Supermarkets all sell fresh cuts of meats and animal organs, like spleens, especially for your pets. French dog owners are less obsessed with the macho image of "all-meat" for their hounds; they feed their dogs well balanced meals which include lots of vegetables. On the other hand, your average citizen is likely to offer your over-weight beagle a few sugar cubes at the zinc bar of your local café. *Vive la contradiction!*

Dogs are allowed in restaurants and most public places, although they must be leashed in parks and "bagged" in the Métro and on trains. For an assortment of dog bags, go to Samaritaine. As long as you are not leasing a furnished apartment for a short period of time, there is no problem renting apartments if you have pets. No extra fees. There are animal *auberges* for vacation time, and numerous chic dog salons, where the poodles recline on mock Louis XIV fauteuils. There are several taxi services for pets, as well as pet ambulances.

On the rue Mâitre Albert, in the 5e, there is an animal *dispensaire* for inexpensive veterinary services. Otherwise, call: *SOS Véterinaires*, Tel: 48.32.93.30 This recording gives the telephone numbers for Paris and the suburbs where emergency veterinary care can be obtained. The French S.P.A. shelters homeless pets, many of which are abandoned along the autoroutes during vacation times. Beware—some are not healthy and not vaccinated.

Société Protectrice des Animaux
La Boutique SPA
BP 44
95333 DOMONT Cedex

It is relatively easy to bring dogs and cats into France. Although a valid health certificate, showing a recent rabies vaccination, is required, chances are you won't even have to show it at the airport when you arrive, but you may have you show it when you leave the country. But it's ill-advised to arrive without one. Technically, animals without proper certification can be deported or destroyed! If you're planning to pass through or visit the U.K. with a pet, be advised that a strict, six-month quarantine is enforced for animals, vaccinated or not! This can be a terribly cruel and costly surprise, so inquire first if you have any doubts. Pets can travel on international airlines, in approved kennel cages, for the price of a piece of extra baggage. (The only airlines, by the way, that charges nothing for kennels is Air France.) On regularly scheduled flights, animals travel in the hold of the plane in temperature-controlled and well-lit storage areas. Be wary of charters.

There are some regulations though that should be carefully noted. Dogs under the age of three months old and cats under six weeks are prohibited from international travel. You cannot bring more than three animals at one time, only one of which can be a puppy or a kitten. Rabies vaccination certificates must state that the vaccine had been administered more than 30 days and less than one year prior to the date of departure. Birds are limited to two psittacidaes and ten birds of small species with health certificates issued within five days of departure. All other animals require special import permits from the Ministry of Agriculture. Fortunately, the bottom line is that living and traveling in France with pets generally poses few problems, and can even be an easy and agreeable way to make acquaintences quickly.

The Streets
It should be pointed out that the infamous problem of *un*curbed dogs, which had given Paris a bad name for many years, has been somewhat rectified. Although the law states that you have to curb your dog, directing him to do his *besoins* (needs) in the *caniveau* (gutter) off the curb—and there are even cute graphic reminders painted onto certain sidewalks—you used to have to hop-skip-and-jump to

avoid landing in a rude pile. The city has recently launched a clever and graphically-pleasing poster campaign designed by famed-illustrator Sempé to remind dog owners of their civic responsibilities. Now, in the nicer neighborhoods at least, the city cleans up with the use of a technician with a green designer suit on a converted motorcycle equipped with a high-powered vacuum cleaner. Much of the eye-sore has been aspirated away. As of October 1991, there is a new law that allows you to be fined on the spot for not curbing your dog.

While on the subject, Paris has other ways of keeping itself clean. You may wonder why water gushes out of sewers and runs through the gutters so often—even when it's not been raining. Paris street cleaners, mostly Africans in green municipal jump suits, open valves of clean, but undrinkable water and direct the flow up or down street, by positioning soggy bolts of tied-up cloth. Then they sweep with their green plastic-branched brooms, loose papers, *mégots* (cigarette butts), trash and unclaimed dog-doo into the moving stream, which drains into the city sewers and eventually into the Seine system for recycling. You can visit the impressive sewers, *Les Egouts de Paris*, daily at Pont de l'Alma in the 7e. Every address in Paris has an equivalent one underground. This complex, unlit network was extensively used by Resistance fighters during the Nazi Occupation.

For humans, Paris streets are equipped with automatic, self-disinfecting pay toilets. For two-francs, you gain access to a futuristic compartment whose cleanliness and comfort is guaranteed.

The Métro

The Paris Métro (RATP) has been in existence since the turn of the century. It truly plays an essential role in the life of the city and is filled with its own character, energy, and mythology. The system has 13 lines that reach 322 stations, the newest being La Defence beyond Pont de Neuilly, and the final destination, opposite Vincennes, on the Number 1 line. You can get nearly everywhere in a relatively short period of time for a reasonable price in relative safety and security on the Paris Métro. Don't be afraid of it. At times it gets a bit overcrowded, odoriferous, noisy, and confused, but on the whole the Paris underground subway system is among the best in the world. It'll be one of your greatest resources.

Whether you live in Paris or intend to commute by train from the Paris suburbs, you should purchase a monthly pass, *une carte orange,* which allows unlimited travel within five specific zones. The five circular zones are organized in concentric circles with Paris-proper consisting of zones 1 and 2. The other three zones extend far into the suburbs. A single ride (one yellow—turquoise as of 1992—magnetized ticket) costs 5,50 FF. If not buying the *carte orange* or the weekly equivalent, *coupon jaune* (49 FF), buy a *carnet* (pack of ten individual tickets, for 34,40 FF. This is a substantial savings over the purchase of individual tickets at 5,50 FF. The same card is also valid on Paris buses and *le métro* and on the Regional Express trains (R.E.R.). The *carte orange* costs 190 FF for two zones; three zones costs 247 FF, four zones for 342 FF, and five zones 516 FF. This is a real bargain. Your first time, you need a photograph of yourself, easily obtained from the instant photo booths located in many stations, and the orange card with plastic sleeve that you get at any Métro station ticket window. A yearly *carte orange* ticket *(la carte intégrale)* is also available. You are supposed to carry the magnetized ticket in a little slot in the sleeve and inscribe the number of the card onto the ticket. Failure to do either can cause you a fine upon verification. The same is true for the lack of a picture. The card is strictly for the use of the person whose name and picture appear on the card. Periodically, controllers stake out Métro stations and selected cars, usually at the beginning of the month, when some decide to rough it by not renewing their *carte orange* for the month.

One Métro phenomenon you're likely to observe is gate-hopping. A fair amount of people duck under or jump over the turnstiles either to avoid payment or because they are too lazy to get out their *carte orange.* RATP officials have reduced some of this by installing quick-moving stop gates that make cheating harder. Often people sneak in for free behind someone who has paid. So, if someone pushes in behind you or asks to pass through the turnstile with you, don't be alarmed. If by some odd chance you get caught without a ticket, speak your mother tongue, play dumb and innocent, and when asked for your name and address, remember, you're from Oshkosh. If you *are* fined, though, you may be asked to pay from 85 FF to 230 FF on the spot for jumping over, sliding under, or riding without a valid ticket. If you cannot pay or refuse to pay immediately, the controller will write you a ticket (PV, *proces verbal)*, for which there is of course a supplementary fine. You are supposed to send in the payment. A commonly controlled station is Franklin D. Roosevelt on the *Champs-Elysées* where controllers hide behind the *guichet* booth waiting for cheaters.

Be aware of the "last Métro" phenomenon. For a city the size and complexity of Paris, it is surprising that the métro doesn't remain open all night. The Métro runs till about 0h50, and you must keep this in mind if you want to get home the easiest and cheapest way. Be careful about catching the Métro on one line but missing your transfer. If you miss the last Métro you'll have to either find a taxi, walk, "stay over" or, when completely desperate, sleep in a Métro station (which is funky but not recommended, but tolerated) until the first train at 5h45. The disco scene revolves around the first Métro concept. Otherwise, you can try the *Noctambus* (see Buses).

How to Use the Métro
The Métro is easy to use, once you've mastered the symbols employed to indicate exits, transfers, and train directions. First of all, Métro lines are named after their end points, i.e. the Porte de Clignancourt line is called *Direction Porte de Clignancourt;* and the same line traveling in the opposite direction is called *Direction Porte d'Orléans*. Naturally, it serves all the stations in between. Signs indicating *direction* are white. For transferring from one line to another, orange signs on the *quai* (platform) marked *correspondance* indicate the path to other *quais* and other *directions*. You can usually switch to a métro heading the opposite direction for free, though in some smaller stations there are separate turnstiles. Blue signs marked *sortie* point you in the direction of the exit, and often you'll have a choice of exits, all emerging onto different streets or different sides of the street. When meeting friends at a métro station, make sure to specify which exit and whether you will meet underground or above ground. In every big station, you will find a *plan du quartier* (neighborhood map) on the platform, but all métro stops have maps at the ticket office exit. When with a group, if one of you gets left behind, a good policy is to get off at the next stop and wait for your friend to arrive. Then continue.

The Bus
The sign of a real Parisian is the mastery of the bus system. Many new residents take a long time before attempting to use buses. The Parisian Bus System is excellent, although its efficiency suffers from the generally congested traffic situation. The bus does have the advantage of allowing you to see more of the city than traveling underground by Métro. And there are still some lines with buses that have open, trolley-like back sections. Aside from the pollution, these are fun. *Paris par arrondissements* has maps of individual bus routes, otherwise stops are indicated on maps inside the Métro, at bus stops, and in large black letters on the side of each bus. Buses use the same tickets as the Métro, which are cancelled in the machine located at the front of the bus.

Don't cancel your *carte orange!* Just flash it by the driver. The driver also sells individual tickets which must be punched (*oblitéré*) upon boarding and are only good on the bus. If you do not have a *carte orange*, traveling long distances on the bus is more expensive, because you must buy a new ticket for every *section* through which you travel. There are about six or seven *sections* for a bus going from one side of Paris to the other, of which you can see clearly indicated on the maps at bus stops and inside the bus. When standing at a bus stop, signal the driver if you want to be picked up. Inside the bus, there are red stop request buttons located on the aisle posts. Several lines have incorporated new vehicles which you can enter via the middle doors without showing your card to the driver.

Most buses, whose numbers are indicated at stops by black numbers on a white circle, run every day of the year from about 5h30-0h30. Buses whose emblem is a white number on a black circle generally run only from about 6h00-20h30 Monday through Saturday except holidays.

When the number on the front of the bus has a slash through it, the bus runs through only half of the route. This short range service usually happens only at rush hours and on certain routes. If you're a late nighter, familiarize yourself with the Noctambuses which leave the Châtelet-Hôtel de Ville area (avenue Victoria) every hour from 1h30-5h30 for 15 FF and traverse Paris in every direction. The mob scene to get on these can be intimidating, but the service is safe and reliable. Here's a complete list of night buses, all marked with the sign of a black owl in a yellow circle:

A:	Pont de Neuilly
B:	Levallois Mairie
C:	Clichy Mairie
D:	Saint Ouen Mairie
E:	Pantin Eglise
F:	Les Lilas Mairie
G:	Montreuil Mairie
H:	Vincennes Château
J:	Porte d'Orléans
R:	Rungis Marée

For more information contact:
RATP Info
53ter, quai des Grands Augustins
75006 PARIS
Tel: 40.46.41.41

Taxis

In general, Paris taxis are readily available and reasonably priced. However, finding a taxi in Paris is different from finding one in, for example, New York. Paris taxi drivers frequently do not feel obliged to stop for you if they don't have a passenger. When you do get them to stop, if your destination doesn't appeal to the driver, he will tell you so and drive off. Although relatively orderly, taxi stands can be competitive scenes—stand your ground. When ordering a taxi between 18h-21h, don't be surprised to find 20 or 30 FF already on the meter. French taxis, when ordered, start counting from the moment they set out to fetch you. It's always a better idea to find the number of the taxi stand closest to where you live, work, or usually need taxis. The system of lit bulbs on the roof of txis indicates if the taxi is in service, is already carrying a fare, or is free. Hailing a cab mid-block is practically unheard of.

Taxi Stands By Arrondissement

• 1° Métro Concorde	42.61.67.60
• 1° Pl Châtelet	42.33.20.99
• 1° Pl André Malraux	42.60.61.40
• 2° Place des Victoires	42.33.12.94
• 2° Pl de l'Opéra	47.42.75.75
• 2° 19 bd St. Denis	42.36.93.55
• 3° rue Bretagne, St. Denis	42.78.00.00
• 4° Métro rue Rambuteau	42.72.00.00
• 4° Métro St. Paul, rue de Rivoli	48.87.49.39
• 5° Place Maubert	46.34.10.32
• 5° Pont de la Tournelle	43.25.92.99
• 5° Pl des Gobelins	43.31.00.00
• 6° Métro St Germain	42.22.00.00
• 6° Pl Alphonse-Deville	45.48.84.75
• 6° Observatoire	43.54.74.37
• 7° Tour Eiffel	45.55.85.41
• 7° Pl du Palais Bourbon	47.05.03.14
• 7° 27, bd de Latour-Maubourg	45.51.76.76
• 7° Métro Latour-Maubourg	45.55.78.42
• 7° Pl de l'Ecole Militaire	47.05.00.00
• 7° Métro Solferino	45.55.00.00
• 7° Pl Léon-Paul-Fargue	45.67.00.00
• 7° Métro rue du Bac	42.22.49.64
• 8° Pl Rio de Janeiro	45.62.00.00
• 8° Pl St Augustin	47.42.54.73
• 8° Rond-Point des Champs-Elysées	42.56.29.00

- 8° Pl des Ternes — 47.63.00.00
- 9° Square de Montholon — 48.78.00.00
- 9° Métro Richelieu-Drouet — 42.46.00.00
- 10° Métro Goncourt — 42.03.00.00
- 11° Métro Ménilmontant — 43.55.64.00
- 11° Pl de la Nation — 43.73.29.58
- 11° Pl Léon-Blum — 43.79.00.00
- 11° Métro Père-Lachaise — 48.05.92.12
- 12° Pl Félix-Eboué — 43.43.00.00
- 13° Métro Glacière — 45.80.00.00
- 13° Pte d'Italie — 45.86.00.44
- 13° Pl Pinel — 45.86.00.00
- 13° Carrefour Patay-Tolbiac — 45.83.00.00
- 14° 1, av Reille — 45.89.05.71
- 14° Métro Alésia — 45.45.00.00
- 14° Pte d'Orléans — 45.40.52.05
- 14° Pte de Vanves — 45.39.87.33
- 14° Métro Plaisance — 45.41.66.00
- 14° Pl Denfert-Rochereau — 45.35.00.00
- 15° Pont Mirabeau — 45.77.48.00
- 15° Métro Bir Hakeim — 45.79.17.17
- 15° Métro La Motte-Picquet — 45.66.00.00
- 15° Pl de Breteuil — 45.66.70.17
- 15° Mairie annexe du 15° — 48.42.00.00
- 15° Métro Convention — 42.50.00.00
- 15° Pl Charles-Michels — 45.78.20.00
- 15° Pte de Versailles — 48.28.00.00
- 16° Pl Clément-Ader — 45.24.56.17
- 16° Métro Muette — 42.88.00.00
- 16° Pl Jean-Lorrain — 45.27.00.00
- 16° av Victor-Hugo-Etoile — 45.01.85.24
- 16° Métro Porte Dauphine — 45.53.00.00
- 16° Pl de Barcelone — 45.27.11.11
- 16° Gare Henri-Martin — 45.04.00.00
- 16° Pl de la Porte d'Auteuil — 46.51.14.61
- 16° Pl du Trocadéro — 47.27.00.00
- 16° Métro Passy — 45.20.00.00
- 16° Pte Molitor — 46.51.19.19
- 16° Métro Jasmin — 45.25.13.13
- 17° Pl Aimé-Maillard — 46.22.40.70
- 17° Pl du Maréchal-Juin — 42.27.00.00
- 17° Pte de Clichy — 46.27.90.06
- 17° Métro Villiers — 46.22.00.00
- 17° Pte de St-Ouen — 42.63.00.00
- 17° Pl de la République de l'Equateur — 47.66.80.50
- 17° Pl Charles-de-Gaulle — 43.80.01.99
- 17° Pte d'Asnières — 43.80.00.00

Here is a space for you to add your own: _____

France's sophistication in com-munications is impressive. On the whole, you will see that the telecommunications field is one of the most advanced areas of French industry. The Post Office *(La Poste),* formerly the PTT *(Postes Téléphones, Télégraphes)* has been separated admini-stratively from the dynamic and expanding France-Télécom, the nationalized telephone comp-any, in an effort to increase efficiency. France has worked hard to bridge new technology and *la vie quotidienne* (daily life). France-Télécom, has brought the latest technological developments into the home with the Minitel, an on-line computer and screen accessed through the telephone system which is at once a visual tele-phone book, a reservation net-work, a research library, a home shopping tool, a direct means of written communi-cation with other users, and more. Extensive use of the Minitel as a fax, printer, modem, etc. is already in use. Minitels can be obtained free from the local telephone office in your *arrondissement.* (See Minitel).

The Public Telephone Booth (*Cabine téléphonique)*

Over the last several years most public coin-operated phone booths have been replaced with a new type that accepts only micro-chipped cards, called the *Télécarte,* which can be bought in post offices and *tabac,* in units of 50 or 120 for 40 FF and 100 FF respectively. Buy one right away; they're very practical! Plus, it's getting increasingly difficult to find a public phone that takes coins (local calls require a one franc coin).

All Paris and the close suburbs have numbers begin-ning with 4 (the more distant suburbs begin with 3 or 6). Calls to other parts of France require the prefix 16. Inter-national calls must be preceded with 19. In both cases, wait for a second dial tone and then dial your number. On the last remaining coin phones, you'll get a round blinking sign or beep on the phone when your money is about the run out. Shove in more coins—one, two, or five franc pieces are accepted. Otherwise, your *télécarte* will let you speak to anyone in the world as long as you still have units left on the card.

In the Sixties and Seventies, broken phones were occasionally discovered which allowed free unlimited international calls to go through undetected. When the word got around, lines would form with foreign students at all hours of the night to call families and friends around the world at no charge. These wonderful little finds have all but disappeared with the new telephone card. The advantage of the card is that there is no money to deal with. Each unit costs 73 *centimes* and units are deducted electronically from the micro-chip *(puce)* of the card automatically at a rate which depends on where and when you're calling. One minute to the United States or Canada costs about 15 FF. But this depends on the time of day and day of the week. Rates in France have traditionally been rather high, but France-Télécom has made great efforts to both increase service and cut rates. Nonetheless, if you get cut off or have disturbing interference on the line, don't count on asking the operator for credit. It's not an option. To use *télécarte* phones, pick up the receiver, slide in the card, arrow facing forward, close the *volet* (sliding mechanism), wait for a dial tone, and make your call. After hanging up wait about five seconds; the *volet* will open and a beep will sound, reminding

you not to forget your card. Note that these cards have become collectors items in France much like baseball cards in America. The card with the Van Gogh portrait is very popular as are the cards commemorating the 1992 winter Olympics in Albertville.

The chart on the following page indicates national and international telephone dialing codes.

Calling the French provinces from Paris:
Dial 16, wait for the tone, dial the number.

Calling between the provinces:
Dial the number; no 16 needed.

Calling the Paris area from the provinces:
Dial 16, wait for the tone, dial 1, and then the number.

Making an international call from anywhere in France:
Dial 19, wait for the tone, dial the country code, the city code and the number. To call the U.S. collect or with an AT&T calling card, after 19 dial 0011 to get an AT&T operator. The code for MCI from France is: (19) 0019 then wait for operator. The code for Sprint is: (19) 0087 then wait for operator. Collect calls can be made with any of these three services. France-Télécom offers its own *Carte Pastel* for direct dialing France from overseas or nationally.

Getting international information:
Dial 19, wait for the tone, dial 33-12 and the country code.

Lodging complaints:
Dial 13.

International Country Codes

Afghanistan: 93	Bermuda: 1809
Albania: 355	Burma: 95
Algeria: 213	Bolivia: 591
American Virgin Islands: 1809	Botswana: 267
Angola: 244	Brazil: 55
Antilles: 599	British Virgin Islands: 1809
Argentina: 54	Brunei: 673
Australia: 61	Bulgaria: 359
Austria: 43	Burkina Faso: 226
Azores: 351	Burundi: 257
Bahamas: 1809	Cameroon: 237
Bahrain: 973	Canada: 1
Bangladesh: 880	Cap Vert: 238
Belgium: 32	Cayman Islands: 1809
Belize: 501	Central African Republic: 236
Benin: 229	Chad: 235

Chile: 56
China: 86
Cyprus: 357
Colombia: 57
Comores: 269
Congo: 242
Cook: 682
Costa Rica: 506
Cuba: 53
Czechoslovakia: 42
Denmark: 45
Djibouti: 253
Dominican Republic: 1809
Egypt: 20
El Salvador: 503
Ecuador: 593
Ethiopia: 251
Falkland Islands: 500
Faroe Islands: 298
Fiji: 679
Finland: 358
Gabon: 241
Gambia: 220
Germany (East): 37
Ghana: 238
Gibraltar: 35
Greece: 30
Grenada: 1809
Greenland: 299
Guadeloupe: 590
Guam: 671
Guatemala: 502
Guinea: 224
Guinea Bissau: 245
Guinea Equatorial: 240
Guyana: 592
Haiti: 509
Hawaii: 1808
Honduras: 504

Hong Kong: 852
Hungary: 36
India: 91
Indonesia: 62
Iraq: 964
Iran: 98
Ireland: 353
Iceland: 354
Israel: 972
Italy: 39
Ivory Coast: 225
Jamaica: 1809
Japan: 81
Jordan: 962
Kenya: 254
Korea: 82
Kuwait: 965
Laos: 856
Lesotho: 266
Lebanon: 961
Liberia: 231
Libya: 218
Liechtenstein: 41
Luxembourg: 352
Martinique: 596
Macao: 853
Madagascar: 261
Madeira: 351
Malaysia: 60
Malawi: 265
Maldives: 960
Mali: 223
Malta: 356
Mauritius Island: 230
Mauritanie: 222
Mexico: 52
Mongolia: 976
Montserrat: 1809
Monaco: 93

Morocco: 212
Mozambique: 258
Namibia: 264
Nauru Islands: 674
Nepal: 977
Netherlands: 31
New Zealand: 64
Nicaragua: 505
Nieves: 1
Niger: 227
Nigeria: 234
Norfolk Island: 6723
Norway: 47
Oman: 968
Uganda: 256
Pakistan: 92
Panama: 507
Papua/New Guinea: 675
Paraguay: 595
Peru: 51
Phillipines: 63
Poland: 48
Portugal: 351
Puerto Rico: 1809
Qatar: 974
Romania: 40
Rwanda: 250
Samoa US: 684
Samoa Western: 685
Sao Tome e Principe: 239
San Marino: 39
St Vincent: 1809
St Kitts: 1809
St Helene and Ascension: 247
St Lucia: 1809
Saudi Arabia: 966
Senegal: 221
Seychelles: 248

Sierra Leone: 232
Singapore: 65
Somalia: 252
Solomon Islands: 677
South Africa: 27
Spain: 34
Sri Lanka: 94
Sudan: 249
Surinam: 597
Sweden: 46
Swaziland: 268
Switzerland: 41
Syria: 963
Taiwan: 886
Tanzania: 255
Thailand: 66
Togo: 228
Tonga: 676
Trinidad and Tobago: 1809
Tunisia: 216
Turks and Caicos Islands: 1809
Turkey: 90
United Arab Emirates: 971
United Kingdom: 44
Uruguay: 598
U.S.S.R: 7
U.S.A.: 1
Vanauatu: 678
Vatican City: 39
Venezuela: 58
Vietnam: 84
West Germany: 49
Yemen: 969
Yugoslavia: 38
Zaire: 243
Zambia: 260
Zimbabwe: 263

Telephone Skills in French

Those first few calls can be traumatic. It's especially difficult to integrate your French into dialogue when you cannot see the other person and can't rely on gestures. Here are a few simple telephone dialogue patterns for the uninitiated:

How to ask for someone:
- *Bonjour, est-ce que je peux parler avec...?* (Hello, can I speak with...?)
- *Bonjour, puis-je parler avec..?* (Hello, may I speak with...?)
- *Bonjour, est-ce Monsieur* (Mademoiselle, Madame) *...est là?* (Hello, is...there?)

Answering the telephone:
- *Allô.* (Hello.)
- *Ne quittez pas.* (Don't hang up, or, hang on.)
- *Il/Elle n'est pas là.* (He/she is not here.)
- *Vous vous êtes trompé de numéro.* (You have the wrong number.)
- *Qui est à l'appareil?* (Who's calling?)
- *Est-ce que je peux laisser un message?* (Can I leave a message?)
- *C'est* (your name) *à l'appareil.* (It's...calling.)
- *Comment ça s'écrit?* (How is that spelled?)
- *Je suis desolé(e).* (I'm sorry.)
- *Répétez, s'il vous plaît.* (Please repeat that.)
- *Lentement, s'il vous plaît.* (Slowly, please.)

Minitel

The Minitel is a small, on-line computer with multi-services that can be connected to any French telephone line and can be accessed internationally via modem hook-up. The basic telephone directory service which has virtually replaced the telephone book in France is available free of charge to anyone possessing a telephone. Although the basic service, the information directory, obtained by simply dialing 11, is free for the first two minutes, other services such as banking, shopping, research, ticket reservations, dating services, porno, etc. accessed by dialing 36.14, 36.15, 36.16, and 36.17 prefixes on the phone, followed by different *serveur* codes on the Minitel unit, are charged by the minute directly to your bi-monthly telephone bill. Prices vary for different services, ranging from 37 *centimes* a minute to over 3 FF, with some highly specialized services costing much more. Rates are listed at the beginning of the connection. So be careful with this fascinating, seductive, and vastly useful tool...and toy.

Throughout Paris you will see a strange host of billboards advertising Minitel services. These begin with the access numbers plus a usually catchy code, the most embarrassing one for Anglo-saxons being 36.15 CUM, a service for singles to meet, talk, play, seduce, sometimes marry. The 2000-plus porn-oriented services, better known as *messageries roses,* have generated some controversy; the State has tried to limit "unhealthy" use of the Minitel while it reaps the huge financial benefits of electronic quasi-porn.

User's Instructions

To use the Minitel, turn on the unit, dial the code number on your telephone, wait for the Fax-like tone, type in the rest of the code on the Minitel, and then press *Connexion fin* on the Minitel keyboard. Now, you're on-line. The rest should be self-evident. To break the connection and stop the billing clock, but not erase the information on the screen, touch *Connexion fin.*

Though France Télécom doesn't have a satisfactory guide

for the Minitel, you may want to pick up *Télémat France* at a nearby *kiosque* (49 FF). Though saturated with tacky and tasteless ads, it is a helpful listing. *Libération* publishes a mini-directory from time to time as well. You can consult the guide to services when connected to the Minitel, but that costs. Here is a sampling of some of the more useful access codes. The list grows daily.

3615 AF
Air France information.
3615 AHP04
Tourist activities and resources in the Haute-Provence Alps; cultural animation, leisure activities, thermal spas, etc. Accommodation guide.
3614 AIRTEL
National and international airline schedules and airfares.
3615 AMNESTY
A good way to join Amnesty—this connection lists their accomplishments, the when and where of their protest marches, who their religious contacts are, plus educational games and even the possibility to aid prisoners.
3616 ASFA
Traffic conditions and highway information.
3615 ASTRO
This service lets you know your sign, or your Chinese sign, your horoscope of the day, or of the year.
3615 BBC
British and international news broadcast in English by the BBC.

3615 BHV
Information, bargains, services, and job offers of the Bazaar de l'Hôtel de Ville.

3615 CAP 2
Municipal libraries in Paris.

3614 CASE
French health or thermal, seaside and tourist resorts: facilities, leisure activities, list of accommodations.

3615 CORUS
Information on 150 mountain resorts.

3615 DICO
The first dictionaries available by Minitel: orthography, synonyms, conjugations.

3614 ED
Administrative and emergency phone numbers and addresses.

3614 EMS
Chronopost—fast mail service.

3615 EPARGNER
This service is essentially the same as the first two, though slightly less expensive, making it practical for frequent use.

3614 EVAZUR
Tourist guide to the Cote d'Azur and the Midi. Useful addresses: hotels, restaurants, camping sites, discos.

3617 FAX
In order to send a message by fax, you type in the fax number and the correspondent, then the message for a fee, via Minitel, will arrive by fax.

3515 FL
Information concerning river tourism.

3615 FLORITEL
Send some flowers—to anywhere in France. Prices range from 100 FF to 1500 FF, plus 30 FF delivery charges.

3615 FL
Information on river tourism, walks and river cruises.

3615 FNAC
A listing of all existing CD's, though no listing of which are available on the market, and no way to order them.

3611 FUAJ
Information on all youth hostels in France.

3615 GAULT
Listing of 2500 selected Paris restaurants with Henri Gault's opinions on the best ones.

3615 HORAV
Airport guide: parking, services, hotels. Flight departure and arrival times.

3615 INVESTIR
The stock market—live.

3615 ITOUR
National directory of tourist bureaus by region, department and town.

3615 JDF
The stock market with advice on how to invest your money.

3615 KITI
Guide to cultural sites, monuments and French castles by department and site.

3615 LIBE
American and international news in English direct from USA TODAY.

3615 LOCAT
Looking for an apartment? Find one through classifieds and agencies on the Minitel.

3615 METEO
Weather forecast.

3615 MICHELIN

To establish a detailed itinerary, to know the prices of tolls, hotels, restaurants on the road: this service can answer all these questions. Takes about ten minutes.

3614 NATURISM

Information on *naturisme* and naturist holiday centers (nudist colonies).

3615 PARISCOPE

This allows you to reserve your seat at a movie theatre.

3615 PAT

Tourist and medical information on French thermal resorts, oceano-therapy, regeneration.

3615 RANDO

Guide of walking trips in France. List of maps and guides.

3615 RATP

This connection is helpful in determining the best means of transport (Métro, bus) to use and how long it will take you. About four minutes is average.

3616 SEALINK

Times and prices for ferries to England and Ireland.

3615 SNCF

While indicating the station of arrival and departure, and the chosen date of your journey, this service offers all the possibilities of travel. For instance, you can reserve your ticket and pick it up later at either an SNCF window or a travel agency, on the condition of having kept the reference number that the Minitel provides. The catch? This service is always blocked up during rush hour, but the average time to reserve two tickets from Paris to Marseille is about six minutes.

3615 T7J

Not only does this give a listing of all the TV programs but also a large list of wines for sale.

3615 TMK

This service allows you to order your groceries via Minitel, and delivered to your door the same day—for a 60 FF charge if your purchase is less than 1200 FF—or the next day for 45 FF. If your purchase is over 2000 FF, delivery charges are free. Order before 10h if you want it delivered the same day, and after 10h to choose the day you want it delivered. Pay by credit card or check, but make sure to order the catalogue, or you will spend most of your costly time browsing the selection on the Minitel.

3615 UPI

International news in English.

3617 U.S.ACCESS

News in English; yellow pages for New York and Boston

3617 VOCALE

If the person you're calling is absent, then type your message on the Minitel and it will be delivered by a synthesized voice at the time of your choice. You can also send a song, if you wish.

3616 VOYAGEL * FRANCE

Formalities, addresses and practical information (hours and days of banking, shopping,etc.) to enable foreign tourists to have trouble-free holidays.

The Post Office (PTT) (La Poste)

Although the French postal service has been rated tenth among the twelve EEC countries in Europe, you will probably be both impressed and frustrated by your experiences concerning the mail. The latest PR slogan for *La Poste* is *Pas de probleme*. First, you will have to get used to longer lines than you're probably accustomed to. The French post office handles so many functions that sending a simple letter sometimes gets caught in the shuffle of all the rest. *La Poste* handles long distance telephone calls, telegrams, an express mail system called Chronopost, the entire array of letter and package possibilities, plus numerous financial and banking functions such as savings accounts, money markets, cable or wire transfers of funds, payment of telephone bills, distribution of major mail house catalogues, retirement plans, checking accounts, tax consulting, investment plans, housing funds, mortgages and more. *La Poste* is in direct competition with commercial banks. Of eight windows *(guichets)* open in an average post office, sometimes only two or three will be equipped for sending letters or packages—marked *Envoi de lettres et paquets*—but it is becoming more frequent to have other windows open for more services.

La Poste
Hours: Monday-Friday: 8h-19h.
Saturday: 8h-12h.
Closed Sunday

The Main Post Office is open 24 hours a day, 7 days a week:
52, rue du Louvre
75001 PARIS
Tel: 40.28.20.00

A Few Helpful Terms

une lettre recommandée (registered letter): the French use this rather expensive means not so much for security as to have proof that a particular letter, document, bill or administrative measure was executed. Post offices tend to be cheap with the forms so you often have to wait to get to the front of the line to fill in your registered letter form. When picking up a registered letter, you must bring (in person) your *avis* (notice) plus valid identification that has a picture. If you want someone else to fetch it for you, you must file a form ahead of time or send that person with his or her identification plus yours. The post office will only hold a registered letter for 15 days, so be careful when leaving town on holiday.

avec accusé de réception (return receipt requested): this can be added to the registered letter if you want proof that your letter was in fact received on a certain date. Note: there is no such thing as insuring your letters or parcels, however, items sent *recommandée*—if lost, stolen, or damaged—can be reimbursed up to 750 FF. But you will never meet anyone who has ever collected.

lettres: All letters should be marked LETTRE to insure that they go first class. Aérograms are 4,20 FF for the whole world. The basic 10 gram air mail letter to North America and the Middle East is 3,50 FF. The price for postcards is the same. The French often send post cards in envelopes, a habit that seems bizarre to North Americans. In any case, they usually put the same postage as a letter, in that it then goes as fast as a letter. In that postal rates change periodically, it's a good idea to request from your local post office a rate sheet upon arrival.

pli non urgent (PNU) (Third class mail): This is cheaper but considerably slower, especially for items mailed near the end of the week in that PNU ìtems do not travel on weekends.

parcels: Packages require more work to send in France than in many other countries. First of all, they need to be packaged in a special way, so you are better off just buying the ready-made boxes at the post office. Also, first class letters and packages are limited to two kilos (4.4 pounds). Books and packages are limited to five kilos (11 pounds). For heavier items, you are obliged to take your wares to a special window at the main post office of any *arrondissement* or the Central Post Office at 52, rue du Louvre in the first *arrondissement.* This post office, it should be noted, is the only 24 hour/7 days a week postal facility in Paris. This is useful when you have applications and other materials that need to be postmarked by a particular date. Enquire about special postal *sacs* for sending books and *classe economique* for cheaper air mail service. A new *colissimo* domestic service for packages up to ten kilos has been introduced.

Chronopost: Chronopost is the French Post Office's Express

Mail service. Letters sent to North America by Chronopost arrive in 48 hours, guaranteed. Packages can also be sent by Chronopost. A letter will cost you about 200 FF. Minitel provides information on everything you ever wanted to know about Chronopost—3614. EMS. Items sent via US International Express Mail arrive via Chronopost, and can be delivered to a post office box, whereas Federal Express or DHL parcels cannot.

poste restante: If you find yourself in France without a reliable address, remember that you can always receive mail by having it sent to the post office of your choice marked with your name and *poste restante*. Other options include the American Express Office (Métro: Opéra) or Western Union.

Media

Television

French television has progressively loosened up and expanded over the last five years. Some would argue that the quality has diminished. Not so long ago there was no pro-gramming before noon so that kids wouldn't be fixed to TV sets. And there were few emissions after midnight. In general, this is still true of several of the channels.

There are principally four French television stations and one subscriber station currently available to Parisian viewers, although new cable options are being installed all the time and many neighborhoods have already been connected. Thus, CNN, Sky, BBC, Eurovision, MTV, and other networks are available. The channels are: TF1, Antenne 2, FR 3, and M6. Up until April 1992 there was the fifth channel, La Cinq, a highly visible private station that, after five years of operation, was shut down following battles to remain solvent. The station was hit by management problems and claims that it was killed by oppressive government regulations and taxes. Channel 4 is Canal Plus which you must pay for to receive, except for certain programs during the day which are transmitted *en clair* (unscrambled). One of these *en clair* moments includes a 7h or 8h (depending on the season) transmission of Dan Rather's CBS Nighly News from the previous evening. Dan is of course speaking English, but subtitles have been added for French viewers. It can be fun to watch your shifting perceptions of American life and media as you live overseas and begin to see the world in a wider, more international scope.

TF1 has been privately owned for only several years after a rather major battle on the subject. The programming is solid but a bit conservative. The news gathering and reporting is generally untenacious.

Antenne 2 is wholly State-owned, more liberal and more progressive in its programming. It programs many special events, interviews and cultural happenings. The news, however, isn't much better than TF1. There is an excellent film series

on Friday nights in V.O. *(version originale)*—often in English. This follows Bernard Rapp's literary talk show *Apostrophe,* which famed Bernard Pivot gave up in 1991 to initiate his *Bouillon de Culture.*

FR3 shares much of its programming with Antenne 2 but adds a lot of regional transmissions, news, documentaries, and some excellent environmental programming. FR3 has certainly come up substantially in the last few years.

Canal Plus shows a lot of films, many of which are second rate. It also provides a fair amount of American sports coverage otherwise unavailable in France.

La Cinq, the most American of French channels, went off the air on April 13, 1992. By the time you read this, a replacement station may have been created.

M6 has a lot of entertainment, show biz and video clips. Some good programming here, despite the lack of promotion and general low visibility.

There's a seventh channel filled with wonderfully enriching cultural programming, but is only available on cable, although at several times during the week its programs are seen on FR3. CNN is also available via cable, or on FR3 on Saturday evenings, and a number of Paris' better hotels receive it for their guests. Cable should reach all of Paris by 1993, but for now only limited areas of the city do receive it, along with more than 20 other cable stations. This is an area of rapid development in Europe.

Video/TV

If you buy a television *(télé)* or VCR video player in France don't forget that you can only receive French channels. A U.S. or British video player usually will not work with a French set, which is in the PAL standard. Britain and the rest of Europe uses SECAM, while North America and Japan use NTSC. Multisystem video players and recorders (*magnéto-scopes*) are sparse and expensive although the prices are coming down. The FNAC carries both a multisystem video and TV. Some North Americans opt for two VCRs and two TV sets.

French law requires a special annual users tax *(redevances)* for TV and video owners. Electronics stores are obliged to report all sales to the government, so quick-witted and laissez-faire consumers pay in cash and give fictitious addresses; although the tax rate has come down some, you will still probably find yourself with around 500 FF to pay each year. Prerecorded video films are readily available but expensive, with little in English. Check FUSAC for new places to rent. An old standby has been Reels-on-Wheels, which, both sells and rents English and American films (on PAL only), and delivers and picks up, too. However, readers have reported abrasive and less than helpful service, so be wary. The American Women's Group in Paris at 49 rue Pierre Charonne also has a video club worth investigating.

Radio

French radio bands were strictly controlled in the seventies. The airwaves were certainly not free. Numerous unofficial pirate stations were hidden around the city. Most radio emissions now come from one centralized building complex in the sixteenth *arrondissement* called the *Maison de la radio*. When

Mitterand came into power, radio in France was decontrolled. Scores of little radio stations sprung up at once. Many represented ethnic groups, alternative attitudes, or regions. The result was a glut on the airwaves; it became difficult to pick up clear signals except for the huge and powerful commercial radio stations RTL, Radio Luxembourg, Radio Monte Carlo, NRJ and a few others. So, new rules were clamped on. Things have leveled out now. Radio programming can be quite original in France, and if you are used to turning the dial to hear a different style of music, you may be pleasantly surprised to hear a Chopin Nocturne followed by Led Zeppelin followed by John Coltrane. It seems that to the French, either quality transgresses the bounds of style or the art of the smooth "segway" is still to be learned.

The irreverent expat DJ from New Jersey, Bart Platenga, whose former show Wreck This Mess had been heard on the feisty Radio Libertaire on Tuesdays at 16h30, writes: "Paris radio is more open and unpredictable in general than American or British radio. Just spin the dial & one gets an amazing variety of sound. But Paris radio is formating fast. Their station id's are VERY inventive, often better than the music they play. While in America there is lots of talk about nothing, in Paris there is too much talk about significance. The French like to talk ABOUT music. That's why you'll hear five minutes of music & then fifteen minutes of discussion about it. Perhaps that's why jazz is popular."

Here is Bart's list of Paris' major FM radio stations.

FRANCE INTER–87.8
French variety & cultural chandelier chats (a 3 minute Leon Redbone song commands a 15 minute panel discussion). Unadventurous forays into culture Muzak from this state-run station.

RADIO ORIENT–88.6
Arab pop. If we understood the lyrics, maybe it wouldn't seem so exotic.

KISS FM–89.0
Wallpaper Muzak demographically aimed at the spineless upward-bound consumers who dance to Pink Floyd and Madonna with no discernable change in step.

RADIO LIBERTAIRE–89.4
Anarchist federation's Voice Without Master. Eclectic embrace of world's disinherited and disaffected. Some of Paris' best blues, jazz and alternative info.

FIP PARIS–90.4
Commercial-free sublime simmer of soothing woogie music from Barbieri to Mingus, Lester Young to Neil. Mellifluous DJ's, casual traffic (26 updates daily), weather, news interruptions.

CANAL 9–90.9
Leans heavy on plod-plod ballady pop. Best: *Intérieurs Nuits* (live personal column with secret, sexy and perverse announcements), Fri. 23h–1h.

FRANCE MUSIQUE–91.7
Though this state-run station is mainly devoted to classical, it wanders into jazz, ethnic and experimental sounds.

RADIO CVS–92.1
Ding-a-ling songs that make you want to stuff Malobars in your ears.

TROPIC FM–92.6
Truly one of the cream. Joyous equatorial notes that are eclectic and human. Great creole-juju-mambo-salsa-zulu-ethno-pop-reggae bubbling stew.

ICI & MAINTENANT–93.1
Decent stuff, depending on the show. Unique dedication to listener call-ins. Best: Spiral Insana (experimental, cut-up), Tues. 17h–18h30. Shares frequency with Radio Aligre.

FRANCE CULTURE–93.5
France Culture (perhaps the only station in the world exclusively concerned with culture) broadcasts serious cultural topics 24-hours-a-day.

RADIO FRANCE MAGREB–94
Arabic music with an edge.

FUTUR GENERATION–94.4
The pop future as seen from the cyber-souls of E.T. fans.

RADIO SHALOM–94.8
Vegas comes to Tel Aviv.

RADIO TOUR EIFFEL–95.2
Some good, cool jazz that is unfortunately hindered by incessant interruptions.

RADIO COURTOISIE–95.6
This station is national-Catholic and interview-heavy (and we mean heavy). Shares frequency with Radio Asie.

SKYROCK–96.0
This giant describes itself as "chewing gum for the ears." Chain-talking DJ's vaccinated with phonographic needles whack off crappy, headless recordings.

PACIFIC FM–97.4
Describes itself as *"la radio évasion"* (escapism radio). Intriguing mishmash of junk and gems from all over the world: from gut-wrenching segues of airhead nostalgia (John Denver) to real Delta blues.

RADIO BEUR–98.2
Arab pop & ethno-music with integrity. Best: Raîkoum (Raî), Monday 16h30-18h:

RADIO PORTUGAL–98.6
Is schmaltzy sentimentality just a universal affliction? French with a Portuguese accent.

RADIO LATINA–99.0
Solid and adventurous jazz daily like Cecil Taylor compositions actually allowed to stretch and explore.

REUSSIR FM–99.6
Why succeed when you can fail so effortlessly. Station of "professional info & business communication."

Obviously looking for its niche among the career-oriented. Shares frequency with Jazzland.

RADIO CLASSIQUE–101.1
Commercial-free, 24-hour-a-day classical music. One exception is the financial news, Mon.–Fri. 7h–8h30.

NRJ–100.3
The giant which boasts 5 million listeners. A fair selection of pop, house and rock.

RADIO NOVA–101.5
Everything from urban-warfare rap, love-funk and acid garage-jazz to zulu. Easiest station to pop on anytime.

FUN RADIO–101.9
Noisy like your worst pinball nightmare on speed. Pop without pulp. Bump without bang.

OUI FM–102.3
Overrated computer-generated rock format that's white as nose candy. Trendy guitars and a bit of self-serious rock NOOZ.

RTL–104.3
News bulletins on the hour, every hour. The concept here is accessible, popular and lively—in short, close to millions of hearts nationwide.

EUROPE 1–104.7
News, soft rock, festival coverage, almanacs and DJ-hosted *variété* and entertainment programming. Very informal tone.

RADIO NOSTALGIE–105.1
Lots of dippy, purring come-on *chanteurs & chanteuses*. All the romantic squish of a sponge dipped in cheap perfume.

FRANCE INFO–105.5
Around-the-clock, state-run, commercial-free, nationwide news. Broadcasts in all French cities, albeit on different frequencies. Almost as up-to-the-minute as a wire service.

TABALA–106.3
Paris' Afro station plays mix of African, Caribbean and black American music with African news.

RADIO TOMATE–106.7
Small "associative" radio, collective idealism, alternative info. Best: Konstroy (alternative rock) Sun 17h–19h; *Poésie* (*engagé*, dub & ghetto poetry) Fri 19h–20h30; Radio Mango (Antilles culture) Fri 20h30–0h.

For news and information in English you can tune in to a range of international English news services, each with its particular ideology. One American professor in Paris used to profess that there was only one real way to learn what's really happening in the world: listen to BBC World Service, Voice of America, Radio Tirana (Albania) English Service, and Radio Moscow English Service and average them out. With the new evolution of the world political order, this system needs revamping. In any case, it's both revealing and amusing tuning in to alternative sources of information.

For a foreign city, Paris has a healthy variety of English-language publications. Here is a descriptive listing of what's being published regularly here in English. Those of you who are looking for the city magazine *Paris Passion* should note that the mag folded in 1990 following a take-over by London *Time Out.*

International Herald Tribune: Daily newspaper written and compiled by local staff with the *New York Times* and *Washington Post,* catering primarily to the international business community. American sports coverage on Mondays. The Money Report in the weekend edition. 8,50 FF at the kiosk or 515 FF for a three-month subscription for students or teachers in France.
International Herald Tribune
181, ave Charles-de-Gaulle
92200 NEUILLY SUR SEINE
Tel: 46.37.93.00
Publisher: Lee HUEBNER
Director of Promotions: Randy WEDDLE

Wall Street Journal Europe: Published daily out of Brussels, specializing in financial and economic news with a focus on European news and money markets.

Wall Street Journal Europe
9, rue de la Paix
75002 PARIS
Tel: 42.96.96.44

*USA Today:*The international edition is coordinated in London. This four-color daily brings American news, sports, and events to Europe. No Paris office.
USA Today
10 Wardour St.
LONDON WIV3HG
Tel: (44)(71)734-3003

The European: English-language weekend newspaper with a particular take on European issues now under new ownership after the death and demise of its founding publisher, the late Robert Maxwell. Based in London. 15 FF every Friday.
The European
38, rue de Bassono
75008 PARIS
Tel: 47.23.55.18
FAX: 40.70.01.30
Bureau Chief: Elisabeth MOUTET

Paris Free Voice: A monthly community-oriented free newspaper with a circulation of over 18,000. Cultural news, features, and local color. Published since the late Seventies by community leader, blues guitarist, and Parsons professor of photography, Bob Bishop, out of his basement office in the American Church. Inexpensive and effective classified advertising.

Paris Free Voice
American Church
65, Quai d'Orsay
75007 PARIS
Tel: 47.53.77.23
Editor/Publisher: Bob BISHOP

France-USA Contacts(FUSAC): A well-organized and ubiquitous semi-monthly circular of classified advertisements and useful tips devised, produced and distributed by John and Lisa Vanden Bos. Distributed free in both Paris and New York. Free bulletin-board center open from Monday to Friday 10h-19h, Saturday 12h-17h. Métro: Gaité or Edgar Quinet.

France-USA Contacts (FUSAC)
3, rue Larochelle
75014 PARIS
Tel: 45.38.56.5
FAX: 45.38.98.94
Editor: John VANDEN BOS

Paris-Anglophone: Annual directory of all English-speaking professional, commercial and cultural activities in Paris. A handy tool for job-seeking and an invaluable mailing-list for entrepreneurs. Sponsored by France-Télécom. 135 FF.

Paris Anglophone
B.P. 29
94301 VINCENNES CEDEX
Editor: David APPLEFIELD

Boulevard: A flashy monthly with topical articles on the French corporate world and the upper echelons of French society. Calendar of events.

Boulevard
Mediatime France
8, rue Simon le Franc
75004 PARIS
Tel: 40.29.95.55
FAX: 40.29.94.45

Speak Up: An attractive and well-edited monthly magazine and cassette designed for French readers interested in keeping up with the times and reenforcing their language skills.

Speak Up
Loft Internationale
1, rue Lord Byron
75008 PARIS
Tel: 42.25.65.20
Fax: 45.63.61.44
Editor: Isabelle RIPPON

Vocable: Geared towards French readers wanting to maintain and improve their foreign language skills. English edition available at many kiosks and bookstores.

Vocable
4, rue de Cerisoles
75008 PARIS
Tel: 47.20.74.16

Publications/ Newsletters

AAWE
24, rue A. Perdreaux
78140 PARIS
Director: Catherine GODDARD
Tel: 42.56.05.24

AIUA
150, av Victor Hugo
75116 PARIS
Director: Olivier HAERTIG

American Chamber of Commerce
21, av George V
75008 PARIS
Director: Ann LE CHARTIER

Democrats Abroad
10, av de Messine
75008 PARIS
Tel: 45.63.11.52
Contact: Joseph SMALLHOOVER

France-Amèrique
23, rue Edouard Nortier
92200 NEUILLY
Director: Françoise
DE CREMIERS

France File
Association of British & American
Residents in France
17, rue de la Baume
75008 PARIS
Tel: 44.13.40.25
Fax: 44.13.40.26
Directors: Amy SLOANE-PINEL,
Robert BROWN

Franco-Amèricaine
38, av Hoche
75008 PARIS
Director: Jacques
MARCHANGISE

Franco File
15, av Victor Hugo
75116 PARIS
Fax: 47.55.17.02

International School of Paris
96 bis, rue du Ranelagh
75016 PARIS
Director: Maurice PEZET

International Fund Investment
(a world investment magazine)
181, ave Charles-de-Gaulle
92200 NEUILLY SUR SEINE
Tel: 46.37.93.11
Fax: 46.37.21.33
Editor: Martin BAKER

Message
17, rue des Apennins
75017 PARIS
Director: Lynne CHAILLAT

The Planet
The American University of Paris
31, Avenue Bosquet
75007 PARIS
Advisor: Mark HUNTER

"Welcome to Paris"
119, rue de Longchamp
92200 NEUILLY
Director: Dominique AMELINE

WICE
20, bd du Montparnasse
75015 PARIS
Tel: 45.66.75.50
FAX: 40.65.96.53

Literary & Art Journals

Frank: An International Journal of Contemporary Writing & Art: Has been publishing fiction, poetry, literary interviews and contemporary art since 1983. Available at literary bookshops in Europe and North America. Edited by fiction-writer David Applefield.
150 FF/$30 for four issues.
Frank: An International Journal of Contemporary Writing & Art
B.P. 29
94301 VINCENNES CEDEX
Tel: 43.65.64.05

Paris Transcontinental, A Magazine of Short Stories, edited by Sorbonne professor Claire Larriere and local fiction writer Albert Russo. Hosts a Short Story Contest for fiction of 5,000 words or less, the first-prize winner receiving 1000 FF(or $200 US) and publication, or a scholarship to the Annual WICE Paris Writers Workshop.
Paris Transcontinental
Institut du Monde Anglophone
Sorbonne Nouvelle
5, rue de l'Ecole de Médecine
75006 PARIS

Raw Vision: Periodical specializing in art brut and primitive art from around the world, published in London.
Raw Vision
Sandra Kwock-Silve, Paris editor
22, rue de Turin
75008 PARIS
Tel: 43.87.55.08

Revue Noire: African Contemporary Art International Magazine. Bi-lingual.
Revue Noire
8, rue Cels
75014 PARIS
Tel: 43.20.28.14
Editor: Simon NJAMI

Art International: One of the world's finest quarterlies in English on contemporary art. Edited in Paris by Jill Lloyd and Michael Peppiatt. Well-researched and well-written articles with high-quality reproductions.
Art International
77, rue des Archives
75003 PARIS
Tel: 48.04.84.54

Other English-language Press Represented in France

Here is a rather complete list of major networks, stations, newspapers and magazines in France. For purchasing English and American magazines and newspapers, W.H. Smith, FNAC

Internationale, and Brentanos are good sources. The monopoly press distributor NMPP, which runs all Paris kiosks and is owned by the multinational French publisher Hachette, has its own international press shop:

NMPP
111, rue Réaumur
75002 PARIS

Radio and TV

American Broadcasting Company (ABC)
Tel: 45.05.13.73

British Broadcasting Company (B.B.C.)
Tel: 45.61.97.00 (television)
        45.63.15.88 (radio)

Central Broadcasting System (CBS)
Tel: 42.25.26.52

Cable News Network (CNN)
Tel: 42.89.23.31

Canadian Broadcasting Corporation (CBC)
Tel: 43.59.11.85

New Zealand Press Association New Zealand TV
Tel: 43.27.02.75

Radio Canada
Tel: 43.59.11.85

Radio France Internationale
Tel: 42.30.30.62

Tokyo Broadcasting Systems
Tel: 42.66.15.55

Newspapers

Los Angeles Times
Tel: 49.24.96.69

New York Times
Tel: 42.66.37.49

The Observer
Tel: 42.74.60.86

The Sunday Times
Tel: 47.42.73.21

The Wall Street Journal
Tel: 47.42.08.06

Washington Post
Tel: 43.59.56.16

Magazines

Business Week
Tel: 42.89.03.80

Newsweek Magazine
Tel: 42.56.06.81

Time-Life
Tel: 44.01.49.01

U.S. News & World Report
Tel: 47.20.84.83

Although France is a traditionally Catholic country, religion does not play a highly visible role in Parisian life or values. Church and State formally separated in 1905, and the debate over public *(laïque)* vs. parochial education in France flares up periodically. As does the heated and recurrent issue of racism and anti-semitism.

The Paris area, of course, has some of Europe's most astonishing cathedrals and churches. Attending Mass in Notre Dame or l'Eglise de St. Germain-des-Prés, for example, can be memorable. Just being in the presence of the stained glass windows at Chartres is a spiritual experience.

As in all big cities, the opportunities for worship are numerous. Here's a list of what Paris offers in English.

American Church in Paris
65, Quai d'Orsay
75007 PARIS
Tel: 47.05.07.99
Pastor: Dr. Thomas DUGGAN
(services for all Protestant denominational)

**American Cathedral
of the Holy Trinity**
Church of the Holy Trinity
23, ave George V
75008 PARIS
Tel: 47.20.95.30
(Episcopalian/Anglican services)

Christian Science Church
36, bd St. Jacques
75014 PARIS
Tel: 47.07.26.60

**Church of Jesus-Christ
of Latter-Day Saints**
23, rue du Onze Novembre
78110 LE VESINET
Tel: 39.76.55.88
Leader: James JOHNSON

Church of Scotland
17, rue Bayard
75008 PARIS
Tel: 47.20.90.49
Reverend: Bruce ROBERTSON

**Consistoire Israëlite de Paris
(synagogue)**
44, rue de la Victoire
75009 PARIS
Tel: 45.26.90.15

Emmanuel Baptist Church
56, rue des Bons-Raisins
92500 RUEIL MALMAISON
Tel: 47.51.29.63 or 47.49.15.29
Pastor: Dr. B.C. THOMAS

Great Synagogue
44, rue de la Victoire
75009 PARIS
Tel: 45.26.95.36

International Baptist Fellowship
123, ave du Maine
75014 PARIS
Tel: 47.49.15.29 or 47.51.29.63

La Mosquée (Moslem)
Place du Puits de l'Ermite
75005 PARIS
Tel: 45.35.97.33

Liberal Synagogue
24, rue Copernic
75016 PARIS
Tel: 47.04.37.27
Rabbi Michael WILLIAMS

Living Word Christian Fellowship
21, rue Gallieni
78230 LE PECQ
Tel: 39.76.75.88

Quaker Society of Friends
114, rue de Vaugirard
75006 PARIS
Tel: 45.48.74.23

St. George's Anglican Church
7, rue August-Vacquerie
75016 PARIS
Tel: 47.20.22.51
Chaplain: Martin DRABER

St. Joseph's Roman Catholic
50, ave Hoche
75008 Paris
Tel: 42.27.28.56
Father Marius DONNELLY

St. Mark's Anglican Church
31, rue du Pont Colbert
78000 VERSAILLES
Tel: 39.02.79.45
President Chaplain: Rev. Martin

St. Michael's Church
5, rue d'Aguesseau
75008 PARIS
Tel: 47.42.70.88
(Anglican)
Venerable Brian LEA

Unitarian Universalist Fellowship of Paris
1, rue de l'Oratoire
75001 PARIS
Tel: 42.78.82.58

Health Services

Although France has a highly impressive and widely democratic system of socialized medicine, this might not undo the feelings of loneliness and despair if you fall sick in a foreign country where you are not sure where to turn for sympathy or help. This feeling is compounded, of course, if you are unsure about your language skills. For that reason, services in English have been included here. If you feel like braving the language barrier, you will find that almost any pharmacist is eager and willing to give you advice and to recommend remedies. He or she may go so far as to give you the number of a doctor around the corner. Pharmacists play an essential intermediary role between doctor and patient. And pharmacies are not cluttered with all the non-medical goods found in North American and many British drug stores. Medication comes with two-part stickers on the packaging *(vignette)*. One part is peeled off and stuck on the orange and white *feuille de soins* used for reimbursement from the *Sécurité Sociale*, the national health administration. Prescribed drugs are reimbursed at 75%. Don't be surprised, however, that treatment varies from one country to another. You may find yourself using methods you had never even conceived of at home. For instance, the French are keen on the use of suppositories, for many different problems, including a cough. Pharmacists are even trained to know about the mushrooms you find in the woods and will offer free advice on the delicious and deadly.

A lot of misunderstanding about French medical practices is a matter of aesthetics and style. French doctors' *cabinets* (offices) are surprisingly unclinical in feel, and doctors, particularly specialists, appear more like professors than physicians. Doctors' offices in France are not teeming with paramedical practitioners nor do doctors' offices maintain extensive medical records. With children, medical records are maintained in a *carnet de santé* (health book) which accompanies the child throughout his/her early life. Very little lab work is done in doctors' offices, and the white-coat sterility associated with North American and Scandinavian medical facilities is virtually absent. One does not get the feeling of being dynamically treated, however, there is no denying that French medical procedures are wisely oriented towards prevention instead of intervention. Because the *Sécurité Sociale* reimburses most of the cost of visiting any doctor of your choice, people don't usually wait until they're seriously ill to see a doctor.

Don't be overly judgmental if the waiting room is drab, there is no air-conditioning and the doctor inspects you in an alcove of his study. The French are not highly obsessed with the aesthetics of hygiene.

A normal consultation should run about 100 FF. Many doctors don't require appointments and simply receive walk-ins during fixed hours.

Hospitals

The American Hospital of Paris *(Hôpital Américain de Paris)*: This is a famous, private hospital which employs British, American and French doctors on its staff and is partially bilingual. F. Scott Fitzgerald, among others, spent time here in the pre-renovation days drying out "on the wagon."

It is much more expensive than the French hospitals, but offers excellent health care with a style that you may recognize and appreciate. You can pay with dollars and credit cards. Those covered by Blue Cross-Blue Shield have their hospitalization covered, provided they fill out the appropriate paperwork first.

The American Hospital of Paris
63, bd Victor Hugo
92202 NEUILLY SUR SEINE
Cedex
Tel: 46.41.25.25
Fax: 46.24.49.38

Another hospital which employs English-speaking doctors and is noted for serving the anglophone community:

Hetford British Hospital
3, rue Barbès,
92300 LEVALLOIS PERRET
Tel: 47.58.13.12

Medical Practitioners

Practitioners in France are either *conventionné* (abiding by the *Sécurité Sociale* system's schedule of fees) or *non conventionné* (charge higher rates). Note below that WICE publishes a detailed booklet on health in Paris, the best source on the subject. As for recommendations, The American University of Paris' medical brochure recommends the following English-speaking doctors. Otherwise, asks friends and colleagues.

General Practitioners

Dr. Hubert Gamon
20, rue Cler
75007 PARIS
Tel: 45.55.79.91

Dr. Claude Guichard
37, rue du Départ
75014 PARIS
Tel: 43.22.22.96

Dr. Stephan Wilson
44, ave de Ségur
75015 Paris
Tel: 45.67.26.53

Dr. Francis Slattery
42, rue de Bellechasse
75007 PARIS
Tel: 45.55.16.52

Chiropractor

Marc Tourneur, D.C.
44, rue Laborde
75008 PARIS
Tel: 43.87.81.62

Dentists

Dr. Gauthier
47, ave Hoche
75008 PARIS
Tel: 47.66.33.25

Dr. Chagari
22, rue Cler
75007 PARIS
Tel: 47.05.40.10

Dermatologists
Dr. Marchal
40, ave Bosquet
75007 PARIS
Tel: 45.51.04.40

Dr. Metter
29, ave Franklin Roosevelt
75008 PARIS
Tel: 43.59.88.17

Gynecologists/Abortion
Dr. Richet
109, rue de l'Université
75007 PARIS
Tel: 45.51.82.32

Dr. Tatiana Oppenheim
17, bd du Temple
75003 PARIS
Tel: 48.87.22.63

Dr. Sarrot
6, ave Sully-Prudhomme
75007 PARIS
Tel: 45.56.03.30

Laboratories
Laboratoire Trivin-Vercambre
14, rue Dupont des Loges
75007 PARIS
Tel: 47.05.84.37

Laboratoire Lobar-Philippe
(x-rays only)
199, rue de Grenelle
75007 PARIS
Tel: 47.05.51.87

Ophthalmologist
Dr. Linda Abitbol
131, rue St. Dominique
75007 PARIS
Tel: 45.55.65.45

Optician
Walter's Paris
107, rue St. Dominique
75007 PARIS
Tel: 45.51.70.08
(20% discount on frames, lens & contacts for university students)

Psychiatrists/Psychologists
Emmanuel Ansart, M.D.
43, rue La Bruyère
75009 PARIS
Tel: 48.78.04.60

Barbara Cox
115, rue du Théâtre
75015 PARIS
Tel: 45.75.74.61

Mary Larounis
65, Quai d'Orsay
75007 PARIS
Tel: 45.50.26.49

Docteur H.R.S. Nagpal
65, rue Pascal
75013 PARIS
Tel: 47.07.55.28

Nancy Sadowsky
12, rue Marie Stuart
75002 PARIS
Tel: 42.33.10.07

Joseph Shesko
4, rue Michel Chasles
74012 PARIS
Tel: 43.47.19.72

Sports Medicine
Dr François Manier
64, rue de Rennes
75006 PARIS
Tel: 45.44.03.21

Free A.I.D.S. Testing Clinics
Centre Anonyme et Gratuit des Medécins du Monde
1, rue du Jura
75013 PARIS
Tel: 43.36.43.24

Centre Medical de Belleville
218, rue de Belleville
75020 PARIS
Tel: 47.97.40.49

Dispensaire (City Health Clinic)
3-5, rue de Ridder
75014 PARIS
Tel: 45.43.83.78

Hôpital La Pitié Salpétrière
47, bd de l'Hôpital
75013 PARIS
Tel: 45.70.21.73

Reproductive Health
A prescription is necessary for contraceptive devices and drugs. There is no age limit. Male contraceptive condoms (*préservatifs*) and female contraceptive sponges (*ovules*) are available without prescription. Family planning centers provide information on contraception. Among others, Le Planning Familial has centers at 10, rue Vivienne, 75002 PARIS, Métro: Bourse, Tel: 42.60.93.20, and at 94, bd Massena, 75013 PARIS, Métro: Porte-de-Choisy, Tel: 45.84.28.25. Do-it-yourself pregnancy tests are available in pharmacies at a cost of about 60 FF. Ask for G-Test, Elle-Test, or Predictor. When positive, these tests can be believed absolutely. When negative, they should be repeated five to seven days later. Abortions are legal in France.

Free, anonymous courses of treatment for venereal diseases are offered by the Institut Prophylactique, 36, rue d'Assas, 75006 PARIS, Métro: Saint-Placide, Tel: 42.22.32.06; 8h00-15h00 Monday through Friday and Saturday 8h30-12h00; and by the Institut Alfred Fournier, 25 bd Saint-Jacques, 75014 PARIS, Métro: Saint-Jacques, Tel: 45.81.46.41.

Other Health-Related Services

Support Groups
AIDS Support Group
American Church
65, Quai d'Orsay
75007 PARIS
Tel: 45. 50.26.49.

Alcoholics Anonymous
3, rue Fréderic Sauton
75005 PARIS
Tel: 47.05.07.99

Alcoholics Anonymous
American Church
75007 PARIS
Tel: 46.34.59.65

Alcoholics Anonymous
American Cathedral
23, ave George V
75008 PARIS
Tel: 47.20.17.92
Recorded Information: 46.34.59.65
(Saturdays at the American
Hospital: 46.41.25.25)

American Aid Society of Paris
Talleyrand Building
2, rue Saint-Florentin
75382 PARIS Cedex 08
Tel: from 9-12, call 42.96.12.02
ext. 2717; other hours, call ext.
2667 (Office of American Services)
President: Mme Dorothy LOBL
(helps U.S. citizens who encounter
problems in France)

American Women's Group
(address soon to change)
49, rue Pierre Charron
75008 PARIS
Tel: 43.59.17.61

**British and Commonwealth
Women's Association**
7, rue Auguste Vacquerie
75016 PARIS
Tel: 47.20.01.36

Canada Welcome
24, bd Port Royal
75005 PARIS
Tel: 43.37.43.96

Europ Assistance
23-25, rue Chaptal
75445 PARIS Cedex
Tel: 42.85.85.85

International Counseling Service
65, Quai d'Orsay
75007 PARIS
Tel: 45.50.26.49
Mon.-Sat: 9:30-1:00pm

Weight Watchers France
18, rue Jean Pierre-Timbaud
BP 87
78392 BOIX-D'ARCY CEDEX
Tel: 43.57.65.24
Director: D. BROTHERS

**WICE (Women's Institute for
Continuing Education)**
20, bd Montparnasse
75015 PARIS
Tel: 45.66.75.50
Offers courses (in English) in
Career & Personal Development,
Arts & Humanities, Living in
France, Women's Support Group.

For further information on
AIDS (*SIDA*), there is a round
the clock telephone information
service at Tel: 47.70.03.00 from
10 a.m.-7 p.m. and at Tel:
47.70.98.99 from 7 p.m.-11
a.m. More information may be
obtained by consulting the
Minitel at: 3615 AIDS. Or this
service may be written to, at:
AIDES, 6 Cité Paradis, 75010
PARIS.

For more information re-
garding English-speaking medical personnel, a good resource is
Health Care Resources in Paris, a
comprehensive guide in English.
Contact WICE, Tel: 45.66.
75.50 to order a copy.

Pharmacies

To match a prescription from home be sure to have the following information, since finding the equivalent may be difficult: an up-to-date prescription with the medication's trade name, manufacturer, chemical name, and dosage. If you don't speak French, you may have an easier time if you go to the English and American Pharmacy, since they are used to having to match prescriptions. The pharmacists, aside from speaking English, tend to be very helpful. In most pharmacies, for many prescription drugs, you will be asked to give your address. This is normal.

Pharmacie Swann
Anglo-American Pharmacy
6, rue de Castiglione
75001 PARIS
Tel: 42.60.72.96

British and American Pharmacy
1, rue Auber
75009 PARIS
Tel: 47.42.49.40

Pharmacie des Champs
(24-hour pharmacy)
84, ave des Champs-Elysées,
75008 PARIS
Tel: 45.62.02.41

Air France *Service Vaccin*
Square Max Hyman
75015 PARIS
Tel: 43.20.13.50; Minitel: 3615 AF
(For vacinations and health cards)

At night and on Sundays you can call the local *commissariat de police* for the address of the nearest open pharmacy and that of a doctor on duty. You can also check the door of a closed pharmacy for the address of the nearest open one. Note: if you cannot find a prescribed medication at a local pharmacy or you've been told that there is a *rupture de stock* (out of stock), try calling or visiting the *Pharmacie Centrale des Hôpitaux*, 7 rue Fer à Moulin 75005 PARIS, Tel: 43.37.11.00 *poste* 299, Métro Gobelins, 9:30-17:30. This is the central supplier for Paris hospitals.

Natural Medicine

The French are great believers in traditional medicines. *Homéopathie* (homeopathic medicine) uses only herbs and other natural products in very care-fully compounded mixtures whose composition is fixed by law. In many cafés, *infusions* (herbal

indications	ailments treated by the product
voie orale	by mouth
gelules	capsules
mode d'emploi	directions for use
posologie	dosage
gouttes	drops
effets secondaires	eventual side effects
sirop	liquid or syrup
poudre	powder
ampoules	small glass containers
sachets	small packets of soluble powder
cuillère à soupe	tablespoon
comprimés or *pillules*	tablets or pills
cuillère à café	teaspoon
suppositoires	suppositories
contre-indications	warnings (when medicine should not be used)
ne pas depasser la dose préscrite	do not exceed prescribed dosage
mal des transports	motion sickness
le rhume	cold
la toux	cough
la diarrhée	diarrhea
les maux d'oreilles	earache
mal de tête, migraine	headache
l'indigestion	indigestion

teas) are served, largely for complaints such as nervous-ness, weakness, etc. A few of the calming herb teas available in most cafés are *tilleul, camomille, menthe* and *verveine*. There are also a number of *fortifiants* (tonics, mild stimulants) available in pharmacies, as well as preparations for just about any common ailment. Pharmacies specializing in homeopathic medicine will be clearly marked and can be found throughout the city.

Health Insurance
Before coming to France, you should find out whether or not you are insured overseas and in what instances. Certain firms will expect you to pay your bills

Medical Emergencies

Police Secours: Tel: 17.
Pompiers (Fire): Tel: 18.
Ambulances Municipales:
Tel: 47.05.44.87.
Rapid transport to the closest French hospital emergency room.
SAMU ambulances:
Tel: 45.67.50.50.
Life-threatening situations; detailed information will be required by phone.
Ambulances de l'Assistance Publique: Tel: 43.78.26.26.
Handles transportation from one hospital to another.
Burns (severe): Tel: 42.34.12.12.
Hôpital Cochin, 27 rue St. Jacques, 75005 PARIS.
SOS Médecins: Tel: 47.07.77.77.
24-hour emergency medical house calls—150 FF before 19h00, 275 FF after 19h00.
SOS Dentistes: Tel.43.37.51.00
24-hour emergency dental help. Similar prices.
Association des Urgences Médicales de Paris: Tel: 48.28.40.09.
Sends a doctor in an emergency.
Anti-Poison Center:
Tel: 40.37.04.04.
24-hour service.
Poison Control:
Tel: 42.05.63.29.
SOS Rape: Tel: 42.34.82.34.
SOS Help: In English.
Tel: 47.23.80.80.
Crisis hotline nightly, 15h-23h.
SOS Help: In French.
Tel: 46.08.52.77.
SOS Drug Center:
Tel: 45.81.11.20.

in France and then the reimbursed after you send them the receipt *(feuille de soins)*. It may take several months for the reimbursement to come through.

French law requires that students have complete medical coverage during their stay in France. Copies of official documents attesting to this fact are required when you request a student visa from the French Consulate in your home country and by the *Préfecture de Police* when you apply for your *carte de séjour*. The law requires that the medical plan provide for the following coverage: hospitalization in Europe, short and long-term, outpatient treatment, visits to the doctor, dentist and laboratory expenses, pharmaceuticals, medical repatriation (transportation back to country of residence), medical recommendation. Most national health plans in Europe meet these requirements. Many private plans in the United States and Canada do not. However, if you have substantial coverage by your health plan in North America (inquire for the U.K. and the rest of Europe) and can get a clause to include a provision for medical repatriation, you may meet the necessary coverage requirements. Several American university programs do provide a special student health insurance plan for students who require it. Students and non-students who are not covered by an employer but who legally reside in France can also take advantage of the French *Sécurité Sociale* (referred to in conversation as the *Sécu*) by paying the annual fee. Inquire at the office of the *Sécurité Sociale* in your *arrondissement* for information.

Insurance Exemptions for Students: Those covered by European National Health plans (e.g. French Social Security or British National Health), International Organizations or a particularly extensive private plan in North America, may apply for an exemption. You must send a copy of your insurance policy to the Administration or Bursar of your program when paying the tuition fee to determine if your coverage meets exemption requirements. Note that you will need official copies of your insurance policy translated into French to apply for your visa and your *carte de séjour*. Usually, exemptions must be approved prior to registration or you may be enrolled in your program's plan automatically.

Housing/Accommodations

Street Signs and Addresses

In French, your address and phone number are your *coordonnées* (literally, 'coordinates'). Some addresses may seem strange at first, but you'll learn these nuances rapidly. You can live on a *rue*, an *avenue*, a *boulevard*, an *impasse*, a *cour*, a *passage*, a *parc* or a *chemin*. The street number may be a regular whole number like 34 or 7 or 178, but it may also have an extra bit, *bis* or *ter*, which means that the house is attached or adjacent to the property that takes the whole number. Other aspects of the address: *bâtiment* (building name or number), *escalier* (stairway), *étage* (floor), *code* (door code), *à droite* (to the right) or *à gauche* (to the left). When visiting someone, always get as much of this information as possible. People usually will tell you something like this: *J'habite au 35, Boulevard du Montparnasse, escalier C au fond de la cour, quatrième étage à gauche* (I live at 35, Boulevard de Montparnasse, stairway C, at the back of the courtyard, fourth floor, on the left). If you see *Cedex* at the end of an address, it simply means that the address is a post office box and the mail is kept at the post office. Most buildings have either a door code, which is activated at night, or a buzzer system outside the building, called an *interphone*. There will always be a button to activate the door and, on the inside, a lit button to turn on the timer for the lights in the stairwell. When going to someone's house, always ask if there is a door code, since many buildings now have them on all day and night.

Hostels

Here are three *hotels de jeunesse* (something between a proper hotel and a youth hostel) in the center of Paris:

Le Fauconnier
11, rue Fauconnier
75004 PARIS

Le Fourcy
6, rue de Fourcy
75004 PARIS

Maubuisson
12, rue des Barres
75004 PARIS
Reservations and information for all three hotels can be sought at Le Fauconnier, or by calling: Tel: 42.74.23.45. Fax: 42.74.08.93.

Short Term Housing Options

Miles Turner's *Pauper's Paris* is a great resource for good, value hotels and student hostel listings. Here are a few:

Café Couette
8, rue d'Isly
75008 PARIS
Tel: 42.94.92.00
French "bed and breakfast" association which has rooms throughout France. Ninety francs for single and 120 FF for double room.

Ligue Française des Auberges de Jeunesse (LFAJ)
38, bd Raspail
75007 PARIS
Métro: Sèvres-Babylone
Limited to three-day stays for holders of the YHA (Youth Hostel Association) card, but very cheap.

Hôtel Studia
51, bd St. Germain
75005 PARIS
Tel: 43.26.81.00
Excellent location at Place Maubert. 244 FF with a *douche* (shower) and *petit déjeuner* (breakfast).

Finding an Apartment

Probably the most frustrating aspect of living in Paris is the hassle of searching for a place to live. The options are numerous, from finding other people to live with to cloistering yourself in your own small room. Remember, however, that the competition at certain times of the year can be extremely tough and that only those who rise early and call first will have a chance. The competition is at its worst during September and October when the Parisians come back from a month of vacation and students need to find accommodations.

The simplest and cheapest way to find accommodations is to look for individuals who have apartments or rooms to rent. In some cases, avoiding the agencies will save you a lot of paperwork, not to mention paying high commission fees, which can easily be as much as a month's rent, and a required two-month deposit plus one month's rent in advance. There are several newspapers you can consult which list housing ads *(petites annonces)* from individuals. *J'annonce* comes out weekly on Wednesday morning and *De Particulier à Particulier* comes out every Thursday morning. These two papers also have Minitel services which are updated daily. The French daily *Le Figaro* also has extensive listings. To recognize ads not placed by agencies, look for the words *propriet. loue*. For those who yearn for the security of going by the book, you can make an appointment with someone at the City Hall of your district to receive free legal advice. This service, called AILAP, can be used to verify your contract or lease and any other "suspicious" extra fees your landlord or landlady may conveniently—and convincingly—inform you after signing the contract. Other alternatives include "renting" the services of a *hussier de justice* (notary) from a housing agency for about 100 FF/hour before you move into your new apartment. He will insure that everything is done to the letter, and in under a couple of hours.

France USA Contacts, a twice monthly give-away, and the *Paris Free Voice,* community newspaper, list housing opportunities as well as all sorts of services and some job opportunities. These are available at most English language bookstores, public places and restaurants. The *International Herald Tribune* also advertises apartments but these tend to be rather up-market.

Here is a sample housing ad followed by a translated explanation.

17eme ROME. 4p. cuis. bns.
ref.nf. 4300 44435111

17th *arrondissement* near Métro Rome, 4 rooms, kitchen, bathroom, newly remodelled. 4300 FF a month. Call 44.43.51.11

Column Headings in the Newspaper

Immobilier	Real Estate
Achats et Ventes	Wanted/Offered for Sale
Location Offres/Demandes	Offered/Wanted to Rent
Meublé	Furnished
Vide	Unfurnished

Helpful Terms

agences s'abst.	no agencies
asc. (ascenseur)	elevator
bns. (bains)	bathrooms
bal. (balcon)	balcony
boxe	parking space
calme	quiet street, building
carac. (caractere)	with character
caution	security deposit
chgs. (charges)	supplementary monthly fee in addition to rent
chb. (chambre)	bedroom
chambre de bonne	maid's room
chambre indépendante	independent room
charm.	charming
chauf. cent.	central heating
com.	agent's commission
cft. (confort)	"comfort"—i.e. private bath, carpeted rooms, equipped kitchen
coq. (coquette)	cute
cour	courtyard
dche. (douche)	shower
et. el. (étage élevé)	high floor
eq. (equipped)	equipped with major appliances
except.	exceptional
garçonnière	bachelor's apt; small studio or room
grenier	attic, room under roof
imm.	building
imm. mod.	modern building
imm. nf.	new building
imm. p de t	cut stone building
imm. rec.	new building
imm. anc.	old building

interméd.	agent
jar./jdn.	garden
kit.	kitchenette, usually not windowed
loue, je loue	I am offering for rent (i.e. no agency)
lux.	luxurious (carpeting)
loyer	the rent
m2 (métre carré)	square meter (about 10 square feet)
moq.	wall-to-wall carpeting
part à part	private party to private party; no agency
p. (pièce)	room, not including bathroom
poss. (possibilité)	possibility of
pr. cpl.	for a couple only
poutres apparentes	beamed ceilings
rav. (ravissant)	delightful
ref. nf. (refait neuf)	newly remodeled
r. (rue)	street
slle. (salle)	large or formal room
salle de réception	large living room
salle à manger	formal dining room
salle d'eau	sink
salle de bains	with shower or bath
ss. (sans)	without
stdg. (standing)	"status" or "high class" building, fashionable address
gd. stdg., tr. gd. stdg.	more of the above
studio	one room apartment, usually with bath and kitchenette
s/ (sur)	on
tél	telephone
terr.	terrace
ttc (toutes charges comprises)	all charges included
w.c.	toilet, in room separate from bath and sink; water closet

There are also many bulletin boards scattered all over Paris. Try the following for finding housing:

The American Church in Paris: 65, Quai d'Orsay, 75007 PARIS, Métro: Alma-Marceau or Invalides. Tel: 47.05.07.99. Open Monday-Saturday 9h-22h30; Sundays 9h-19h30.

FUSAC (France-USA Contacts) Bulletin Board: (*Centre d'annonces et bureau*): 3, rue Larochelle, 75014 PARIS, Métro: Gaîté or Edgar Quinet. Open from Monday to Saturday 10h-19h, Saturday 12h-17h. Tel: 45.38.56.57. Fax: 45.38.98.94.

The American Cathedral: 23, ave Georges V, 75008 PARIS, Métro: Georges V, Alma-Marceau. Tel: 47.20.17.92.

Shakespeare and Company: 37, rue de la Bûcherie, 75005 PARIS, Métro: St. Michel. Open noon-midnight seven days a week.

Centre d'Information et de Documentation Jeunesse: 101, Quai Branly, 75015 PARIS, Métro: Alma-Marceau.

Many *laveries* (laundrymats), *boulangeries* (bakeries), large grocery stores (Prisunic, Monoprix, etc.) and gyms also have bulletin boards.

Short Term Housing Agencies

Mr. and Mrs. Z. Szabo (proprietor, therefore no agency fee) 7, rue Charles V 75004 PARIS Tel: 42.72.49.02

Types of Housing Contracts

• Short term furnished contracts can be for one year or less and are renewable at the option of the landlord.

• Long term unfurnished contracts are for three years and are hard for landlords to break without a just reason. Both can be broken by the renter with 1-3 months notice, depending on the agreement.

Housing Insurance

French law requires that anyone occupying space in France (an apartment, a maid's room, a studio or a room in someone else's home), be covered by property insurance. The landlord will assume that you have proof of this coverage. Such insurance, known as *"Multirisques Habitation,"* also covers personal liability for the insured party and his/her spouse, children and domestic animals. Renters are responsible for any fire or water damage originating from their apartment—not just for their premises, but for the entire building. This is so well known that your landlord may not ask for it, but you are legally liable so this must not be overlooked.

Furnished/ Unfurnished Apartments

First, consider the amount of time you are planning to stay in Paris. When looking through rent ads, note whether the apartment is furnished or unfurnished. If you are only staying for a short time, a furnished place will be much more suited to your needs, even though the rent may be higher. If you plan to stay for a while, however, consider taking an unfurnished place since you can most likely obtain a standard three year lease *(un bail de trois ans)* and will want to get set up with your own stuff. The advantages of having a three-year *bail* (lease) include a set percentage over which your rent may not increase annually, the right to sublet for one year, and the right to break your contract if you give your landlord three months notice by registered letter *(lettre recommandée avec accusé de réception)*. On the other hand, you have the right to six months notice from the landlord before having to move out, and the reasons for asking you to leave are limited by law.

When you do find an apartment, the *propriétaire* (landlord) will want a *caution* (security deposit) as well as some proof that you are financially able to pay the rent. A letter from a parent or sponsor stating financial support will normally suffice. So will a bank statement or pay slip. You will probably be asked to sign a lease. Under French law, minors (under 18) cannot sign contracts, and if you are under this age the landlord or his agent may insist that your parents or some responsible adult sign for you. If you must sign a lease, ask for an *état des lieux* or an *inventaire détaillé* (detailed inventory) of the apartment and its contents, and make two copies. This way the landlord can't hold you responsible for damage done to the apartment before you moved in. In any case, you should keep in mind that some landlords and almost no agencies will accept a guarantee of financial support from outside of France, since tracking down the tenants to pay for damages would be impossible.

The French Apartment
L'entrée

Often the best apartments are in the most unlikely places, so don't be influenced by the building's street-side appearance; the grungiest looking building with a seedy stairwell may have a beautiful garden in the courtyard and an entirely different look behind the front door. On the other hand, a well-kept entranceway with *bourgeois* details, polished brass, etc. indicates immediately that the building is of high *standing*, a term the French have borrowed.

La Cour

Most French urban structures are built in a square, around a courtyard. The Paris everyone can see is but a portion of what it contains: behind the average front door may be a formal garden complete with fountain, a stone-paved walkway leading to a private residence, hidden behind the walls of the *bâtiment* (building) or parking lot. It may also be just a playground for the children of the *concierge* or a passageway to the back section of the building.

Le/La concierge

The *concierge* in Paris, almost always a Portuguese or Spanish wife and husband team cram-med into a tiny apartment in the entranceway of the better Parisian apartments, plays a unique role in daily French life. He or she is the onsite representative of the organization or group of owners in an apartment building (*syndic*). He/she knows all, hears all, tells all, and is an essential person to get along with. Their principal tasks include shining the brass in the entranceway, distributing the mail in the building, cleaning the stairwells, doing minor repairs, carting out the garbage cans, receiving packages, etc. When you move in, and at Christmas, it is a good idea to tip your *concierge* as much as you can afford (100 FF is normal) and according to the amount of extra work you make for them. *Concierges* are very valuable allies and very powerful enemies. If problems arise over such things as noise after 22h, your concierge can often prevent or instigate much unpleasantness.

Le WC (les toilettes)

WC means "water closet," and that's what it is, a closet-sized space with a toilet. The WC (also called *le water*, pronounced as if the word was French) is very often its own separate room. Although this may seem odd at first, it's rather practical. The WC is colloquially referred to as *les chiottes* (the crapper). Other classic bathroom functions are performed in the *salle de bains*.

La salle de bains

Bidet: You may be perplexed on your first trip to a French bathroom to find this little fixture. Historically designed to serve aristocratic women as a hygienic aid, today the *bidet* can be used for lots of things, from relieving the pain of hemorrhoids, hand-washing delicate clothing, bathing a baby, or soaking your feet. Fresh water enters the fixture through a vertical spray in the center of the bowl, through a flushing rim or integral filler or through a pivotal spout that delivers a horizontal stream of water. A pop-up drain allows you to fill it with water.

Le bain/La douche: Expect anything. Although on the rise, showers are not as classically standard in daily French life as baths. Consider yourself lucky if you end up with a large enough space to stand up and lather up, let alone possess a shower curtain. This seemingly essential bathroom fixture is not seen as essential to the French. Invariably, a shower is improvised via a metal hose running from the bathtub spout, and dexterity is a must to prevent splashing, especially since you will probably not have a place to hang the nozzle on the wall. But washing your hair with one hand has got to be character-building. In the older buildings you'll have to get used to tiny tubs, sitting tubs, and other microscopic means of washing. It's all great fun. But remember to be careful. You are responsible for water damage to any and all floors below if it comes from your apartment (See *Housing Insurance*).

La Cuisine

Parisian kitchens tend to be an exercise in space utilization. They often have tiny but efficient appliances, especially refrigerators *(le frigo)* and gas stoves. Unfurnished apartments almost never come with appliances, and often don't even have kitchen cabinets. Get used to the *chaudiere*, the hearth of the French home, the gas apparatus that heats on command the water for the kitchen and bathroom. An appliance that you may not be familiar with: *la friteuse*. Also note that Parisian kitchens are very often where you house your washing machine or dryer, if you have one.

Moving In

When you have found your apartment and are ready to move in, keep in mind that the electricity and gas will probably have been turned off. Contact your local EDF-GDF office (*Electricité de France/Gaz de France*) to reactivate the service. Bring proof of address—your rental agreement, for example. And make sure to take the meter reading as you move in to avoid being charged for previous tenant's bills. You might need these to avoid paying for renters before or after you as well as proof in the case of dispute over cost of electric and gas.

To obtain a telephone, call *renseignements téléphoniques* (information—dial 12) to find out at which PTT *(Postes-Téléphones-Télégraphes)* office or France-Télécom office in your *arrondissement* you must make your request. The surest bet to have the service and number activated is to go in person. Expect a wait of seven to ten days. If there is already a phone, the landlord may insist that you list the number under your name, which is a smart move, since you would not want to pay for the previous tenant's calls, making your first bill an unpleasant surprise. If the phone is under the landlord or previous tenant's name, your access to 19 (calls out of the country) or 16 (calls out of the Paris region) may be blocked. If you are sharing the apartment with other people, it is always best to restrict the phone to local calls. For four people calling internationally, it is not uncommon to have bills up to 6,000 FF ($1,100 US) or more. As an alternative, reserve long-distance calls for your *télécarte* (see *Communications*), so you can gage how much you are spending, since it is more costly to telephone from France than from North America or Asia.

If you want an itemized bill of all calls (*une facture detaillée*) you must request this from the start. It's 20 FF a month extra. The bill comes every two months and you have two weeks to pay. Late bills are subject to a 10% penalty. And it's virtually impossible to contest items on the bill.

Moving Out

Before leaving, ask for a *relevé spécial* (special reading) of the electricity, gas and telephone from the local EDF-GDF and PTT center listed on your bills. At the EDF-GDF center, your charges can be computed immediately from the meter readings, though the telephone company takes about one or two days. Don't forget to return your phone, or you will be billed for it.

Room with a French Family

You can also rent a room in an apartment with a French family or, more often, an individual *propriétaire*. This housing arrangement usually consists of a private room with limited access to the kitchen, telephone and bathroom facilities. Each situation offers varying degrees of privacy. Some landlords have more than one room to rent in their apartments, making it possible for two students to live together. Others have large rooms that can be shared by two people. There are varying degrees of comfort (private or shared bathroom, television, personal phone) and the price fluctuates accordingly. Landladies and couples are usually interested in some cultural exchange, which can help enable the student ease his/her way into daily French life. This is an arrangement that can often be made through your particular school's housing office. AUP and several other university programs make extensive housing arrangements of this kind.

Chambre de bonne

The most inexpensive form of accommodations is usually a *chambre de bonne* or *chambre de service* (maid's room). This is usually a converted maid's room on the top floor of a bourgeois apartment building. It often has a separate entrance from that of the landlord (very often a 6th or 7th floor walk-up) via a service entrance. It is usually a small room for one person with a sink and a hot plate. Many independent rooms do not have private showers or full kitchens, but shared shower and bathroom facilities are usually available in the hallway. Some landlords offer the use of the shower in their apartment. This doesn't sound too glamorous but it can have its charm for a while. With simple accommodations you can focus more time and money on Paris itself.

Au Pair

Another alternative to finding an apartment is to look for an *au pair* position. *Au pair* arrangements are available primarily but not exclusively for female students. This work often consists of baby-sitting, housework, English lessons, mother's helper chores, collecting children at school, or any combination thereof in exchange for room and board and a small salary. It often entails some evening or weekend work. Students must generally have some knowledge of French and be willing to work a regular schedule. Though the conditions of such positions can vary, the following agencies will arrange *au pair* positions. They require that students be at least 18 years old and under 30 years of age, have a valid student visa and be enrolled in classes, and will ensure that students are paid pocket money (not salary) of about 1500 FF a month plus room and board in exchange for up to 30 hours a week of work. For full-time students with a heavy workload, it is wise to find *au pair* work not more that 10-20 hours per week. You should keep in mind that *au pairs* are often treated as paid help rather than members of the family. The quality of this experience depends wholly on the household that you work in. Some experiences can be wonderful, especially when the host family is not only friendly, open, and instructive, but also has a country house in Normandy or Burgundy or asks you to accompany them on vacation to the Alps or Riviera.

During the school year, a minimum stay of three months is required. The regular program stay is normally one year, but it can be extended to a maximum of 18 months. A student may stay with more than one family during the *au pair* period, but the total stay cannot exceed 18 months.

There are also summer *au pair* programs of one to three months. In these cases, the requirement that the *au pair* be taking French courses is waived if the student has completed at least one year of college-level French studies.

Most families provide their *au pair* with a *carte orange*, a monthly pass valid for the Métro, buses and suburban trains, but they are not always required to do so by the Ministry of Labor regulations. The family must declare the *au pair* as *stagiaire aide familiale* to the French Social Security Administration (URSSAF) and make the monthly contribution (*cotisation*) so the *au pair* will receive social security benefits in case of illness or accidents.

After arrival in France with a visa, the classic *au pair* must apply within eight days for a residence permit (see section on Residence Permits and *cartes de séjour*).

Along with his/her work contract, the classic *au pair* must present evidence of registration in a French language school (Alliance Française, the Sorbonne, etc.). Evening classes are not acceptable.

Having obtained an *au pair* position, the *au pair* returns to the *Service de la Main d'Oeuvre Etrangère* to receive a temporary work permit *(autorisation provisoire de travail)*. The permit is normally valid for six months and is renewable.

Accueil Familial des Jeunes Etrangères: 23, rue du Cherche-Midi, 75006 PARIS, Métro: Sèvres-Babylone. Tel: 42.22.50.34. Open Monday-Friday from 10h-16h and Saturday from 10h-noon.

Arche: 7, rue Bargue, 75015 PARIS, Métro: Volontaires. Tel: 42.73.34.39. Open Monday-Friday from 9h 17h.

Géolangues: 25, rue de Navarin, 75009 PARIS, Métro: Place Clichy. Tel: 45.26.14.53. Open Monday-Friday from 9h30-18h30.

Inter Séjour: 179, rue de Courcelles, 75017 PARIS, Tel: 47.63.06.81. Open Monday-Friday 9h30-17h30.

Relations Internationales: 20, rue de l'Exposition, 75007 PARIS, Métro: Ecole Militaire. Tel: 45..50.23.23. Open Monday-Friday from 9h-12h30 and from 14h-18h30.

Here are a few more places to try when looking for housing and/or *au pair* positions:

A.C.I.S.J.F.
63, rue Monsieur-le-Prince
75006 PARIS
Tel: 43.26.92.84
Métro: Odéon
Hours: Monday and Wednesday only 2-6 pm; closed August

Alliance Française
101, bd Raspail
75006 PARIS
Tel: 45.44.38.28
Métro: Rennes, St. Placide
(For their students only) Hours: Monday—Friday 10 a.m.-6 p.m.

Institut Catholique
21, rue d'Assas
75006 PARIS
Tel: 45.48.31.70
Métro: Rennes
Hours: Monday-Friday 9:30 a.m.—5:30 p.m. (closed 12—2:30) Saturday 9:30—12:00 Open all year round except Saturdays in July and August.

Foyer le Pont
86, rue de Gergovie
75014 PARIS
Tel: 45.42.51.21
Métro: Pernety
(Six-month students only. And while financed by the German Government, the Foyer is open to others as well) Hours: Monday—Thursday 9 a.m.—5 p.m., closed 12 noon—2 p.m. Friday 9 a.m.—12 noon.

A.P.E.C.
39, rue Gounod
92210 ST CLOUD
Tel: 46.02.90.83

Cité Universitaire

This lovely campus complex has rooms available at very reasonable rates in 30 different *maisons* (houses) for university students (under 30) studying in Paris. If you are an architecture buff, you might want to investigate the two *maisons* designed by Le Corbusier: the Swiss Foundation and the Franco-Brazilian Foundation. Make sure to call or write far in advance of your arrival date if you are considering this option. Rooms go fast, and can only be booked for a year-long period. A single room goes for 90 FF per day, and 1200 FF per month; monthly double room rates are 1500 FF, depending on the *maison*. This could also be a good alternative to a hotel while you are looking for other accommodations—rooms are available to anyone with an International Student Identity Card at 80-100 FF per night during the summer and in September before the beginning of the school year. Accommodations are usually provided in the *maison* of the country from which the student originates;

some houses prefer graduate students only. A list of all the houses is available from the central office at the following address:

Cité Universitaire
47B bd Jourdan
75014 PARIS
Tel: 45.89.13.37

Or try contacting one of the following directly:

Fondation des Etats-Unis
Cité Universitaire
15, bd Jourdan
75690 PARIS Cedex 14
Tel: 45.89.35.77 (administration)
Tel: 45. 89.35.79 (students)
Director: Terence MURPHY

Maison des Etudiants du Canada
31, bd Jourdan
75014 PARIS
Tel: 40.78.67.00

Neighborhoods

To give you an idea in advance of the difference between neighborhoods, a general idea of Paris' principal areas and a brief, subjective description of each of the 20 *arrondissements* has been included. Use the map on the next page to locate these areas. Note that 75005 means Paris 5th *arrondissement*, etc.

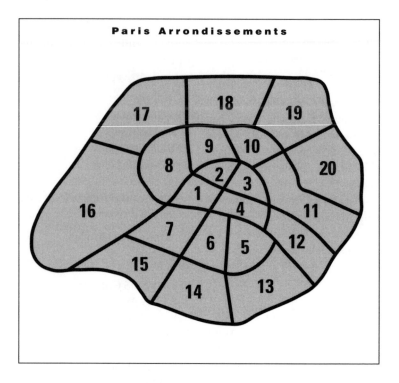

Paris Arrondissements

Neighborhoods/*Quartiers*

Opéra: 1st, 2nd and 9th *arrondissements*
Les Halles: 1st
Le Marais: 3rd and 4th
Ile Saint-Louis: 4th
Quartier Latin: 5th
Saint Germain: 6th
Champs de Mars/Invalides: 7th
Etoile/Faubourg St-Honoré: 8th
Bastille: 11th, edge of 12th
Chinatown: 13th
Parc Monceau: 17th
Montparnasse: 14th and 15th
Victor Hugo/Palais de Chaillot: 16th
Montmartre: 18th
Belleville/Ménilmontant: 19th and 20th.

Paris by Arrondissement

There is of course quality housing with charm in every *quartier*, but a notion of each area might be helpful in deciding where to look and what to consider. The following comments should be especially useful when having to select a neighborhood sight unseen. One of your first purchases in Paris should be a small square red or black book called *Plan de Paris par Arrondissements*, which includes detailed maps, a street and Métro index, and bus routes. This is indispensable for finding your way around Paris. Trust this advice, you'll need a *plan*. Carry it at all times.

1er—Central Paris, well connected by Métro and bus. Tends to be pricey and very busy. Not a great place if you have a car. Châtelet is very congested, but very central. Chic and trendy around Les Halles. The park Palais-Royal is a bastion of undisturbed Parisian elegance.

2e—Also central but more commercial in the sense of wholesale outlets. Sentier is the core of Paris' garment district. You may find unusual places to live here but it's more the exception than the rule. The parts near the Opera and Madeleine are very high rent districts and not especially inviting as far as daily Parisian neighborhood life. The streets between Les Halles and the Grands Boulevards are some of the oldest, truly Parisian and enchanting you'll find. The rue Montorgeuil, the oldest market street in Paris, is worth a detour. Also contains the fashion-chic Place des Victoires.

3e, 4e—Very central with many lovely little streets, cafés, shops, etc. Congested, but worth it. Expensive. The Marais has lots of living advantages. One of the most desirable areas of Paris, for those who insist on old buildings with character and multicultural exposure.

5e—Left Bank, the Latin Quarter. This is where you get both the chic and the classy. The areas down by St. Michel are tight and noisy but you can't beat the location. The areas closer to the 13e are more residential, well connected to the center of Paris and very pleasant. You can't go wrong in the 5e. Tends to be expensive, but great little finds are not impossible.

6e—Left Bank, St. Germain des Prés, Odéon. This is for the wealthy and artistic. Many bookshops, galleries, cinemas, classy cafés, restaurants and publishers. Between St. Germain and the Seine, prices are sky high. The 6th extends to Montparnasse and to Duroc. Lots of wonderful little streets. Very desirable.

7e—Tends to be expensive, high class and residential. Also houses many government ministries. Not very lively at night, although very pleasant and pretty. The street behind Les Invalides, the avenue de Tourville, is the most expensive property in the French version of Monopoly. The Esplanade des Invalides offers sprawling lawns that are not off-limits for frisbee-playing and picnicking.

8e—Right bank. Financial and corporate territory. Champs-Elysees. Very high rents and a lot of pomp. Lots of motion and money. Some surprisingly quaint and quiet streets. The rue St. Honoré has to be a highlight for extravagant Sunday window shopping.

9e—This includes Pigalle and Clichy. More *populaire*, meaning working-class. This can be fun. Depends on particular street and apartment. Don't exclude this. The covered passageways wait to be discovered.

10e—There are some great spots near La République and along the St. Martin canal, although along the major boulevards and St. Denis, an element of tackiness and sleaze is present. Definitely worth checking out. Less expensive than nearby 3e and 4e.

11e—Not too far from things and still filled with great finds, but hurry up. Close to the Bastille on one end and Nation on the other. The 11e has a lot to offer without the pretentions of the Marais. Excellent for artists.

12e—Similar to the 11e; up and coming around Bercy and Gare de Lyon, areas that were rather run-down and depressed. Not the most beautiful district, but you may find more space for less francs here than elsewhere. New construction tends to be hideous.

13e—The heart of Chinatown. Here you can find quaint streets with little houses next to horrible rows of Miami Beach style high rises. Some excellent, authentic Chinese restaurants. The areas near the 5e are very desirable.

14e—Denfert, Montparnasse, Porte d'Orléans. On the major north south axis. Many popular neighborhoods and great markets. Without a doubt some of the best residential living in Paris.

15e—Highly sought-after residential district among Parisians. Comfortable and not without its share of trees. The parts near the Seine host an unlikely outcrop of Japanese tourist hotels (to be avoided). The rue du Commerce captures the essence of daily Parisian family life.

16e—Etoile, Trocadéro, etc. Perhaps the most boring and bourgeois area of Paris, yet one of the richest spots on earth. Many students end up here, attracted by the nearby Champs-Elysées, prestigious address and safety (a mistake). The streets, although pretty, are dead quiet at night and there is nothing to do. Street life is absent except around the rue de Passy.

17e—The most schizophrenic district of Paris. Half as bourgeois as the 16e, Parc Monceau is absolutely lovely—to stroll around. The other half is *populaire*, real and even funky. A bit far from the heart of things but this could be worth it if you want to really experience Paris life. Prices vary dramatically.

18e—Kind of far from central districts, although this depends if you're on a good Métro line. More immigrants than elsewhere. Less expensive, so you definitely can get more for your money. Lots of things to discover. Touches Montmartre.

19e—Probably the least known of all the Paris districts, mainly because it is so isolated. Not very convenient in most cases, but again, you may find a great space near a Métro. Check it out.

20e—A lively mix of races and ethnic groups, Africans, Antilleans, etc. Some excellent work spaces and artists' atelliers. Less expensive than the middle of town, working class, and less prestige, but it all depends on what you want.

21e—Not yet a reality, but discussion and some advanced advertising is already circulating. This district will include parts of the north east quadrant of Paris around the canals near La Villette and Pantin where new neighborhoods are being carved.

A Word
on the *Banlieue*

You may find yourself living in the Parisian suburbs, which can be either pleasant or grim, depending on your expectations and the actual town you're in. The closest suburbs which touch Paris, and are well-served by Métro and bus lines, are called the *proche-banlieue*. The most "exclusive" and desirable include Neuilly, Boulogne and St. Cloud to the west, and St. Mandé and Vincennes to the east. The little towns in the Vallée de Chevreuse, served by the RER, are the most desirable southern *banlieues*. The towns to the north tend to be the poorest and what the French would describe as sad *(triste)*. The northern suburbs and scattered others have experienced increases in crime, drugs, and delinquency in public places and housing projects called *cités* or *zones*. Bands or gangs of bored youth called *les casseurs* from these suburbs have on occasion invaded student demonstrations and vandalized and looted sections of Paris. The "Red Suburbs" signify the municipalities governed by the Communist Party and include Montreuil, Bagnolet, Bobigny, Kremlin-Bicêtre, Malakoff, etc. These communities, although not very different from the others, tend in theory to cater to the needs of the working class. In towns like Montreuil, which houses the headquarters for the CGT (powerful left-wing worker's union), there are large Arab and African communities. Apartments and work-spaces here can be cheaper and more spacious than anywhere in Paris. The more distant suburbs *(grandes banlieues)*, such as Versailles, St. Germain-en-Laye and Chantilly, are served by RER and commuter trains. The eastern line of the RER has recently been extended to Marne la Vallée to better serve the newly opened EuroDisneyland. The choice to live in the suburbs is a highly personal one depending on how important it is for you to be in the vicinity of Paris with its cafés and night life. The suburbs tend to be quiet at night and provincial in feel. Often there seems to be little difference in being 10 kilometres or 200 kilometres from Paris. Several Paris suburbs, nonetheless, offer very vibrant cultural programming such as the Banlieue Jazz and Banlieue Bleues Festival in Seine St. Denis, the Children's Book Fair in Montreuil, and the public theater in Bobigny.

As 1992 approached and arrived—the portentous date for the member countries of the European Economic Community (EEC) to coordinate and consolidate many aspects of their local economies and commercial and cultural sectors into one united entity—French banking laws and practices have not yet really loosened up as hoped. Plans are materializing for a single European Ecu currency, which following the historic meetings in Maastricht in 1991 is expected to affect France by 1996 should the needed constitutional amendments be ratified in time. In the next few years, regardless, French banks will have to begin offering more complete services for international customers at competitive prices. Your reactions and experiences with French and international banks in France will undoubtedly vary depending on what you're accustomed to. Remember one thing—France has never really been a service-oriented society. Things do not run around the omnipresent operating practice that the customer is always right. Although money and financial gain play an important role in France, as in all Western societies, the French are unwilling to sacrifice everything for the sake of profit. A shopkeeper may refuse to stay open slightly after closing time, even to make a sale. Businesses often don't answer phones at lunchtime. Real estate brokers will wait for you to call back. All this can be both enchanting and annoying. Learn to be enchanted—the quality of daily life wins out over more aggressive commercial practices. Take the longer meal.

In banks, you will probably not have a personal first-name-basis relationship with your banker. He or she will not close each transaction with a drippy but sincere "Have a Nice Day." You will experience this everywhere from banks to restaurants. If you receive moderately polite and efficient service in a bank consider yourself lucky. And don't expect toaster ovens or Walkmans for opening an account! Patience is not a commodity found in abundance when the thick Plexiglass *guichet* (window) service is involved. No one in any particular branch of any bank will ever have the authority to credit your account one *centime* without first passing on your written request to *la direction* (management) of the bank. All operations, complaints, modifications and verifications are slow and tedious and, when possible, should be avoided. It is a good idea to get yourself known by at least two bank employees at your branch. That way when one is *en vacances* (on holiday) you still have a chance of better service if needed. This will save you time and aggravation in that a number of bank operations run smoother when you're recognized and don't have to provide identification each time. Over the last five years, France has become highly *informatisée* (computerized) in everything from banking to dating. *Guichets automatiques* (automatic tellers for withdrawing cash) abound. Between your *Carte Bleue* bank payment card and the Minitel, the private citizen in France essentially has access to all sectors of commercial life. This computerization comes as much from the French love of form (or, systems and structures) and aesthetics (or, style) as from a search for greater efficiency. So, service in France is improving in business as less and less is required from human interaction.

As for banking you'll probably have a few early questions: How do I change money? How can I receive money from abroad? What do I need to open a bank account? Which banks are the best for students? Where can I cash travelers checks? And what about credit cards in France? These are all answered in the pages to come.

A society's relationship to money reveals much about that society. If you're coming from the United States, where banking (except currency conversion in small banks) is a relatively easy and flexible activity, you may be frustrated at first when even attempting simple transactions. In France, the banks are a highly regulated industry. The State has played an increasingly present role in matters of banking since 1983, when Mitterand nationalized the industry. There are a handful of huge and omnipresent banks that have hundreds of branches all over Paris and in a majority of towns in the provinces. The largest French banks, and thus the ones with the most branch offices, are Crédit Agricole, Banque Nationale de Paris (BNP), Crédit Lyonnais and Société Générale. These are the most visible and the easiest to work with concerning overseas transfers, but they don't necessarily provide better service than the smaller banks. When selecting a bank, first consider the branch's location in terms of convenience to your home, place of work, or school. Here are a few key banks well-adapted for foreigners, where you'll be able to change money and ask questions. Insist on service. If you're displeased, go elsewhere; there are plenty of banks and almost as many answers to your questions as there are banks. Don't forget that in France the post office *(La Poste)* also serves as the largest banking facility in the country, issuing checking, savings, and money management accounts that are often advantageous with regards to income taxes. One reason *La Poste* is popular is that every post office is a branch, the hours extend from 8 a.m. to 7 p.m. (till noon on Saturdays), and every transaction is confirmed with a receipt by mail. This makes for easy bookkeeping. One snag: *La Poste* often requires that its banking customers have *résident* status.

American Express International
11, rue Scribe
75009 PARIS
Tel: 47.77.77.07
Travel agency, exchange service, clients' mail and travelers' checks. Open 9h-17h Monday-Saturday for clients mail, currency exchange and travelers checks and 9h-17h30 Monday-Friday for travel agency. In cases of stolen credit cards during hours of closure, call 47.77.72.00. For lost travelers checks call AMEX in Brighton, England at telephone number (19)05.90.86.00 (free call—all 05 calls, *numeros verts,* are automatically collect). American Express *green* card holders, that is, the normal card, can write checks off their accounts up to $1,000 per week, and for those with gold cards, the limit is $2,000 per week.

Crédit Commercial de France (CCF):
115, Champs-Elysées
75008 PARIS
Métro: George-V
Hours: Open every day, 8h30-20h and in July, August and September on Sundays from 10h15-18h.
Tel: 40.70.27.22 or 40.70.77.17

Banque Nationale de Paris (BNP)
Place de l'Opéra
at rue du Quatre Septembre
75002 PARIS
Métro: Opéra
24-hour VISA automatic cash machine and automatic changer for foreign notes.
Tel: 42.66.23.89

Barclays Bank
33, rue du Quatre Septembre
75002 PARIS
Métro: Opéra
9h30-16h, Monday-Friday
and Rond-Point des Champs-Elysées
75008 PARIS
Métro: Champs-Elysées-Clemenceau
Barclay checks only, and travelers checks. 7,50 FF commission on checks up to £100.

Crédit Lyonnais
55, av des Champs-Elysées
75008 PARIS
Métro: Franklin Roosevelt
Tel: 45.62.96.15
Espace CL: 40.82.56.56

Banking Hours: generally 9h00-16h30 or 17h00 on week-days, closed on weekends. Foreign banks close at 16h00. The currency exchange closes for lunch.

Foreign Currency Exchange: Open nightly on weekdays until 20h00 at the Gare St. Lazare and the Gare de L'Est, everyday at the Gare du Nord and Gare de Lyon until 21h00 and 23h00, respectively. Many banks also have exchange windows, usually open during select hours (never during lunch). The Crédit Commercial de France, 113 ave des Champs-Elysées, is open on Saturdays from 8h30-20h00. Many private exchange services have opened all over the city, most in response to the five million tourists who came for the bicentennial and the flood of new Japanese visitors in France. One change outfit with a major presence in Paris is Exact Change with 17 key loca-tions (4, bd St. Michel, 75006 is the main address), noted for its English speaking tellers and its competitive rates. These are usually reliable in terms of rates and commission and advantage-ous in terms of hours. Another popular one is called Cheque-point (Head Office, 150, av des Champs-Elysées), which accepts Eurocheques and personal checks drawn on British bank accounts. Remember you can always negotiate a slightly better exchange rate with these walk-up change bureaus, especially if you're changing large sums. If they won't budge, go elsewhere. Be wary of individual money changers in that numerous travelers and students have reported being victims of short change artists. Some have even ended up with fists full of worthless Polish *zlotes*.

Opening an Account

There has been some ambiguity as to the procedures for foreign-ers to open accounts in France. This stems from the curious fact that rules, regulations and form-alities vary greatly from not only bank to bank but between branches of the same bank. As a student or new resident, you'll want to remember that the way you're handled is highly discretionary. So, it's to your advantage to present yourself well, convey stability, respecta-bility and the certainty and regularity of deposits. If you hit a snag, don't fight or lose sleep; try another branch, or another bank—there are plenty.

In most cases, you'll be asked for a *carte de séjour* and proof of address (EDF/GDF strikes again). However, even this fluctuates. One Société Générale manager stated confidently "just a passport will do." The BNP, although one of the largest banks, tends to require a lot of paperwork. The Société Générale may ask for fewer documents to begin with, but tends to be cautious in issuing checkbooks and *Carte Bleue* bank payment cards. Some of the smaller banks like B.R.E.D. may prove to be the easiest in opening up accounts and offering services but have fewer branch offices. Many banks will only let you open accounts if you live or work in the neighborhood of the branch.

For your first two years in France you will be entitled to a *compte non-résident* (non-resident account) unless you are from an EEC country. Previously, the *compte non-résident* limited you to making deposits from outside of France. These regulations have been dropped. So essentially there is no difference between a *compte non-résident* and a *compte résident* for deposits up to 50,000 FF. You

can withdraw and deposit funds of any currency without limit. Note that although it's easy to deposit foreign currency checks and cash, hefty and seemingly illogical fees and commissions may be debited from your account and a delay of up to four weeks may occur before payment is completed. In most cases, you'll receive your *chéquier* (check book) in 2-3 weeks, and, if you request one, your *Carte Bleue* bank payment card. Cards must be picked up in person while check books may be sent to you via registered mail at your expense. When you leave France, you might want to maintain your account in that after two years you'll qualify for a *compte résident*. This is easier than starting everything over should you decide to return and an easy way to settle bills that arrive later.

Checking Accounts

The personal check plays a vast role in daily French life. You will most certainly want to open *un compte-chèque* (a checking account) and *carnet de chèques* or *chèquier* (check book), in that paying by check is the most widely accepted and easiest form of handling your affairs in French, although this is being seriously challenged by the almost omnipresent *Carte Bleue*. Everywhere from restaurants to gas stations, the personal check is readily accepted. You can even pay for your monthly Métro pass with a check. All stores accept checks. The post office accepts checks, too. You will often, but not systematically, be asked to show some form of identification when you pay by check. The reason for the widespread acceptance of checks stems from the fact that checks in France are not negotiable or even cashable as they are in the US, Canada, and to a great extent, the U.K. Most checks in France are *barrés*, meaning they have two lines or bars pre-printed across the front of each check. This simply signifies that the check cannot be signed and re-endorsed for payment to a third party. All checks thus must be deposited into the bank account of the person whose name appears on the face of the check. So, be wary of accepting a personal check from someone if you do not have a bank account yourself. You will not be able to go to the maker's bank and cash the check. It must be deposited. This means that all payments by check are officially recorded and thus are easily controlled by bank inspectors, accountants, and eventually the

fisc (tax collectors). Most salaries in France are paid directly into the employees bank account via *virement* (electronic bank transfer). Similarly, bank mortgages, utility payments, telephone bills, etc. are often deducted automatically from the recipient's account. A *relevé de compte* (R.I.P.) is the printed form at the top of your monthly statement that gives all the codes of your account, bank and branch. These are demanded of you when payment is to be wired directly into your account. This obviously limits the mobility of money in French society, but it also restricts seriously the degree of fraud and the frequency of bounced checks or bad checks (*chèque en bois*—wooden check). It can be difficult to stop payment on a check (*faire opposition à un chèque*) and French law is unrelenting concerning writers of bad checks, although as the economy tightens more and more bad checks are in circulation. The strictest penalty is being declared to the national Banque de France, where your name goes on a list of people not allowed to have checking accounts in France. On the following page is a sample *chèque*.

Banque Nationale de Paris
B.P.F. **88 F**

Payez contre ce chèque non endossable sauf au profit d'un établissement bancaire ou assimilé :

quatre vingt / huit francs

A Frank Boodo, SARL
PAYABLE
PLACE MAUBERT
19 RUE LAGRANGE
75005 PARIS

A Paris
le 15 mai 1992

tél (1) 43 29 77 31
compensable à   PARIS
chèque n°

Savings Accounts

Un compte d'épargne sur livret (savings account) can also be opened. Most banks will pay modest interest on funds left in savings accounts for extended periods. Your current balance will be noted in *le livret* (passbook) after each deposit or withdrawal. In France, many people also have a P.E.L. (*Plan d'Epargne Logement*), a government-subsidized, low-interest bearing savings account designed to accrue credits toward a future low-interest loan to be used exclusively for the purchase of a house or apartment or a home improvement project. Minimum monthly deposits of 300 FF for at least five years are required to benefit from this account. *La Poste* also offers other beneficial savings plans.

Credit Cards

In France the *Carte Bleue* (CB) offered by each bank has truly become an institution in daily life. The French attraction for computerized systems has been married to this centralized form of payment. The CB (part of both the VISA and Mastercard/Eurocard network) is widely accepted, although it is not really a credit card; it's a payment card. Purchases and automatic cash withdrawals are debited from your checking account. Thus, you do not really get true credit. You do not receive a monthly credit card statement and you cannot run up large bills. You do not have a credit line other than the overdraft limit permitted by your bank. Your use of the card is debited automatically. The idea of real credit, that great and abusive invention that permits people to live painlessly beyond their means, is still rather foreign in Europe. The main advantage of the *Carte Bleue* is its surprisingly wide acceptance.

You can pay your tolls on the *autoroute* with your CB; you can pay all your supermarket purchases with your CB as well as automatic underground parking lots; you can even stick your CB into a ticket machine in selected Métro stations to buy your monthly *Carte Orange*, or purchase a museum admission ticket in the lobby of the Louvre with your CB. The list continues. CB cards now contain not only a magnetic band which permits users to draw up to 1800 FF per week cash from any bank's automatic teller machines, but also a circular micro chip *(puce)* into which your four digit access code (PIN) is inscribed. This system has eliminated the need for customers to sign bills as many restaurants, gas stations, hotels, etc. now have portable, cordless machines that read the *puce* and check it against the number the customer punches in. CB cards sometimes malfunction and need to be rubbed with a clean cloth. When using the automatic tellers note that they only accept cards issued on French banks, so don't stick your Visa, Mastercard, or American Express cards into one of them. It may retain the card and you'll have to return the next day with your passport to retrieve it. Cards eaten by machines in the Métro, etc. take several weeks before being returned to your bank branch.

All major credit card companies are represented in France. Here are phone numbers in case of lost or stolen cards:

American Express
Tel: 47.77.70.00
Lost cards: 47.77.72.00

Diners Club de France
Tel: 47.62.75.00 (Info)

(Mastercard) Eurocard
Tel: 45.67.53.53
Lost cards: 45.67.84.84

(Visa) Carte Bleue
Tel: 42.25.51.51
Lost cards: 42.77.11.90 (Paris)
(16) 54.42.12.12 (provinces)

Transferring Funds From Abroad

Getting Cash Fast

One of the most important questions you may someday have about banking is: "How can I get money quickly from home?" Despite assurances made by many issuing banks in other countries, the majority of money orders and interbank checks—and all personal checks—must normally be cleared through the issuing bank before they can be credited to your account. This can take weeks. Other, possibilities include:

• Wire transfer: the sender can wire money directly to a French franc account, specifying the branch name and the address of your bank—this normally takes 48 hours. Always note the *siège* (branch) number and *clé* R.I.B. (bank code). Having money telexed to your Paris bank account can be done quickly if the issuing bank is directly affiliated with the receiving bank so that the money does not have to go through intermediaries. For example, money telexed from the Crédit Lyonais in New York will go directly into your account in a Parisian branch if the branch name and account number are specified. If you plan to receive a regular transfer of funds over a period of time, and if the issuing bank is not directly affiliated with your bank in Paris, count on the transfer to take as long as four weeks. Therefore, it is a good idea to ask your home bank if it is affiliated with a French bank before you open an account. Most banks have an electronic bank transfer system called SWIFT, which doesn't always live up to its name, in that although the actual transfer takes one day, some banks may take a day to send the order from one branch to a larger one, and then another to process the transfer. When weekends and holidays interfere money can be slowed down tremendously. Depositing foreign fund checks into a French bank account can take weeks to clear and cost you high fees. It's usually better to group small checks and deposit them together than individually. On some occasions a small sum like ten dollars or ten pounds might cost you less not to deposit. Depositing *Eurochèques* in either French francs or foreign currency will cost you at least 30 FF per check plus the commission and exchange charge and TVA sales tax.

• American Express: if you have no account in France, a wire transfer can be made through American Express—one of the most rapid systems. A "Money-gram" allows one to send or receive cash instantly; the minimum being $100 US and the maximum being $2,000.US. You will be unable to transfer more than $1000 US to a resident of France. Transfers to residents of over $1000 US must go through their French bank accounts and will take about two weeks to clear with a transfer charge being levied. This is to control, for tax purposes mainly, the flow of large amounts of money to and from residents of France. The

American Express Bank on the Champs Elysée is not for currency exchange. At the rue Scribe address, you can draw French cash against your American Express card.

• Bank checks in francs: have the sender purchase a bank check drawn in French francs at your Paris bank's foreign branch and send it to you through the mail.

• Pray

Taxes

To help you understand the complicated French tax laws, Price Waterhouse offers a booklet entitled *The French Pocket Tax Book* as well as legal and tax advice, available at: 18, Place Henri-Bergson, 75008 PARIS. Tel: 42.94.45.45. For a discussion of TVA (sales tax) see the section on Duty Free. For a discussion of income taxes see Pineau and Kelly's book, *Working in France.*

Here's a quick lexicon of French fiscal taxes and fees:

impôt sur le revenu: income tax—tax returns due each year usually in February or March. Payments are made on an annual, trimesteral, or monthly basis. For an average income count on about one month's salary in income taxes.

TVA (taxe sur la valeur ajoutée): sales tax—built in tax of 18.6% on most goods and services. 33% on luxury items. 5.5% on books. There is talk of creating a unified TVA for Europe set at 15%.

taxe foncière: property tax—an annual tax on the value of land and housing to be paid by the owner.

taxe professionnelle: professional tax—a sum levied on all businesses for the right to conduct business based on surface space being used for professional purpose.

taxe d'habitation(impôts locaux): municipal housing tax—an annual local tax imposed on housing payable to the town by both owners and renters.

vignette: motor vehicle registration sticker—purchased each autumn at any *tabac* in the *département* in which the vehicle is registered. Price is based on year of car and size of engine.

Doing Business/ Forming a Company

This is potentially complicated—for assistance, consult the U.S. Embassy Foreign Commercial Service at 2, ave Gabriel, 75382 PARIS CEDEX 8, Tel: 42.96.12.02, FAX: 42.66.97.83. Additionally, information and support can be obtained from the American Chamber of Commerce in France, 21, av Georges V, 75008 PARIS, Tel: 47.23.80.26 or 47.23.70.28. The Chamber of Commerce publishes a business directory and a magazine called *Commerce in France* and a pamphlet on small companies in France as well as its directory of members. A third resource is the French-American Chamber of Commerce located at 7, rue Jean Goujon, 75008 PARIS, Tel: 42.56.05.00. For a list of Lawyers see *Paris Anglophone.* One Canadian lawyer who specializes in assisting foreigners set up working papers, business plans, and legal status is: Daniel Laprès, 11, rue Jules Chaplain, 75006 PARIS, Tel: 43.26.77.90. For accounting and TVA help you could try Raymond Laudui at Fiduciaire Union, Tel: 42.55. 60.22.

Student Employment
Part-Time

American and other foreign students in France can, under certain conditions, obtain a temporary work permit *(autorisation provisoire de travail)* for part-time *(mi-temps)* work during the summer vacation months or during the regular school year. Students at the Sorbonne's *"Cours de Civilisation Française,"* the Alliance Française, the Institut Catholique and at any other school which does not provide French Social Security medical care coverage of students are not eligible for temporary work permits.

Part-time work during the school year is limited to a maximum of 20 hours per week, and during the summer vacation, a maximum of 39 hours per week. Each year, the French Government issues instructions during the last trimester of the academic year governing part-time employment from June 1 of the current year through May 31 of the following year.

Part-Time Employment During the Summer Vacation

The following categories of foreign students can be considered for summer employment if they have completed one year of study in France.

• Students pursuing higher (university) studies, including *établissements d'enseignements supérieur, facultés, grandes écoles* and *écoles de preparation aux grandes écoles.*
• Students, 16 years and older, in secondary and technical schools (*colleges* and *lycées*).
• Students aged 14 and 15 (light work only).

Summer work cannot exceed three months and must fall within the time frame of June 1 to October 31, except for a maximum of 15 days each for the Christmas and Easter holidays. The work period for students aged 14 and 15 is limited to one-half of their school vacation time.

Part-Time Employment During the School Year

Part-time employment during the academic year is restricted to foreign students attending French universities and other institutions of higher learning. A student must submit his or her current card *(carte d'étudiant)* in order to be eligible. Secondary and technical school students are not eligible.

Temporary work permits are usually given to students who do not have sufficient private resources to pursue their studies. Thus, recipients of grants and those who have sufficient means are not authorized to have temporary work permits. Students wishing to work part-time during the school year must, in addition to the usual documents (see below), submit a letter justifying the need to work as a student.

The part-time work must fall within the academic year. The temporary work permit is valid for three months and may be renewed upon presentation of evidence of continuing studies.

Where To Apply for a Temporary Work Permit

Foreigners attending French universities in Paris should apply at:
Ministère du Travail
Service de la Main d'Oeuvre Etrangère
80, rue de la Croix Nivert
75015 PARIS
Tel: 45.31.10.03/40.56.60.00
Hours: 9:30 a.m.-11:30 a.m. and 1:30 p.m.-4:30 p.m. Métro: Commerce.

Documents Required

The student should present the following:
• Valid residence card *(carte de séjour)*
• French university student card *(carte d'étudiant)*
• Letter from an employer stating the following:

-name and address of applicant
-position of job description
-number of hours to be worked
-wages offered
-place of work
-length of employment

In addition to the documents listed above, students in French secondary and technical schools must present a letter from their parents authorizing them to work if they are under 18, and foreign students aged 14 and 15 must furnish proof that their parents are legally residing in France. Also, students in secondary and technical schools must present a *certificat de scolarité* in lieu of a *carte d'étudiant.*

You will probably also be required to prove that you are not a French *boursier* (French State Scholarship Recipient) by picking up a waiver form at: CNOUS, 6 rue Jean Calvin, 5e, Métro Censier. Open 13h30-16h. This might seem silly but it's necessary while being simple to obtain.

Otherwise, three-month work permits are issued to students at CIEE at 1, Place de l'Odéon 75006 PARIS for the fee of 500 FF. In that regulations and fees are subject to change, it is wise to always verify latest information.

For complete and detailed information on career and employment opportunities in France, along with model resumés and cover letters and pointers on interviewing in French, consult *Working In France,* by Carol Pineau and Maureen Kelly (Frank Books, 1991).

WORKING IN *France*

The Ultimate Guide to Job Hunting and Career Success à la française

Carol Pineau & Maureen Kelly

Upon arrival, one may be struck by the charming inconveniences of the Parisian shopping system. Although large supermarkets and mall-style complexes are cropping up all over—especially the suburbs—one who has spent time in North America might find French supermarkets both fascinating and annoying. These places tend to be an enigma of grandeur and chaos. Contradictions galore—lots of space with spotty selections, bright aisles and poorly maintained shelves, great slogans and surly or ill-trained service. First and foremost, remember to bring along your own shopping bags, basket or backpack. Only thin and tiny baggies are given away for free. They are practically useless for any major shopping. Stronger ones are available in supermarkets but will cost you at least 2 FF. One must also consider the flow of time, as most businesses close between noon and 14h or between 13h-15h and most small shops and grocery stores are closed on Mondays. One of Paris' greatest resources though is its proliferation of wonderful little shops and street markets. The lack of many large supermarkets (*grandes surfaces*) in convenient Paris locations often means having to frequent these small neighborhood shops, which necessitates organization and a deeper understanding of Paris fare and habits as well as waiting to be served in line after line. Though these circumstances may discourage one at first, taking part in the markets and different shops is a valuable way of enjoying a very basic and material aspect of the culture. The subtle varieties one finds in these shops prove to be intriguing as you'll discover that the merchant *(commerçant)* is an expert in his or her field and can give you all sorts of interesting tips. Going frequently to the same baker or butcher can also be helpful as merchants are very quick to remember a face. This is one direct way of participating fully in daily Parisian life.

The larger supermarkets tend to feel like open air markets that have been roofed in and stocked with army sized quantities. The largest chains are Codec, Monoprix, Prisunic, Inno, Continent, Carrefour, Casino, Mammouth, Uniprix, and Felix Potin. And, Ed, the cut-rate bargain brand chain. Often the food section is upstairs or in the basement of a department store. In French supermarkets don't expect much service. There are no baggers and your tender goods can get smashed as you scramble to bag them yourself as they pile up at the end of the mat and the check out person rushes you to pay up so he or she can move on to the next person. Don't try to make a special request in the meat section; there is no meat manager, nor will the produce manager mark down the bunch of bruised bananas that you've located. A typical response to your question "Where can I find spaghetti sauce? might be "I don't know" or "We don't carry it." Don't be surprised if a store clerk doesn't try to find what you're looking for or that no one is mopping up the splattered jar of pickles. No one ushers you to your car, and the shopping carts are rigged up to a system whereby you feed a ten franc coin into a locking mechanism to release it. You get the coin back when you return it and re-lock it onto the others. The internal organization of food and products may be disorienting to you at first. The grocery sections often flow directly into housewear, hardware, clothing, and garden centers in the really large stores. If your image of Parisian grocery shopping has been riveted to the quaint cheese shop followed by the beautiful bounty of the *pâtisserie*, you should treat yourself to a hectic visit to a massive supermarket in the *banlieue* (suburbs) to fully appreciate the daily or weekly habits of the *Français moyens* (middle class), where industrial *croissants* are purchased in cellophane packs of 15.

Les Commercants (little shops)

There is, obviously, a wide range of shops in each Parisian neighborhood and the differences are sometimes very subtle, especially when food is concerned. This explains the chain of names one often sees on the awnings of shops. For example, a *Boulangerie-Pâtisserie-Confiserie* will have bread, pastries, and fine candies.

Boulangeries

Most *boulangeries* sell prepared sandwiches, mini pizzas, quiches, onion tarts and *croque-monsieurs* (the classic French common food available at all hours in all cafés, consisting of two slices of buttered toast, a slice of ham with grilled cheese on top—the *croque madame* is the same thing topped with a sunny-side up egg) on the streets for about 15 to 20 FF. They'll microwave food for you upon request.

It'll take some time before you become agile with all the many nuances in the French *boulangerie*. The bread alone will stun you in its variety. The following are a few main items:

Baguette: (flour, water, yeast and salt), weight (250 grams) and price (3,80 FF) are all government regulated and nationally uniform in weight and price.

Demi-baguette: half a *baguette*, around 1,70 FF.

Pain au levain: sourdough bread. Usually found in health food or specialty stores and relatively expensive. Sold by weight. Delicious with fresh butter.

Bâtard: same weight as a *baguette*, but shorter and less elegant, made from the squatty end of the rolled out dough.

Boule: round loaf, either small or large.

Chapeau: small round loaf topped with a *chapeau* (hat).

Couronne: ring-shaped *baguette*.

Le fer à cheval: horseshoe-shaped *baguette*.

Ficelle: thin, crusty *baguette*.

Fougasse: a flat, rectangular-shaped bread made of *baguette* dough filled with onions, herbs, spices or anchovies.

Miche: large, round country-style loaf.

Pain de campagne: can be a white bread dusted with flour, giving it a rustic look (and a higher price) or a hearty loaf that may be a blend of white, whole wheat and rye flour with added bran. Also called *baguette à l'ancienne* or *baguette paysanne*. It comes in every shape, from a small, round individual roll to a large family loaf.

Pain complet: bread made partially or entirely from whole wheat flour.

Pain fantaisie: "fantasy bread"—any imaginatively shaped bread.

Pain de mie: a rectangular, white and crusty sandwich loaf used for toast.

Pain aux noix and *pain aux noisettes:* unsweetened rye or wheat bread filled with walnuts or hazelnuts.

Pain aux raisins: rye or wheat bread filled with raisins.

Pain de seigle: closest thing to pumpernickel bread in a *boulangerie*. Two-thirds rye and one third wheat flour.

Pain au son: a dietetic bread that is "quality-controlled," containing bran flour.

Pain Viennois: milk and sugar are added to the *baguette* dough for a finer texture.

Pain Brioché: a rich dough made with milk, eggs and sugar. *Brioche* comes in all sizes and a variety of shapes. Proportionately expensive, but a real delight for those lazy mornings. Great to dunk in *café au lait*.

Note: you will often hear customers asking for their bread *"Bien cuit"* (well done and crusty), *"Pas trop cuit"* or *"Bien tendre"* (less baked and doughier). You can also ask for *"une baguette coupée en deux"* (a *baguette* cut in half). This facilitates transportation and prevents the bread from breaking en route. All of your requests, whether they be at the bakery, the cheese shop or the hardware store, should of course be accompanied by a smile and followed by *"s'il vous plaît,"* two things that will go a long way towards making any transaction simpler and easier. Also, get accustomed to carrying your bread in your hand, bag, or under your arm. Bread is seldom wrapped or bagged. Sometimes, in the more bourgeois boulangeries, your *baguette* will come with a square of tissue paper wrapped around the center where you are to grasp the bread. If you ask for a second square of paper you'll probably get a strange look if not an outright *non*. Don't worry, though, in four centuries there are no documented cases of anyone getting sick from unprotected bread.

Note: It's annoying, but that's the way it is—if you ask for your bread sliced on the slicing machine, expect to pay an additional franc or two. Don't even bother complaining.

After bread, the most common items in the *boulangerie* include the following:

croissant ordinaire: these are the crescent shaped puff pastry rolls now found all over the world. When the points are curled towards the center, this is the legal indication that the *croissant* has been made with margarine and has not been glazed with butter before baking. Price is always about 50 *centimes* less than the *croissant au beurre*. An interesting historical aside— *croissants* were first made by French chefs in transit for the rulers of the Ottoman Empire; the shape is after the Turkish crescent in the Ottoman flag.

Croissant au beurre: these *croissants* have their tips pointing straight out, signifying their pure butter content. Richer and definitely worth the extra half a franc.

Pain au chocolat: a rectangular flaky pastry filled with a strip of chocolate. If you are lucky enough to catch a batch coming out of the oven, the chocolate will still be warm and soft—a favorite after-school snack for youngsters.

Pain aux raisins: a round, spiral-shaped croissant cooked with raisins and a light, egg cream.

Croissant aux amandes: topped with slivered almonds and filled with a rich almond butter paste.

Chausson aux pommes: a turnover with applesauce inside.

As for individual *gâteaux*, most *boulangeries* that are also *pâtisseries* offer:

Millefeuilles (Napoleon): puffed pastry with pastry cream.

Eclairs: *chou* pastry filled with chocolate or coffee cream.

Religieuse: same as *éclair* but shaped like a nun's hat.

Tartelette aux fruits: small fruit tarts.

Croissants are usually purchased in the morning, cakes in the afternoon or evenings. *Boulangeries* also sell *bonbon* (candy) by the piece to kids, as well as soft drinks and bottled water that are cool but never really cold. It's nearly impossible to get a napkin. Not all *boulangeries* are open on Mondays so expect lines for bread on that day. Also, if you wait too long on Sundays by midday it might get a bit tough to find bread. Most *boulangeries* sell out their bread every day. Some *boulangeries* freeze unsold *baguettes* and re-bake them later at a slight compromise of taste and texture. You can detect this by the pattern of cracks on the sides of the *baguette* crust. Don't make a scene, just change *boulangeries.*

Boucheries

The Parisian butcher shop has a fine array of its own idiosyncrasies. First of all, most butcher shops sell pork, beef, mutton, lamb, veal, liver and some sausages, *pâtés,* poultry, rabbit and game. Specialized poultry like turkeys, pheasant, pigeons and cornish hen should be bought in a *marchand de volaille,* your neighborhood poultry shop. If you see a butcher's shop with nice photos of thoroughbreds on its walls, get the message. Here is where horse meat is sold. Horse is reputed to be the finest meat on the market. Try some. You can buy steaks, roasts, hamburger meat, etc. at your local *Chevaline* shop. They're usually decked out with a gold horse's head over the shop door.

The cuts of meat are particular to France. Steaks are not pre-cut, nor is chopped meat previously packaged. If you're used to thick steaks you have to ask for one *très épais.* French meat is very tasty but on the whole not as tender as U.S. beef. Less hormones though! The superior cuts of beef—*côte de boeuf, entrecôte, filet mignon*—are expensive. Pork, though, is excellent and relatively cheap. As are certain cuts of lamb and mutton. Don't be alarmed by scrawny slabs of lean red meat hanging above bellowed cutting boards on nasty aluminum hooks. The blood-stained butchers cut steaks out of these hanging slabs as they go. Fresher. Here's some helpful vocabulary:

bœuf	beef	*veau*	veal
bavette	tender steak	*blanquette*	stewing meat
bifteck	ordinary thin steak	*escalope*	cutlet
bourguignon	cubed beef stew	*paupiette*	rolled and stuffed
châteaubriand	porterhouse steak	*riz de veau*	sweetbreads
faux-filet	sirloin	*triperie*	tripe
entrecôte	rib steak	*cervelle*	brain
steak haché	ground beef	*cœur*	heart
rosbif	roast beef	*foie de génisse*	calf liver
tartare	ground beef with zero percent fat	*gesier*	gizzard
		langue	tongue
tournedos	filet wrapped in fat	*rognons*	kidneys (note: not to be confused with *reins*, human kidneys)
mouton/agneau	mutton/lamb		
brochette	skewered	*gibier*	wild game
carré	roast rack	*lapin*	rabbit
côte	chops	*lièvre*	wild hare
épaule	shoulder	*marcassin*	baby boar
gigot	leg of lamb	*sanglier*	adult boar
noisette	choice loin		
selle	saddle	*volailles*	poultry
		poulet	chicken
porc	pork	*coq*	rooster
andouillette	pork belly sausage	*coquelet*	young rooster
		poule	hen
boudin noir	blood sausage	*cuisse*	thigh
jambon	ham	*suprème*	breast
épaule	less-expensive ham, comes from shoulder	*dinde*	turkey
		dindonneau	young turkey
		caille	quail
jarret	pork knuckle	*canard*	duck
pied	foot	*magret de canard*	breast of duck
rôti	roast	*oie*	goose
travers	spare ribs	*pintade*	guinea hen

Charcuteries

These are France's delis. The assortment of sliced meats, fish, sea-food in aspic, *saumon fumé*, avocados with crabmeat, *pâtés,* salads, fancy vegetables and prepared dishes like *brandade de morue, hachis parmentier, choucroute* and more are always a savory delight. These stores tend to be expensive but highly pleasurable. They offer a whole gamut of dishes guaranteeing instant culinary success when entertaining or when you want to treat yourself to something tasty and beautiful. When buying cold cuts, order by the number of slices, indicating if you want them *fine* (thin). When buying *pâtés* and *terrines,* you indicate the quantity by where the clerk places the knife. To avoid buying more than you want, state, *"un peu moins que ça, s'il vous plaît."*

Epiceries

Literally "spice shops," these are simply grocery stores that sell a little bit of everything. In most *quartiers* there are independent grocers as well as one or several chains, the old standby being Felix Potin, an institution in Parisian grocery shopping. In recent years, Codec, which has numerous large supermarkets, has taken over many *épiceries.*

The ones owned and operated by North Africans usually stay open late—often until midnight in some of the outlying neighborhoods. This is convenient for finding munchies and beverages late at night.

Poissonneries

The variety of fish available in Paris is remarkable. The French eat a lot more fish per capita than North Americans or Brits. After a number of visits to your local *poissonnerie* you'll learn the names of the fish and decide which ones you like best and which are the best buys. Whole fish are cleaned and scaled by the fishmonger at your request for no extra charge; crab and shrimp often come precooked. Sprigs of fresh parsley are given away too if the customer requests such, especially with the purchase of mussels, which are a particularly French and extremely reasonable meal. Purchase one liter per person. You can scrub the shells quickly and dump the shiny black mussels into a big pot of chopped shallots and garlic with a tad of cayenne pepper; dump in a half a bottle of cheap white wine and steam the mussels until they open. Toss in some chopped parsley at the end and serve.

Seafood Lexicon

fruits de mer	seafood	*poisson*	fish
coquilles		*anchois*	anchovy
St. Jacques	scallops	*bar*	bass
crabe	crab	*cabillaud*	cod
tourteau	rock crab	*morue*	dried salt cod
crustacé	shellfish	*congre*	eel
crevette	shrimp	*calamar*	squid
langoustine	sea crayfish	*haddock*	smoked haddock
homard	lobster	*hareng*	herring
huître	oysters	*lotte*	monkfish
langouste	spiny lobster	*merlan*	whiting
moules	mussels	*raie*	skate
praire	venus clams	*rouget*	mullet
oursin	sea urchin	*sole*	sole
bigorneau	periwinkle	*saumon*	salmon
bulots	whelk	*thon*	tuna
coque	cockle	*truite*	trout

Don't eat the ones that don't open. Drink white wine with the dish and mop up the briny wine and shallot broth with hunks of *baguette*. Two people can have a great time for about 30 FF. Lobster is prohibitively expensive, especially the *langouste* sort which comes in from the *Antilles*. Small, frozen Canadian lobsters are available in good supermarkets at very reasonable prices. Smoked salmon is abundant and excellent. To avoid the very high prices, you can opt for the less expensive sea trout, which resembles salmon in color, texture, and taste.

Crèmeries/Fromageries

Winston Churchill is reported to have once said: "How can anyone govern a country with so many different cheeses?" Some people put the current cheese count at more than 400. The pungent cheese shops offer a wonderful sampling that you should take advantage of. A few things you should learn to appreciate during your *séjour* in France include *chèvre* (goat cheese), especially the fresh *(frais)* ones that are covered in *cendres* (ash). *Fromageries* also sell fresh butter, cut off of huge mountains in chunks, *fromage blanc* (white cheese that falls between sour cream and smooth cottage cheese), *crème fraîche* (a

Dairy Products Lexicon			
Fromage	Cheese	*homogénéisé*	homogenized
vieux cantal		*demi-écrémé*	low-fat milk
or *mimolette*	cheddar	*lait écrémé*	skim milk
fromage frais	cream cheese	*lait stérilisé longue*	
chèvre	goat cheese	*conservation*	sterilized milk
rapé	grated	*lait entier*	whole milk
Gruyère,			
Emmenthal,			
St. Moret	Swiss cheese	*Yaourt*	Yogurt
		maigre	no fat
		nature	plain
Lait	Milk	*nature sucré*	plain but
lait fermenté			sugared
léger	buttermilk	*aux fruits*	with fruit
lait frais	fresh milk		

wonderfully rich, slightly sour cream that is used generously in sauces and on deserts), and fresh milk. In France, you'll find whole and skim milk also in vacuum packed cartons that need not be refrigerated and can last for many months unopened. This milk is labelled *longue conservation* or *sterilisé* and permits you to stock up all at once. Eggs, only brown ones, too are bought in the *crèmerie* in packages of six or by the unit.

A Note on Quality

A friend from California related a story which says a lot about the differing concepts of quality in her country and in France. She set out to make a simple chocolate sauce for a dessert after returning home from a period of time spent in France. It was then that she discovered that Hershey Bars don't melt, they bubble and crack like melted plastic. The cocoa content is less than three percent. The cheapest supermarket brand chocolate in France has at least 20% cocoa. And the chocolate bought in specialty shops can contain as much as 80%! The more cocoa, the higher quality the chocolate—unlike ice cream, where more fat content equals higher quality. So, quality, on the whole, is higher and, with it, importantly, comes a new set of expectations that will change you for life. Your taste buds just might re-awaken. After a year or so in Europe it's doubtful, for example, that you'll be able to chomp on North American chocolate, guzzle the popular St. Louis or Milwaukee beer, or savor bagged and doughy sandwich bread.

Some particularly good chocolateries:

La Maison du Chocolat
225, rue du Faubourg St Honoré, 75008 PARIS
56, rue Pierre Charron, 75008 PARIS

Lenôtre
44, rue du Bac, 75007 PARIS
49, av Victor Hugo, 75016 PARIS
Ile St. Louis, 75004 PARIS

Marquise de Sévigné
32, place de la Madeleine, 75008 PARIS

Léonidas (Belgian)
84 av des Champs Elysées, 75008 PARIS

For the *crème de la crème* of fine sweets and specialty items, a tour of the famous and pricey Fauchon at Place de la Madeleine is a must although the effect has been spoiled a bit by the introduction of banal American products that seem exotic in France. This has been a trend over the last few years, the marketing of North American groceries in France, ranging from nacho chips and salsa to Paul Newman salad dressing. Even Oceanspray fresh cran-berries are now available in Paris in November. More and more shops specializing in the importation of American and Tex-Mex food items have entered the Parisian scene. And the outcrops of corresponding restaurants has continued to flourish since the late 80s.

Food Markets

Paris offers three kinds of food markets: the permanent street markets, the moving open air markets and the indoor markets. In all of these markets, unless you are encouraged to do so, you should not touch the produce which is carefully displayed for everyone's enjoyment. You should, however, feel free to specify exactly what you want and to banter freely with the often flambouyant merchants.

The street markets are open Tuesday through Saturday from 9h00 to 12h30 or 13h00 and normally close for the rest of the day. On Sundays they are open from 9h00-13h00.

•Rue des Belles Feuilles: Begins ave Victor Hugo, 16e. Métro: Victor Hugo.
•Rue Cler: Begins ave de la Motte-Picquet, 7e. Métro: Ecole Militaire.
•Rue Lévis: Begins bd des Batignoles, 17e. Métro: Villiers.
•Rue Montorgueil: Begins rue Rambuteau, 1e. Métro: Les Halles.

Les Halles was formally Paris' central marketplace.

•Rue Mouffetard: Begins rue de l'Epée-de-Bois, 5e. Métro: Monge. One of the oldest and most animated markets in Paris.

•Rue Poncelet: Begins av des Ternes, 17e. Métro: Ternes. Exceptional fruit.

•Rue du Poteau: Begins place Jules Joffrin, 18e. Métro: Jules-Joffrin.

•Rue de Seine/rue de Buci: Begins bd St. Germain, 6e. Métro: Odéon.

The moving markets move from neighborhood to neighborhood, making their appearance on fixed days. They often include clothing and other articles as well as food. These are open from 7h00 to 13h30.

•Alésia: Rue d'Alésia, 14e. Métro: Alésia. Wednesday and Saturday.

•Alibert: Rue Alibert and rue Claude-Vellefaux, 10e. Métro: Goncourt. Thursday and Sunday.

•Amiral-Bruix: bd Bruix, between rue Weber and rue Marbeau, 16e. Métro: Porte Maillot. Wednesday and Saturday.

•Auteuil: Between rue d'Auteuil, rue Donizetti, and rue La Fontaine, 16e. Métro: Michel-Ange-Auteuil. Wednesday and Saturday.

•Avenue de Versailles: Rue Gros and rue La Fontaine, 16e. Métro: Jasmin. Tuesday and Friday. av du Président Wilson, between rue Debrousee and place d'Iéna, 16e. Métro: Alma-Marceau. Wednesday and Saturday.

•Belgrand: Rue Belgrand, rue de la Chine and place de la Puy, 20e. Métro: Gambetta. Wednesday and Saturday.

•Belleville: On the island of bd de Belleville, 11e. Métro: Belleville. Tuesday and Friday.

•Bercy: bd de Reuilly, between rue de Charenton and place Félix-Eboué, 12e. Métro: Daumesnil. Tuesday and Friday.

•Berthier: Angle of av de la Porte d'Asnière and bd Berthier, 17e. Métro: Porte de Clichy. Wednesday and Saturday.

•Bobillot: Rue Bobillot, between place Rungis and rue de la Colonie, 13e. Métro: Maison Blanche. Tuesday and Friday.

•Breteuil: av de Saxe and av de Ségur, toward place Bréteuil, 7e. Métro: Ségur. Thursday and Saturday.

•Boulevard Brune: Between passage des Suisses and 49, bd Brune, 14e. Métro: Porte de Vanves. Thursday and Sunday.

•Boulevard de Charonne: Between rue de Charonne and rue Alexandre-Dumas, 11e. Métro: Alexandre-Dumas. Wednesday and Saturday.

•Carmes: Place Maubert, 5e. Métro: Maubert-Mutualité. Tuesday, Thursday and Saturday.

•Cervantes: Rue Bargue, 15e. Métro: Volontaires. Wednesday and Saturday.

•Cité Berryer: Begins rue Royale in the passage of the Cité Berryer, 8e. Métro: Madeleine. Tuesday and Friday.

•Clignancourt: bd d'Ornano, between rue du Mont-Cenis and rue Ordener, 18e. Métro: Ordener. Tuesday, Friday, and Sunday.

•Convention: Rue de la Convention, between rue Alain-Chartier and rue de l'Abbé-Groult, 15e. Métro: Convention. Tuesday, Thursday, Saturday.

•Cours de Vincennes: Between bd de Picpus and av du Dr. Arnorld Netter, 12e. Métro: Porte de Vincennes. Wednesday and Saturday.

•Crimée: 430, bd Ney, 18e. Métro: Porte de Clignancourt. Wednesday and Saturday.

•Davout: bd Davout, between av de la Porte de Montreuil and 94, bd Davout, 20e. Métro: Porte de Montreuil. Tuesday and Friday.

•Duplex: bd de Grenelle, between rue Lourmel and rue du Commerce, 15e. Métro: Duplex. Wednesday and Sunday.

•Edgar-Quinet: On the island of bd Edgar-Quinet, 14th. Métro: Raspail. Wednesday and Saturday.

•Exelmans: Along place de la Porte-Molitor, beginning av du Général-Sarrail toward bd Exelmans, 16e. Métro: Michel-Ange-Auteuil. Tuesday and Friday.

•Gobelins: bd August-Blanqui, between place d'Italie and rue Barrault, 13e. Métro: Corvisart. Tuesday, Friday, and Sunday.

•Javel: Rue St. Charles, between rue Javel and Rond-Point-St.-Charles, 15e. Métro: Charles-Michel. Tuesday and Friday.

•Jean-Jaurès: 145-185, av Jean-Jaurès, 19e. Métro: Pantin. Tuesday, Thursday and Sunday.

•Joinville: At the angle of rue de Joinville and rue Jomard, 19e. Métro: Crimée. Tuesday, Thursday and Sunday.

•Lariboisière: bd de la Chapelle, across from Lariboisière hospital, 18e. Métro: Barbès-Rochechouart. Wednesday and Saturday.

•Lecourbe: rue Lecourbe, between rue Vasco-de-Gama and rue Leblanc, 15e. Métro: Place Balard. Wednesday and Saturday.

•Ledru-Rollin: Avenue Ledru-Rollin, between rue de Lyon and rue de Bercy, 12e. Métro: Gare de Lyon. Thursday and Saturday.

•Lefèbvre: bd Lefèbvre, between rue Olivier-de-Serres and rue de Dantzig, 15e. Métro: Porte de Versailles. Wednesday and Saturday.

•Maison Blanche: Avenue d'Italie and rue Bourgon, 13e. Métro: Porte d'Italie. Thursday and Sunday.

•Monge: Place Monge, 5e. Métro: Monge. Wednesday, Friday and Sunday.

•Montrouge: Along rue Brézin, rue Saillard, rue Mouton-Duvernet and rue Boulard, 14e. Métro: Mouton-Duvernet. Tuesday and Friday.

•Mortier: bd Mortier, at av de la porte de Ménilmontant, 20e. Métro: St.-Fargeau. Wednesday and Saturday.

•Navier: Among rue Navier and rue Lantier, 17e. Métro: Guy-Moquet. Tuesday and Friday.

•Ney: bd Ney, between rue Jean-Varenne and rue Camille-Flammarion, 18e. Métro: Porte de Clignancourt. Thursday and Sunday.

•Ordener: Between rue Montcalm

and rue Championnet, 18e. Métro: Guy-Moquet. Wednesday and Sunday.

•Père-Lachaise: bd de Ménilmontant, between rue des Panoyaux and rue de Tlemcen, 11e. Métro: Père-Lachaise. Tuesday and Friday.

•Place des Fêtes: Place des Fêtes, alongside rue Pré-St.-Gervais, rue Petitot and rue des Fêtes, 19e. Métro: Place des Fêtes. Tuesday, Friday and Sunday.

•Popincourt: bd Richard-Lenoir, between rue Oberkampf and rue de Crussol, 11e. Métro: Oberkampf. Tuesday and Friday.

•Poniatowski: bd Poniatowski, av Daumesnil, rue de Picpus, 12e. Métro: Porte Dorée. Thursday and Sunday.

•Point du Jour: av de Versailles, between rue Le Marois and rue Gudin, 16e. Métro: Porte-de-St.-Cloud. Tuesday, Thursday and Sunday.

•Porte Brunet: av de la porte Brunet, between bd Sérurier and bd d'Algérie, 19e. Métro: Danube. Wednesday and Saturday.

•Port-Royal: bd Port-Royal, alongside Hôpital du Val-de-Grâce, 5e. Métro: Port-Royal. Tuesday, Thursday and Saturday.

•Pyrénées: Rue des Pyrénées, between rue de l'Ermitage and rue de Ménilmontant, 20e. Métro: Ménilmontant. Thursday and Sunday.

•Raspail: bd Raspail, between rue du Cherche-Midi and rue de Rennes, 6e. Métro: St.-Placide. Tuesday and Friday.

•Réunion: Place de la Réunion, between the place and rue Vitruve, 20e. Métro: Alexandre-Dumas. Thursday and Sunday.

•Richard-Lenoir: bd Richard-Lenoir and rue Amelot, 11e. Métro: Bastille. Thursday and Sunday.

•Saint-Eloi: 36-38, rue de Reuilly, 12e. Métro: Reuilly-Diderot. Thursday and Sunday.

•Salpétrière: Place de la Salpétrière, alongside bd de l'Hôpital, 13e. Métro: St.-Marcel. Tuesday and Friday.

•Télégraphe: Rue du Télégraphe, to the right of Belleville cemetery, 20e. Métro: Télégraphe. Wednesday and Saturday.

•Tolbiac: Place Jeanne-d'Arc, 13e. Métro: Nationale. Thursday and Sunday.

•Villemain: av Villemain, on the island between av Villemain and rue d'Alésia, 15e. Métro: Plaisance. Wednesday and Sunday.

The covered markets are generally open Tuesday through Saturday, from 8h00-13h00 and 16h00-18h30, and on Sunday from 9h00-13h00. Little has changed since the turn of the century in many of these markets.

•Batignolles: 96, rue Lemercier, 17e. Métro: Brochant.

•Beauvau-Saint-Antoine: Between rue d'Aligre and rue Cotte, 12e. Métro: Ledru-Rollin.

•Chapelle: Rue de l'Olive, 18e. Métro: Max-Dormoy. Open until midnight on Friday and Saturday.

•Enfants Rouges: 39, rue de

Bretagne, 3e. Métro: Filles-du-Calvaire.

•Europe: Rue Corvetto, between rue Maleville and rue Treihard, 8e. Métro: Villiers.

•Passy: Angle of rue Boi-le-vent and rue Duban, 16e. Métro: La Muette.

•Porte Saint-Martin: 31 and 33, rue du Château-d'Eau, 10e. Métro: St.-Martin.

•Riquet: 36-46, rue Riquet, 18e. Métro: Riquet. Open until 8:00 p.m.on Friday and Saturday.

•Saint-Didier: Angle of rue Mesnil and rue St.-Didier, 16e. Métro: Victor-Hugo.

•Saint Germain: Among rue Lobineau, rue Clément and rue Mabillon, 6e. Métro: Mabillon.

•Saint-Honoré: Place du Marché-St.-Honoré, 1e. Métro: Tuileries.

•Saint-Quentin: 85 bis, bd de Magenta, 10e. Métro: Gare-de-l'Est.

•Secrétan: 46, rue Bouret, and 33, av Secrétan, 19e. Métro: Bolivar.

•Ternes: Rue Lebon, rue Faraday and rue Torricelli, 17e. Métro: Ternes.

Les Marchés Biologiques (Organic Markets)

These are the equivalent of old-fashioned country farmer's markets. From thirty to fifty independent organic farmers set up stalls on the weekends in Boulogne and Joinville (Parisian suburbs easily reachable by RER). They sell organically grown fruits and vegetables; homemade breads; dried fruits and nuts; *charcuterie*; farm-raised chicken, ducks and geese; and natural wine. There are stands selling things like freshly made pizzas, whole-wheat breads, apple or pear cider, a huge variety of artisanal goat cheeses, sausages, beer, and dried flowers. Go early in the day for a good selection.

•Marché Boulogne: 140, Route de la Reine, 92 Boulogne-sur-Seine. Métro: Boulogne-Pont de Saint-Cloud, or via the No. 72 bus. Open 8h00-16h00 the first and third Saturdays of each month.

•Marché Joinville-le-Pont: Place Mozart, 94 Joinville. Métro: RER Line B to Joinville, then via the suburban No. 106 and 108N buses. Open 8h30-13h00 the second and fourth Saturdays of each month.

•Marché Sceaux-Robinson, rue des Mouille-Boeuf. Métro: RER Line B to Robinson. Every Sunday, 8h30-13h00.

For additional information on these markets, call *Nature et Progrès:* Tel: 47.00.60.36.

Flea Markets (Marchés aux puces) & Special Markets

• Marché de Montreuil: av de la Porte de Montreuil, 12e. Métro: Porte de Montreuil. Saturday, Sunday and Monday. This is probably the least touristy of the flea markets. Located on the eastern edge of Paris at the newly revamped

Porte de Montreuil, this market is noted for its huge, cluttered tables of used clothes. Here, if you're not overly bothered by the idea of rummaging through old clothes and are filled with patience, you may find high quality, although wrinkled, sweaters, skirts, dress shirts, ties, etc. of fine materials for tiny prices. Ten francs for a shirt, for instance. Otherwise, there are loads of old junk, some fine antiques, and piles of useless *bric-à-brac*. You may not be able to bargain quite as much as you imagined, but you usually can get things for 20-30% less than the asking price. It's not incorrect to try in any case. There is talk of closing down the *Marché de Montreuil* in the near future.

• Marché de la Place d'Aligre: Place d'Aligre, 12e. Métro: Ledru-Rollin. Daily from 9h to noon. One of Paris' best and least expensive open air markets.

• Marché de la Porte de Clignancourt (St. Ouen): rue des Entrepots, 75018. PARIS Métro: Porte de Clignancourt. This is the largest and most overwhelming of all Paris flea markets. Careful of pickpockets.

• Marché de la Porte des Lilas: 75019 PARIS. Métro: Porte des Lilas. Sunday and holidays.

• Marché de la Porte de Vanves: av Georges-Lafenestre, 75004 PARIS. Métro: Porte de Vanves. Saturday and Sunday. Particularly strong in antiques, old jewelry, and furniture.

• Marché aux Oiseaux: Same location as the Marché aux Fleurs. Sunday mornings. Bird amateurs from all over bring their birds to sell, trade and exhibit.

• Marché aux Timbres: Métro: Rond Point Clemenceau, 75008 PARIS. Sunday mornings. Stamp collectors unite to trade and sell.

• Marché aux Fleurs: Ile de la Cité, 75001 PARIS. Métro: Cité. Daily assortment of fresh flowers and exotic plants.

Department & Chain Stores

FNAC—leading up-beat cooperative for books, records, photo, video, audio and electronics equipment with *aprés-vente* service all over the city. Also a major outlet for concert tickets. Major locations at Montparnasse, Les Halles, Etoiles, Wagram, the Bastille (music), and bd St. Germain (international store for foreign books and press).

Darty—large appliance chain, wide variety of brands at reasonably good prices. Noted for service, delivery, guarantee, and repair services. Salespeople wear blinding red jackets.

Samaritaine—largest and oldest department store in Paris. It has everything. The rooftop on Building 2 has a great view of the city.

Printemps—major department store with principal location at

Auber/Opéra. All major fashion houses are represented. A view of the Opéra and roofs of Paris can be enjoyed from the rooftop terrace. Also known for its reverse glass-domed restaurant.

Galeries Lafayette—major department store with principal location at Auber/Opéra. All major fashion houses are represented here. Tries to cater to foreign shoppers.

Au Bon Marché—large department store chain that distinguishes itself as being the only Left Bank store of its kind. A bit less visible than Galerie Lafayette and Printemps.

Bazar de l'Hôtel de Ville (BHV)—a stand-by for all your needs. The chaotic basement is particularly well-equipped for hardware and houseware. Good for adaptors and transformers for foreign appliances.

Tati—working-class, department store for inexpensive clothes. Montparnasse and Barbes locations.

Duty-free/Détaxe/TVA (Value added tax)

Sales tax on goods and services, better known as (TVA) in France is steep—18.6% for most consumer goods and services and 33% for luxury items including certain food specialties.(The exorbitant price of gasoline is a result of hidden taxes totalling 74%!) Books, on the other hand, are taxed at only 5.5%. For purchases that are being taken out of the country, a part of the TVA can be recovered *(récupérée)*. Anyone over 15 years old who is a foreign resident when spending less than six months in France can benefit from duty-free shopping. If you have a *carte de séjour* you don't comply with the law, but you can always simply show only your passport when detaxing your purchases. Items which cannot be detaxed are the following: tobacco, medicines, firearms, unset gems, works of art, collectors items and antiques, private means of transport (cars, boats, planes and their equipment), and large commercial purchases. To benefit from the duty-free allowance, ask the vendor at the point of purchase to give you a three-slip form called a *bordereau* (export sales invoice) and an addressed, stamped envelope. Non-EEC Nationals must present the detaxed purchases, the three slips (two pink, one green) and the stamped envelope provided by the shop to the French Customs agents at the airport, border crossings or train crossings. At the airport there is a window marked DÉTAXE where you may be asked to show your purchases. Make sure not to pack your duty free items in your checked baggage before presenting them to Customs in that you risk being denied the tax refund. If you leave the country by train, have your three slips validated by the Customs agent on board. French Customs will keep the pink copies and send them in the envelope directly to the point of purchase, who will then reimburse you the amount indicated on space B3 of the form via check or credit card credit (it is best to do this with your credit card to avoid astro-nomical fees for changing your refund into local currency); keep the green copy for your files. Sometimes you will be reim-bursed at the time of purchase, however, you still must undergo the above process. If you are an EEC resident, you will get a yellow invoice consisting of three copies, two yellow and one green. Upon reaching customs in your country, have all three slips validated by the Customs agent. Send the two yellow slips to the *Bureau des Douanes de Paris*-La-Chapelle, 61, rue de la Chapelle, 75018 PARIS. Keep the green slip for your files. Your purchases, including tax, and from any single store, must at least amount to 1200 FF for foreign nationals or 2800 FF for EEC citizens. The purchases can be cumulative.

Le Café-Tabac (tobacco shop)

Le tabac plays a curious but dynamic role in daily French life. *Le tabac*, clearly marked with a red elongated diamond shaped sign hanging in the street, has a monopoly from the State to sell cigarettes, cigars and tobacco. You cannot buy cigarettes anywhere else in France. In exchange for this privilege, the *tabac*, which is usually also a café, performs certain services at face value, such as selling stamps. If you need some stamps for letters or cards, you can easily buy them from the cashier in a *tabac*. Don't expect total cooperation, however, if you want postal rates for the Ivory Coast. That's not their job. You will find a nearby mail box outside every *tabac* (always yellow and usually divided into two parts—Paris and its sub-urban codes 75, 77, 78, 91, 92, 93, 94 and the rest of the world). A *carnet* of stamps is a unit of ten basic letter stamps for France (currently 2.50 FF) (often sold in little booklets or on convenient, self sticking—

auto-collante—pages). Here is what the standard French letter stamp looks like:

Single envelopes and writing paper can also be purchased in a *tabac*. This is handy when you have to mail something off in a hurry. You have envelope, stamp, and mailbox at hand—but you have to know the postal rates yourself.

Le tabac also handles, in many cases, off-track betting called PMU. *Le tabac* sells lottery tickets (LOTO).

Le tabac sells *timbres fiscaux* as well. This is important in that if you happen to get a parking ticket, you pay for it by purchasing a *timbre fiscal* (State Stamp Tax); paste one portion to the return portion of the ticket and keep the other half as your proof of payment. Similarly, you often need a *timbre fiscal* when you renew your *carte de séjour* and process other official documents. *Le tabac* sells this, although they are frequently out of precisely the denomination you need and you have to walk until you find a better-stocked *tabac*.

If you own a car, you'll soon find out that your annual Car registration tax is paid in December at any *tabac* in the *Département* in which you live, upon presentation of your *carte grise*. You'll receive a *vignette* sticker for your windshield.

Cars/Driving

Coming to Paris as a student you most likely will neither need a car nor want one, but still there are a number of things you might want to know regarding cars, driving and parking in France. Young people in France are in no way as obsessed with cars as are their contemporaries in many other countries, certainly in the U.S. Driving in France is not seen as a symbol of freedom, status and virility although you're certain to encounter a fair amount of nervous drivers with a passion for tailgating, passing on the right, and cheating on left turns. Some French students have cars—traditionally the 1968-style, weak but brave and charming *Deux Cheveaux*—but this is certainly no longer the rule.

The attitudes you may witness among drivers should tip

you off to a lot of things. Although the French are fast and aggressive, relatively few acts of real meanness occur in traffic. The largest difference between French and American urban drivers is a question of morality or principle. If you're waiting on a long line to make a left turn, undoubtedly some feisty guy in a Renault 25 will barrel past you in the on-coming lane, zoom to the front of the line and steal the light. In the U.S., the U.K. or Germany this would cause instant anger because it's a violation and it's unfair. In France, drivers might show discontent too but not out of moral outrage; they'd envy him or at least not fault him for making the most of an opportunity. Opportunism, in general, isn't seen negatively. Other drivers would be angry because he pulled ahead and they were left in the dust, not because he demonstrated a lack of respect for society and its rules. At the risk of over-generalizing, when the French can profit for their own gain and get away with it, they tend to do it. Higher principles are reserved for higher matters than daily traffic.

Parisian drivers are filled with facial and hand gestures. They speed up at lights and breeze past slow cars or j-walkers, but they will never (rarely) hit you. And pedestrians usually stroll across streets with an indifferent gaze.

The *priorité à droite* (yield right-of-way) is often seen as a peculiarity among North Americans, where the opposite is the rule. Essentially, just remember that anyone coming from your right in almost all situations has the right-of-way. Sometimes a car will pull out onto a busy road from a dinky side street. You must yield unless there is a sign that tells you otherwise. Often drivers take unfair advantage of this rule of the road and swing far to the right and loop around to make left turns or merge into another road. The *priorité à droite* seems well-engrained in the Parisian mind-set in that people tend to follow this even when walking. For British drivers and pedestrians, the right-hand system will just take a bit of getting used to. As will the lack of outward, public politeness.

In France, the law requires that seat belts be worn by all passengers. Failure to do so can result in a 230 FF fine for the driver and 500 FF for the passenger. Although this law is a good safety measure, it sometimes can be employed as a pretext for the police to stop cars at random to check identity papers. The law also states that you must carry your *permis de conduire* (driver's license), *carte grise* and *certificat d'assurance* at all times. Failure to present these can mean stiff fines, up to 900 FF. *Briser un feux rouge* (running a red light) is a serious offense that will cost you a minimum of 2000 FF and perhaps an afternoon in court. Crossing a solid white line is also seen as a major fault. U-turns are illegal.

Driver's Licenses

The following information is for U.S. citizens driving in France, and was provided by the Paris *Préfecture de Police.* French regulations distinguish between persons in France on short tourist or business trips (less than 90 days) and those who are here as long-term residents.

If you are a temporary visitor to France, you may drive with a valid U.S. (state) or international driver's license. If a U.S. permit is used, the French government recommends, but does not require, that it be accompanied by an officially recognized French translation (by a *traducteur assermenté).*

If you are a resident of France (holder of a *carte de séjour* or *carte de resident),* you may drive in France with a valid U.S. (not international) license for a one-year recognition period, beginning on the date of validity of the first *carte de séjour.* The license must be accompanied by a translation done by a sworn translator *(traducteur expert-jure).*

Persons with valid driver's licenses from the states of South Carolina, Michigan, and New Hampshire may directly exchange their state driver's licenses for French permits. These states offer a reciprocal privilege of exchange for persons holding French permits. Legislation is pending to make this possible for other states as well.

Apply for a French driver's license *(permis de conduire)* at least three months before the expiration date of the one-year recognition period, to allow sufficient time for the required formalities. Go to your *Commissaire de la République,* or *Préfecture de Police* in Paris. Applicants with licenses from all states other than New Hampshire, Michigan, and South Carolina must take the written *(Code de la Route)* and driving portions of the French licensing examination. All applicants must furnish the following documents:

- *Carte de séjour;*
- *Three passport size photographs;*
- *Proof of current address;*
- *Fiscal stamp of 130 FF.*

In France, almost everyone applies for a license through an *Ecole de Conduite* (Driving School), private companies that practically have a monopoly on the market. Almost no one succeeds in getting a license as a *candidat libre* (independent applicant). You can try, but, due to new laws *préfectures* insist that you show up at the road test with a duo-control car, which needs to be rented from a driving school. Thus with the required 20 hours of classroom and road time, getting your license is time-consuming and costly (from 3000-6000 FF). For the first year though, your national or state driver's license,

along with an International Driver's License, will suffice. This license can be obtained at AAA offices throughout the U.S for $15. It's more work getting one in France.

For more precise information on driving in France and driving lessons contact the legendary, English-speaking Fehrenbach Driving School, 53 bd Henri Sellier, 92150 SURESNES, Tel: 45.06.31.17. Fax: 47.28.81.89.

Replacing Expired, Lost and Stolen Drivers' Licenses

Foreign embassies are not authorized to replace expired, lost or stolen drivers' licenses. If you have lost your driver's license or had it stolen in France, immediately report it to the *commissariat* of police having

jurisdiction over the area where the loss of the theft occurred. The *commissariat* will issue a *Récépissé de Déclaration de Perte ou de Vol de Pièces d'Iden-tité* (Acknowledgement of Declaration of Loss or Theft of Identity Documents). This *récépissé* will generally cover the lack of a driver's license for a few weeks while a replacement is being obtained. The *récépissé* is good for this purpose only in France. In the case of U.S. residents, if the U.S. citizen's home state requires a sworn affidavit or a notarized application for a replacement license, the Embassy's Office of American Services can notarize the application from 9:00 a.m. to 12:30 p.m. Monday through Friday, French and U.S. holidays excepted.

International Driver's Licenses

International driver's licenses, printed in numerous languages, are generally well-recognized in France, and are valid along with your normal driver's license for temporary use in France (less than 90 days). Longer-term residents must comply with the requirements explicated in the section "Driver's Licenses." Residents in Paris should consult their consulates or automobile associations for details on obtaining this license at home. The American Automobile Association (AAA) issues by mail international driver's licenses valid for one year. For an application write to AAA, 811 Gatehouse, Falls Church, Virginia 22042. An international driver's license **cannot** be obtained in France.

Purchasing a Car

When purchasing a car, you need to bring the *carte grise*, the French car registration papers of the seller (on which he has written VENDU, signed it and dated it), to the *préfecture* in your *arrondissement* or *département*. You also need to obtain, at the *préfecture* or *mairie* of the *arrondissement* where the car has been previously registered, a *lettre de non-gage*, which means that there are no *liens* (ties, strings attached) or outstanding debts on the car. For cars over five years old, the law now requires that all such vehicles must undergo a technical inspection and receive a *certificat d'inspection*, which can be obtained for 290 FF from certified service stations by no later than five years to the day from the date the vehicle first appeared in circulation. *Plaques d'immatriculation* (license plates) must be changed by the new buyer within 48 hours after the new *carte grise* has been issued. New plates are stamped out while you wait at most service stations for about 150 FF.

Annual Registration Sticker (vignette)

Vignettes can be purchased in any *tabac*, upon presentation of the *carte grise*, and are renewed annually. Affix it on the inside lower right-hand corner of the *parebrise* (windshield) by December 1 or you risk a fine. The tax varies depending on the size, age and horsepower of the car. Count on 300-400 FF.

Auto Insurance

An unlimited third party liability insurance policy is compulsory for all automobiles entering France. Whether the owner accompanies the automobile or not, the vehicle must be insured. As proof of insurance, the owner must present an international motor insurance card (yellow if the policy is purchased in France, green otherwise) showing that the vehicle is insured in France. A temporary policy is available from the vehicle insurance department of the French Customs office *(la douane)* at the point of entry (border-crossing or seaport). These policies have a validity of eight, fifteen, or thirty days. For those who wish longer-term or additional insurance, the your embassy has a list of English-speaking companies.

If you can prove that you've been insured for two years; you can benefit from a French insurer's *bonus* (discount). For the best rates, check the MACIF and MAAF, two large insurance cooperatives for salaried employees. Again, don't expect snappy service.

Here's one American insurance broker who has been in France for over 25 years and who is noted for his service to English-speaking clients, including general, medical, automobile, fire, accident, and life insurance.

Mr. Reuben Giles
Cerise Assurances—SGB
199-207, rue des Pyrénées
75020 PARIS
Tel: 47.97.64.80
Fax: 47.97.95.42

Documentation of Motor Vehicles

Foreign-registered automobiles entering France by road or ferry are not normally documented by the French Customs at the point of entry. Vehicles shipped to France are treated differently. The shipping company is issued a *déclaration d'admission* by

French Customs at the seaport and this is delivered to the owner with the car.

The French Customs Office decides if foreign license plates can be used in France or if French plates *(plaques d'immatriculation)* are required. In general, cars imported for less than three months can keep their foreign plates; those brought in for more than three months need French plates. After having cleared their vehicles through a French port of entry, foreigners who plan to reside temporarily or permanently in France should consult the local Customs Office to establish the status of their vehicles In Paris, the address is: Bureau de Paris-Douane, Tourisme, 20 Quai d'Austerlitz, 75013 PARIS; Tel: 45.84.33.57.

In addition to license plates, imported automobiles should have a nationality sticker *(plaque de nationalité)* mounted near the rear license plate. These stickers (usually an adhesive plastic disk) can be purchased at most auto accessory stores.

Once an imported vehicle has been processed through the French Customs Office in Paris (or elsewhere, if applicable) the most practical way to document the vehicle or, if necessary, to register it (obtain a *certificat d'immatriculation,* often referred to as *carte grise*) and get license plates is to apply to: Automobile Club de l'Ile de France, 14, avenue de la Grande Armée, 75017 PARIS, Tel: 43.80.68.58. The Automobile Club has offices or representatives in most cities and larger towns in France, but motorists outside of Paris should contact the regional offices in major cities to document their vehicles.

For information on sales and transfers of ownership, consult the embassy of your home country; they have printed material available upon request.

Car Rentals

To rent a car in France you must be at least 21 years old and hold a valid drivers license (at least one year old). A major credit card facilitates matters.

Avis Location de Voitures S.A.
5, rue Bixio
75007 PARIS
Tel: 46.09.92.12 (Res. & Info)

Budget
4, av Franklin Roosevelt
75008 PARIS
Tel: 42.25.79.89

Europcar (National)
5, av Italie
75013 PARIS
Tel: 43.31.58.99

Hertz France S.A.
Tel: 47.88.51.51 (Res. & Info)
Minitel: 3514 HERTZ

InterRent
87, rue la Boetie
75008 PARIS
Tel: 40.74.00.07 (Res. & Info)
Toll Free: 05.33.22.10
Minitel: 3614 IR

Parking

Parking in Paris can be a nightmare. There are just too many cars in Paris for the amount of space. Throughout most of central Paris, on-street paid-parking is the rule. Instead of parking meters, Paris had adopted a system whereby you purchase a paper ticket from a parking meter machine on the block where you've parked, indicating until what time you have paid. This, you leave on your dashboard. The flock of women in blue coats (pejora-tively called in the past *auber-gines*) you'll see parading up and down the avenue writing tickets can rarely be charmed. Now they're called *pervenches* in that they've changed the color of their coats. The basic parking ticket is 75 FF, which skyrockets to 220 FF if unpaid after three months. Parking in an illegal spot is an automatic 230 FF, which becomes 500 FF if unpaid, later to jump to 1100 FF...

At the same time, the style of Paris parking is somewhat chaotic, as you'll habitually see cars pulled up on sidewalks, over curbs, and into other seemingly illegal spaces. This is especially true at night in the Latin Quarter and around Montparnasse. Parisian drivers, who often leave parked cars in neutral *(point mort),* also have the odd habit of pushing cars forward or backward with their

bumpers to make room for their vehicle. One Japanese student observed this and gasped, "In Japan that'd be considered an accident."

If you get towed, call the Police in the neighborhood in which you've parked for the address of the tow yard *(fourrière)*. Be prepared to pay in cash or by French check.

Curiously, there is a tradition in France that all parking fines are waived by the winner after each Presidential election, so if elections are coming up within a year, you might want to hold out on paying, otherwise, better pay promptly to avoid the accumulation of penalties. Parking tickets are, of course, paid by purchasing the timbre fiscal again in the *tabac,* sticking half on the return portion of the ticket and retaining the other for your records. When you receive a note in the mail and a bill for the penalty on unpaid tickets you can no longer *régler* (pay) with a *timbre fiscal;* you must send a check to or visit the *Trésor Public.* Payment schedules for large fines can be negotiated. With the increase of greater European cooperation, tickets given to other EEC cars are forwarded for collection in those respective countries.

If you want to utilize the reduced parking rate for local residents indicated on parking meters, go to the *Mairie* of your *arrondissement* with documentation that you reside there and they will issue you a resident permit in a little plastic pouch which you adhere to the right hand corner of your windshield. There is a place to put your meter receipts next to your residence permit. There is soon to be parking meter subscription cards usable like the *télécartes.*

Motorcycles (Motos)

Paris hosts a proliferation of motorcycles, scooters, *mobilettes* and other motorized two-wheelers. Most of Paris' internal message and delivery services *(coursiers)* move this way.

If you see a rambling mass of motorcycles on a Friday night, don't be alarmed. There's a long tradition in Paris of motorcyclists gathering at 11h at the Bastille and making a giant tour *en masse* along the *grands boulevards.* For those considering scooters and mopeds, a special driver's license is not needed, although helmets are required. Some of these vehicles run on a special gas/oil mixture.

Safety is always relative to what you're used to. Although Paris is a big city and a degree of prudence and common sense should always be applied, it is fair to say that Paris streets, day or night, are relatively safe. In fact, there's little sense in even comparing the safety of Paris to that of any city in the United States. There are fewer dangerous weapons and drugs on Paris streets, nor many desperate and crazed individuals. Nonetheless, one should always be careful and prudent. Incidents do occur. There are cases of muggings, theft and attack. A bigger problem is learning how to remain street-wise while leaving home that defensiveness and massive phobia that you were most likely, and for sound reason, brought up to maintain at all costs. For all practical purposes, you should not be frightened to take the Métro anytime during its operating hours—5h45-1h. In the last few years there has been a slight increase of cases of theft and harassment in certain Métro stations, especially late at night. And, it's true that certain *quartiers* can be a bit intimidating or less reassuring but even here, real danger is minimal but not wholly absent. Women may feel the harassment of being followed or catcalled by bothersome men. As unpleasant as this may be, these encounters are in most cases harmless. Just ignore such advances and carry on. Of course, it's never a bad idea, especially when going out at night into areas you're not familiar with, to have a friend or friends along. If you feel harassed or simply bothered by someone in the street or in a café or club it's best to ignore them at first. If they persist, a clever retort works better than an insult. Try one of these: *"J'attends mon mari," "J'attends ma femme,"* or, *"Est-ce que vous ai donné la permission de me parler?"* Make sure you have these mastered before you attempt them, however. Common sense is the key, but don't forget that Paris just isn't like New York, for example. You need to careful like in all big cities, but not frightened. *Au contraire*, Paris is a city that has a relatively late social life and vibrant street/café life and needs to be negotiated by foot.

Paris is dense; the space between people is often less than in cities in other countries. The social coding between individuals is different. The rules are not always the same. The body language is as distinct as the verbal language. For example, some women have complained that French men in clubs or discotheques become aggressive if they don't get their way after their graciously offered drinks have been accepted. As a rule, you should remember that Americans are more open, verbal and casual than the French in initial social contacts. This difference can lead to misunderstandings which, although not usually unsafe, can be uncomfortable. Some discos attract individuals who want to pick up foreigners.

Areas of town that are known to be a bit less comforting to foreign students, especially women, include the area between Place de Clichy and Barbès-Rochechouart, which delineates the Pigalle district. This area is filled with a lot of porno shops and single men. Being one of the poorer areas of Paris, there are a lot of immigrants, mostly Algerian, Moroccan and African. Although crime is higher here than in the chic parts of central Paris, these ethnic groups usually get an unfair reputation. There is nothing to be frightened about but it's always good to have an idea about where you're going, and to dress more conservatively in those areas.

Street people, called *clochards,* are for the most part harmless, despite their frequent drunkenness, desperate look and sometimes angry-sounding comments. Some of the side streets near the Gare Montparnasse and the desolate back streets of the 14th *arrondissement* had been known to be frequented by drug dealers. More recently the eastern part of the Mairie de Montreuil line has experienced some drug problems, especially Métro Oberkampf. The drug situation in Paris is a fraction of what it is in North American and other European cities, but is growing steadily worse. Far more dangerous than anywhere in Paris are some of the stark concrete HLM complexes in the northern suburbs. There would be little reason for you to head out that way. Also try to avoid the larger Métro stations such as Châtelet/Les Halles late at night, as they can be a refuge for late-night partyers of the slightly dubious type and generally a hang-out for unsavory characters. The same goes for the area around Les Halles/Beaubourg— the rue St. Denis, a notorious sex shop/prostitution street, is not far away. But, in any case, compared to any city in the US, Paris' worst is manageable.

Lost or Stolen Property
If you have lost anything of importance or had it stolen, there are two things to do immediately following the discovery: go to the nearest police station and fill out a report *(déclaration de vol)*, which you will need to make an insurance claim. You may want to check the city's lost and found *(Objets Trouvés)* at 36, rue des Morrillons, 75015 PARIS, Tel: 45.31.14.80 in that papers are often turned in (for lost credit cards or traveler's checks, see Banking). Secondly, pay a visit to your country's embassy and they will provide you with additional helpful instructions including a means to replace your passport.

Police, Law & Authority
By law, every person in France has a legal status and an identity card. North Americans often see the question of "papers" as a psychological hurdle. The United States and Canada do not have National Identity Cards, like most countries in the world. Any policeman has the right to demand that you prove your identity at any time. No real reason or provocation is required. So, it's advisable to carry your passport or *carte de séjour* with you at all times. If you're stopped *(contrôlé)* and you don't have identification or valid papers, say you're a tourist. Don't speak French; smile and be submissive. Show the *agent* (officer, *le flic* in slang) that you respect his power, and in most cases you'll get a banal warning and be sent on your way with a polite salute. But you might have to provide identification within 24 hours or even be accompanied to the local police station. There is a lot of intimidation here. It's better to steer away from any unnecessary encounters with the police.

The relationship that citizens have to authority is different in all countries. In France, the police control the public; in the North American scheme of things one tends to feel that the police works for the public. In France, the police are employees either of the Ministry of the Interior or the Ministry of Defense, thus functionaries of the State, the federal government. The police represents the State. In the US, aside from the FBI or state troopers, the police work for the municipality; they attempt to enforce the law but they are not the law itself. A large psychological difference.

There are several types of police in France. Basically, the *agent de police*, the local officer, is an employee of the Ministry of Interior. The *gendarmes*, the ones you see on the highways out of town and in the small towns, are connected to the Ministry of Defense. The police who ride around in grey-green armored vans and carry Plexiglass shields are the CRS *(Compagnies Républicaines de Sécurité)*, the National Security Police. They are called in to enforce order and maintain security in situations of demonstrations, strikes, riots, protests or upheaval. France experiences numerous national strikes and scores of organized *manifestations (manifs)* (demonstrations) each year. Be prepared to be inconvenienced. En masse, these guys are scary looking. In general, you'll find the police to be polite, formal and mildly helpful. Not more. As already stated, you can be asked for seemingly no reason to *"présentez vos papiers"*—either your passport or your *carte de séjour*. This is a routine called *un contrôle*. You'll see systematic control points in the streets for drivers. From time to time, especially at moments particularly vulnerable to terrorism, you'll see a lot of armed police in the Métro stations as well. Although you may not be used to this, and may even be repulsed by the idea, don't be overly alarmed. Very recently there have been highly visible cases of arrested illegal immigrants, usually black Africans, handcuffed, being escorted to deportation planes at the airport.

Remember, in keeping with the Napoleonic Code, the burden of the proof is upon the accused. For instance, in the case of legal accusations, you can be detained twenty-four hours before you have the right to make a phone call. Yet this concept is just as applicable in numerous sectors of French life; everyday interactions with individuals and administrators are mostly laced with an initial *méfiance* (mistrust). When dealing, for example, with the French tax authorities, even if you are certain that there has been an error, you're obliged to pay first. Justice will follow in due course; the system may be slow, but it is assumed to be right.

A Word on Terrorism
Many visitors have been highly concerned over the past few years with the risks and fears of terrorist activities in Europe. Admitted, there was an atmosphere of uncertainty and distrust in Paris during the Gulf War.

The streets, cafés, and stations were empty and distrusting looks were cast at perfectly innocent Arab or Arab-looking individuals in Paris. Prior to that, there was a short period in Paris in 1985 and early 1986 when an atmosphere of suspicion and terror permeated the air, following the bombings of a shopping complex on the Champs Elysées and the popular working-class department store Tati, near Montparnasse, in which innocent people were killed and maimed. Other than that, many still remember the terrorist attack on Goldenberg's Restaurant on the predominantly Jewish rue des Rosiers. Ironically, two Jews, two Moslems, and two Christians were killed in the blast and the event ultimately served to create a new feeling of inter-religion solidarity in the community. Aside from these selected incidents, the actual risk of being subjected to any danger of this sort is highly remote and should not—at least for the moment—figure into your thinking about life in Paris.

Documentation

Information Available to the English-Speaking Community

The Office of American Services at the U.S. Consulate (2, rue St. Florentin 75001 PARIS, Tel: 42.96.12.02, Fax: 42.61.61.40) provides free of charge the following pamphlets:

• Principal American and Franco-American organizations in Paris
• Notorial Services
• Registration of births and obtainment of birth records for U.S. citizens born abroad
• Citizenship provisions of the Immigration and Nationality Act of 14 November, 1986
• Photograph requirements for passport applicants
• Religious Institutions in Paris
• Private Detective Agencies in Paris
• List of Doctors and Dentists in Paris
• Insurance companies and agents
• OCS Emergency Trust Fund
• Schools
• Stenographer (court reporters)
• Warning about pickpockets
• Taking evidence in France—civil and commercial matters
• List of sworn translators and interpreters in Paris area
• Visa requirements for France
• French sales tax (TVA) Refund Procedure
• Tax accountants and consultants in Paris
• Shipping companies
• Residence permits *(cartes de séjour)*

- Marriage formalities for Americans in France
- Lost or stolen property
- French consulates in the United States
- Student part-time employment in France
- Employment in France
- Divorce
- Banking and foreign exchange facilities
- *Au pair* employment in France
- Obtaining a birth record
- Motor vehicle operations in France
- List of attorneys in Paris area

The British Community Committee, (c/o Mme. Beryl Jones, 17, villa Chaptal, 92300, Levallois-Perret, Tel: 47.58.81.42) provides the following documentation upon request: Digest of British and Franco-British Clubs, Societies and Institutions (free)
Quarterly of British Community Social Events (100 FF)

Association of British & American Residents in France

New on the scene is an innovative, non-profit membership organization intended for native English-speaking expatriates, longer-term residents, and those with an abiding interest in French life and culture. Among its primary objectives is to be a source of timely and objective information on the resources of daily French life concerning both essential and leisure time activities. Its members are encouraged to exchange their experiences, opinions, and discoveries in the areas of gastronomy, travel, shopping, and services.

Secondly, the Association states that it seeks to bring together economic and cultural activity created by expatriates living in France as a means of enriching the community and provide practical discounts, benefits, and services among members. Areas particularly applicable include: hotel accommodations, boutique and department store shopping, wine and cuisine, American and British owned restaurants, books and publications, and art objects. But the list isn't limited.

Four times a year, the Association publishes a handsomely designed and highly informative bulletin for its members called France File, packed with insightful information, reviews, and editorials. Members may submit articles to this forum, rate restaurants and hotels, nominate candidates for the Association's "Integrity Awards," etc. Other features include "Mickey Mouse Watch," a column devoted to activities for children, "Property Line," an unbiased report on the

French real estate market, and "The Disgruntled Traveler," in which members can creatively complain to each other about unsatisfactory services and products in France.

Annual individual memberships are 550 FF while professional memberships for businesses and entrepreneurs offering benefits and services to members cost 850 FF per year.

**Association of British
& American Residents in France**
17, rue de la Baume
75008 PARIS
Tel: 44.13.40.25
Fax: 44.13.40.26
Director: Amy SLOANE-PINEL,
Robert BROWN

After years of being situated in a beautiful building on the bd Raspail, the American Center, a private institution directed by Henry Pillsbury and chaired by Judith Pisar, has relocating to the rue de Pomard at Bercy, a former wine producing village of the last century tucked into the *12e*. Ground-breaking for the new Frank Gehry building started in July 1990 with the center scheduled to open in fall 1993. The American Center, currently housed in a temporary building on the site, is providing some American conferences and language courses.

The American Center
51, rue de Bercy
75592 PARIS Cedex 12
Tel: 44.73.77.77
Fax: 43.07.11.71

The French System

Formal education in France begins for many at the age of three month in the state-run *crèches* (nurseries). These tend to be remarkably well-organized and pedagogically-sound institutions. Aside from the shared colds and minor illnesses, *crèches* seem to offer only positive factors for French society. Mothers return their secured jobs and the kids emerge as well-adjusted individuals. The education of the French palate too begins in infancy, as the toddlers begin to be fed a complex menu of everything from filet of sole to calves brains, artichoke *purée* to *Port Salut* cheese. And Evian or Vittel for a beverage. Between the ages of three and six years, the child can attend his or her neighborhood *école maternelle* (pre-school) which is also state-run and municipally administered.

Classes in French public education up till university runs like this:

Education is compulsory from six to sixteen and is free in state schools. Eighty three percent of children are in state education; the remainder go to private schools, most of which are run by the Catholic Church. Private education does not carry with it much prestige and can even imply the opposite. The French educational tradition emphasizes encyclopedic knowledge and memorization. The rigidness of former years, however, has loosened somewhat and great battles, student strikes, and debates over pedagogic issues have played a major roll in the French political climate since 1968. In general, all children attend the same kind of state day schools, and the tenacious go on to study for the *baccalauréat,* which is roughly equivalent to a level of studies one year beyond the American high school diploma This *bac* is a highly important indicator of a student's potential choices in

Ecole maternelle	*petit, moyen, grande*	3-6 years old
Ecole primaire	*CP (cours préparatoire)*	6 years old
CE 1	(*cours élémentaire* first year)	7 years old
CE 2	(*cours élémentaire,* first year)	8 years old
CM 1	(*Cours moyen,* first year)	9 years old
CM 2	(*Cours moyen,* 2nd year)	10 years old
Collège	*6ème, 5ème, 4ème, 3ème*	11-14 years old
Lycée	*Seconde, Première, Terminale (BAC)*	15-18 years old
Université, Grandes Ecoles, preparatory school or special school		19 +

life. At age 15 or 16 the more academic children go to a *lycée* (high school) to prepare for the *bac*, usually taken at age 18 or 19. The *bac* is more of a means to get into a university than a job qualification in itself. Passing the *bac*, however, is essential for access to all upper-level jobs. Failure is a negative status symbol and source of shame in some socially well-placed families.

There are almost a million university students in France. Unlike the United States, admission to a state-run university is not selective, but guaranteed to everyone who has passed the *bac*. Student/teacher ratios are high. There is little personal contact between professors and students, and professors see their jobs as confined to the classroom. The system is centralized, tightly-controlled, highly politicized, and ridden by life-sapping internal regulations. The Sorbonne's international reputation stems from the quality of the minds who teach there. The archaic organization of the university, however, might dissuade you for life. On the other, hand it might fill you with the sensation of participating in a great and celebrated tradition. Think positive. It has been the focus of many political debates

and upheavals in the past two decades.

In brief, the French university system is organized into three cycles: the *1er*, *2e*, and *3e*. The first cycle is usually two years, and comprises the *DEUG* and the *Licence*. The second cycle, or *Maîtrise*, is roughly equivalent to the American Master's degree. The third cycle, and clearly the most prestigious in the French system, is the Doctoral program, which not long ago offered three different doctoral diplomas. More recently, the long and painfully serious *doctorat d'Etat* was replaced by the *doctorat d'université*, modelled after the American Ph.D. A unique, although disruptive quirk in the university cycle system is the fact that prescribed programs are subject to modification with governmental and ministerial changes. For all questions of recognized transferable credits, you must submit in writing a *dérogation* (appeal) to the universities' *Service des équivalences*. Remember to bring not only transcripts but all original diplomas. French universities need to see the stamped document itself.

In 1968, in keeping with the international climate, there were a series of nationwide demonstrations, walk-outs and riots staged by French university students demanding an overhaul of the dated and archaic university system. Since then the scene has relaxed somewhat and universities have now been split up into smaller, more manageable units. Thus the Sorbonne is now simply a building, beautiful at that, which houses a part of the amorphous *Université de Paris* system. There are a number of programs in Paris run by American colleges which include the possibility of study at one of the Paris campuses. They can also be contacted directly. A complete list of all universities and schools in France, public and private, is published by *L'Etudiant* magazine, called *Le Guide des Etudes Supérieures 1992*. Another source of information are French consulates around the world, which provide information on specific areas of study in France through their Cultural Services office.

Major Paris Universities: *Universités de Paris*

Université Panthéon Sorbonne —Paris 1
12, place du Panthéon
75231 PARIS Cedex 05
Tel: 46.34.97.00

Université de Paris 2 (Droit, Economie et Sciences Sociales)
12, place du Panthéon
75231 PARIS Cedex 05
Tel: 46.34.97.00

Université de la Sorbonne Nouvelle—Paris 3
17, rue de la Sorbonne
75005 PARIS
Tel: 45.87.40.00

Université de Paris- Sorbonne —Paris 4
13, rue de Santeuil
75230 PARIS cedex 06
Tel: 40.46.22.11

Université René Descartes —Paris 5
12, rue de l'Ecole-de-Médecine
75270 PARIS cedex 06
Tel: 40.46.16.16

Université Pierre et Marie Curie —Paris 6
4, place Jussieu
75230 PARIS cedex 05
Tel: 43.29.29.29

Université de Paris 7
2, place Jussieu
75251 PARIS cedex 05
Tel: 44.27.44.27

Université de Paris Dauphine
—Paris 9
Place du Maréchal-de-Lattre-de-Tassigny
75775 PARIS cedex 16
Tel: 45.05.14.10

Institut National des Langues et
Civilisations Orientales
(Langues O or INALCO)
2, rue de Lille
75007 PARIS
Tel: 49.26.42.00

Art Schools
Ecole du Louvre
34 quai du Louvre
75041 PARIS cedex 01
Tel: 42.60.25.50, 42.60.39.26

Ecole Nationale Supérieure des
Arts Décoratifs (ENSAD)
31, rue d'Ulm
75005 PARIS
Tel: 43.29.67.31

Ecole Nationale Supérieure des
Beaux-Arts (Beaux-Arts)
17, quai Malaquais
75272 PARIS cedex 06
Tel: 42.60.34.57

Les Ateliers-Ecole Nationale
Supérieure de Création Industrielle
48, rue Saint-Sabin
75011 PARIS
Tel: 43.38.09.09

Architecture Schools
Ecole d'architecture Paris-Belleville
78-80, rue de Rebeval
75013 PARIS
Tel: 42.41.33.60

Ecole d'architecture Paris-la Seine
14, rue Bonaparte
75006 PARIS
Tel: 42.61.81.11

Ecole d'architecture Paris-La
Villette
144, rue de Flandre
75019 PARIS
Tel: 40.36.79.70

Ecole d'architecture Paris-Tolbiac
5, rue du Javelot
75645 PARIS Cédex
Tel: 45.82.27.27

Ecole d'architecture Paris-Villemin
11, quai Malaquais
75272 PARIS Cédex 06
Tel: 42.60.34.57

Ecole spéciale d'architecture
245, bd Raspail
75014 PARIS
Tel: 40.47.40.47

Grandes Ecoles
The difference between a university and one of the *Grandes Ecoles* is vast. There are about 250 small, autonomous, and elite *Grandes Ecoles*. They train high-level specialists in engineering, applied science, administration and management studies. The entrance exam for French students requires two or three years' rigorous preparatory study in special post-bac classes at the *lycées*. Extremely few foreigners are admitted to the *Grandes Ecoles*. Only 10% of the students are women. These schools turn out a high

proportion of senior civil servants and industrial and business leaders. One of the most prestigious is the *Ecole Polytechnique*, founded by Napoleon to train engineers for the armed forces. It is still run by the Ministry of Defense and is headed by a general. Other *Grandes Ecoles*: *Ecole Centrale, Ecole des Hautes Etudes Commerciales*, and *Ecole Nationale d'Administration*, which trains future high-level political types.

L'Institut d'Etudes Politiques

More than 800 of the 5000 students at *L'Institut d'Etudes Politiques de Paris*, or *Sciences-Po*, are foreign. You must speak and write French to be admitted. There are several possibilities for courses of study:

Those who already have a master's degree in a related field (Political Science, Economics, History, etc.) can enter the *troisième cycle* and obtain a *Doctorat* for further research work in the field or a *Diplôme d'Etudes Supérieures Spécialisées* for preparation for more professional work.

Those who already have three years of university work can enter the *deuxième cycle* by passing an entrance exam. They receive the *Diplôme de l'Institut* after two years of study.

Students having completed some university work: the *Cycle d'Etudes Internationales* is suitable for those on Junior Year Abroad in American University programs; no preparation for diploma.

The *Certificat d'Etudes Politiques* is a one-year program for international students concentrating on studies of modern France, and prepares those who wish to enter the *Deuxième Cycle*.

Further information can be obtained by contacting:

Fondation Nationale des Sciences Politiques
27, rue Saint Guillaume
75341 PARIS Cedex 07
Tel: 45.49.50.50
FAX: 42.22.31.26

Foreign & Exchange Programs Paris

Presently, there are more than thirty university exchange and foreign study programs in Paris in English and a handful in the rest of France. Additionally, there are a number of English-language universities based in or with campuses in Paris, the largest and most complete being The American University of Paris with its 1000 students and 275 courses each semester. The complete list of higher education programs (in alphabetical order) is found below and is followed by a list of schools and alumni associations.

University Programs

For a full listing of elementary and secondary schools, as well as French schools offering English-language instruction, you may consult *Paris-Anglophone.*

Academic Year Abroad
Reid Hall
4, rue de Chevreuse
75006 PARIS
Tel: 43.20.91.92

Alma College
c/o Alliance Française
101, bd Raspail
75006 PARIS
Tel: 45.49.08.16
Director: Mme. BOUNOURE

Allegheny College in Paris
4, rue de Chevreuse
75006 PARIS
Tel: 45.38.52.90

American Business School
15, ave de la Grande Armée
75016 PARIS
Tel: 45.01.96.01
FAX: 40.67.96.96
Academic Director:
Ms. Nazila AMIRKHOSRAVI

American Institute for Foreign Study
10, rue Doctor Blanche
75016 PARIS
Tel: 43.22.11.91
Director:
Mrs. Marthe B. COOPER

American School of Modern Music
117, rue de la Croix-Nivert
75015 PARIS
Tel: 45.31.16.07

American University of Paris, The
31, ave Bosquet
75007 PARIS
Tel: 45.55.91.73
FAX: 47.05.33.49
President: Mr. Glenn FERGUSON
Dean of Academics:
Mr. William CIPOLLA
Dean of Students:
Mr. Paul MARCILLE
Registrar: Ms. DeeDee PEASE
Assist. Dean:
Ms. Charlotte KESSLER
(American university education; B.A./B.S. degree; all classes in English)

American University of Paris, The
Admissions/Development Office
165, rue de l'Université
75007 PARIS
Tel: 45.55.91.73
Director of Admissions:
Ms. Christine BROENING
V. P. for Development:
Mr. John McKEE
V.P. for Finance:
Mr. Rob GROEN

American University of Paris, The
Division of Summer
and Continuing Education
34, ave New York
75116 PARIS
Director: Ms. Susan KINSEY
Summer Program:
Ms. Camille HERCOT
Tel: 47.20.44.99

Bennington College
24, rue de Turbigo
75002 PARIS

Boston University in Paris
(address soon to change)
49, rue Pierre Charron
75008 PARIS
Tel: 45.61.49.23
(offers Masters degrees in
International Relations)

Boston University
Paris Internship Program
International Programs
725 Commonwealth Ave B2
Boston MA 02215
Tel: (617) 353-9888

California State/Denver/CUNY
MICEFA
101, bd Raspail
75006 PARIS
Tel: 45.48.08.95

**Center for University
Programs Abroad (CUPA)**
21, rue Cassette
75006 PARIS
Tel: 42.22.87.50
Tel: (315) 853-6905
Clinton, N.Y, USA
Directors: Elliot CHATELIN/
Pascale BESSIERES

Central College (Iowa)
214, bd Raspail
75014 PARIS
Tel: 43.20.76.09
Director: Inge DRAPPER

**Centre d'Etudes
Franco-Américaines**
84, rue Pixérécourt
75020 PARIS
Tel: 47.97.65.63

Centre Nord Américain
11, rue Pierre et Marie Curie
75005 PARIS
Tel: 43.25.25.45

Chicago Overseas Program
Fondation des Etats-Unis
15, bd Jourdan
75014 PARIS
Tel: 45.89.35.77
Director: Terence MURPHY

Collège Irlandais
5, rue Irlandais
75005 PARIS
Tel: 45.35.59.79

Columbia University
Reid Hall
4, rue de Chevreuse
75006 PARIS
Tel: 43.20.24.83
Director of Studies:
Meredith SYKES

Architecture Program
4, rue de Jarente
75004 PARIS
Tel: 42.78.53.44
Director of Studies:
Meredith SYKES

Consortium of Colleges Abroad
57, rue de Bourgogne
75007 PARIS
Tel: 45.55.84.29

Earlham/Kenyan
Centre F.A. Odéon
1, Pl de l'Odéon
75006 PARIS
Tel: 46.34.16.10

EDUCO/Duke/Cornell
23, rue du Montparnasse
75006 PARIS
Tel: 42.22.34.66

European Master's in International Business
EAP
(Ecole Européenne des Affaires)
108, bd Malesherbes
75017 PARIS
Tel: 47.54.65.78
Director: Mr. Syprum TIJMSTRA

European University
137 ave Jean Jaures
92140 CLAMART
Tel: 46.44.39.39
Director: Mr. Jean -Pierre BAL

European University of America
17/25, rue de Chaillot
75016 PARIS
Tel: 40.70.11.71

Hamilton College
Reid Hall
4 , rue de Chevreuse
75006 Paris
Tel: 43.20.77.77

Hollins College
4, Pl de l'Odéon
75006 PARIS
Tel: 46.34.59.85

Indiana University
Public Adm. Program
C/O ENA
13, rue de l'Université
75007 PARIS

Institute Franco-Américain de Management
19, rue Cépré
75015 PARIS
Tel: 47.34.38.23
FAX: 45.75.87.27
Director:
Mme Marie-France JOSEPH
(B.A., M.B.A. and French *diplôme*

programs; associated with Hartford University, Northeastern University, Boston University and Pace University)

Inter-Univ. Center for Film and Critical Studies
1, Place de l'Odéon
75006 PARIS
Tel: 46..33.85.33
Director: Reda BENSMAIA

The International School of Paris
6, rue Beethoven
75016 PARIS
Tel: 46.24.09.54

MBA Insead
Bd de Constance
77305 Fontainebleau Cedex
Tel: 60.72.40.00
telex: 690 389
FAX: 60.72.42.42
Director: M. Claude RAMEAU
(10 month grad. MBA program)

MBA Institute
38, rue des Blancs-Manteaux
75004 PARIS
Tel: 42.78.95.45
Director: M. George STEWART

Middlebury College
Reid Hall
4, rue Chevreuse
75006 Paris
Tel: 43.20.70.57

New York University
56, rue de Passy
75016 PARIS
Tel: 42.88.52.84
FAX: 42.24.03.73
Director: Mme WALTHER

Paris American Academy
9, rue des Ursulines
75005 PARIS
Tel: 43.25.08.91
and
Pavillon Val-de-Grâce
277, rue St. Jacques
75005 PARIS
Tel: 43.25.35.09
Director: Richard ROY

**Paris Internship Program/
Lake Forest College**
43, rue Lacépède
75005 PARIS
Tel: 45.87.20.51

Parsons Paris School of Design
10-14, rue Letellier
75015 PARIS
Tel: 45.77.39.66
FAX: 45.77.10.44
Director: Keith LONG

Randolph-Macon Study Abroad
74, rue d'Alleray
75015 PARIS

**Reid Hall Centre
Universitaire Americain**
4, rue Chevreuse
75006 PARIS
Tel: 43.20.33.07
(eight American Academic Year
Abroad programs located here)

Sarah Lawrence College
Reid Hall
4, rue Chevreuse
75006 PARIS
Tel: 43.22.14.36

Saint Xavier University—Chicago
Graham School of Management
(executive MBA program)
20, rue de St. Petersberg
75008 PARIS
Tel: 42.93.13.87
Fax: 45.22.12.65
Director: Mr. G. Stephen RYER

Southern Methodist University
Reid Hall
4, rue Chevreuse
75006 PARIS
Tel: 43.20.04.86

Schiller International University
32, bd Vaugirard
75015 PARIS
Tel: 45.38.56.01

Skidmore College
142, rue de Rivoli
75001 PARIS
Tel: 42.36.02.55

Smith College
Reid Hall
4, rue de Chevreuse
75006 PARIS
Tel: 43.21.65.54

Southern Methodist University
Reid Hall
4, rue de Chevreuse
75006 PARIS
Tel: 43.21.65.54

Stanford University
79, ave de la République
75011 PARIS
Tel: 49.23.20.00

SUNY Brockport/SUNY Oswego
Centre Franco-Américain
1, Pl de l'Odéon
75006 PARIS
Tel: 46.34.16.10

SUNY Stony Brook
1, Place d'Odéon
75006 PARIS
Tel: 42.47.06.04

Sweet Briar College
101, bd Raspail
75006 PARIS
Tel: 45.38.79.30

Tulane University/Newcomb
4, rue de Chevreuse
75006 PARIS
Tel: 43.21.35.85

University of Hartford
Business School
15, ave de la Grande Armée
75016 PARIS
Tel: 45.00.98.28
Fax: 47.76.45.13
Paris Director: Ms. Pamela MEAD

Office of Graduate Studies
Paris MBA Program
200 Bloomfield Avenue
West Hartford, CT USA 06117
Tel: (203) 243-4641

University of Illinois at Chicago
Centre Franco-Américain
33bis, rue de Reille
75014 PARIS
Tel: 45.88.26.52

University of
Southwestern Louisiana
I.A.C. Cycle Int'l
71, rue de Fbg. St Honoré
75008 PARIS
Tel: 42.66.66.82/42.66.46.59

Wesleyan University
Reid Hall
4, rue de Chevreuse
75006 PARIS
Tel: 43.22.12.47

Willamette
23bis bd Berthier
75017 PARIS
Tel: 42.67.52.28

Schools
American School of Paris
41, rue Pasteur
92210 SAINT CLOUD
Tel: 46.02.54.43
Headmaster: M. George COHAN

American School-Harriet Bonelli
1, rue Crébillon
75006 PARIS
Tel: 43.25.10.22

British School of Paris
38, Quai de l'Ecluse
78290 CROISSY-SUR-SEINE
Tel: 39.76.29.00
Headmaster: M. D.R. COPE

Cours Bernard Palissy
18-22, rue Eugène-Flachat
75017 PARIS
Tel: 47.55.73.16
Director: M. Siméon DRESSEN

Ecole Active Bilingue
Jeannine Manuel
Ecole Internationale de Paris
70, rue du Théâtre
75015 PARIS
Tel: 45.75.62.98

39, ave de la Bourdonnais
75007 PARIS
Tel: 45.51.20.84

141, ave de Suffren
75007 PARIS
Tel: 47.34.27.72
Directors: Mme Jacqueline ROUB-
INET, Mme Catherine COSTE

THE AMERICAN MBA IN PARIS

A 48-credit Master of Business Administration Degree
taught by the faculty of the University of Hartford

**11 months of intensive study in English delivered for
the seventh consecutive year by the University of Hartford
(established in 1877 - student body of 8000)**

Admission is competitive and selective. The ambiance is
international (39 nationalities represented in 7 years)

**September to April in Paris. Summer on the 300-acre
Hartford Campus located between New York and Boston**

Admission Criteria: Undergraduate Degree,
GMAT and TOEFL

**The University of Hartford also offers a Part-Time
MBA Program (evening classes over a 3 year period)**

For more information on this exciting educational opportunity
Contact: Pamela Meade, MBA

UNIVERSITY OF HARTFORD
BUSINESS SCHOOL

8, Terrasse Bellini, Paris-La Défense 11,
92807 Puteaux Cedex
Tel: 49 00 19 61 - Fax: 47 76 45 13

Ecole Jeanne d'Albert
1, rue Denis Poisson
75017 PARIS
Tel: 45.74.10.95
M. BERBEZY

International School of Paris
Grades K-5
96 bis, rue du Ranelagh
75016 PARIS
Tel: 42.24.43.40

Grades 6-12
7 rue Chardin
75016 PARIS
Tel: 45.27.50.01

Lycée Canadien en France
12, rue du Petit-Thouars
75002 PARIS
Tel: 48.87.97.97

**Lycée International
de Saint-Germain-en-Laye**
230, rue du Fer-à-Cheval
78104 ST-GERMAIN-EN-LAYE
Headmaster: M. Edgar SCHERER
Director (American Section):
Mme Nancy MAGAUD

Marymount School
72, bd de la Saussaye
92200 NEUILLY-SUR-SEINE
Tel: 46.24.10.51
Headmistress:
Sister Maureen VELLON

**Maxim's
(Hotel Management School)**
71, rue du Fbg. Saint Honoré
75008 PARIS
Tel: 42.66.66.82
Fax: 47.42.57.22

**United Nations Nursery
School Association Paris**
40 rue Pierre-Guerin
75016 PARIS
Tel: 45.27.20.24
(international bilingual school for
children 2-6; summer school in
July)

Wilson Learning Performance SA
30, ave Am. Lemonnier
78160 MARLY LE ROI
Tel: 39.16.21.11

**Women's Institute for
Continuing Education (WICE)**
20 bd Montparnasse
75007 PARIS
Tel: 45.66.75.50
(offers courses in Teaching English
as a Foreign Language, Career
Development, Self-Development,
Living in France, Arts, Humanities.
Has career services, a monthly
newsletter, a volunteer service, a
health referral service, and open
houses)

Exchange Programs

**Aspect Foundation
Exchange Programs**
53, rue du Fbg. Poissonnière
75009 PARIS
Tel: 48.00.06.00
FAX: 48.00.05.94
Representative:
M. Helen TONNERRE

**Council on International
Educational Exchange (C.I.E.E.)**
Centre Franco-Américain Odéon
1, place. de l'Odéon
75006 PARIS
Tel: 43.59.23.69 or 46.34.16.10
Director: Mme Andrea MASON

Cultural Crossing
60, rue de Varennes
75007 PARIS
Tel: 45.48.62.51
Director: Mme Polly PLATT

Experiment in International Living
89, rue Turbigo
75003 PARIS
Tel: 42.78.50.03
Director:
M. Gilbert GUILLEMOTO

Fondation des Etats-Unis
15, bd Jourdan
75690 PARIS Cedex 14
Tel: 45.89.35.77 (admin.)
Tel: 45.89.35.79 (students)
Director: M. Terence MURPHY
(residence and cultural center)

Fondation Franco-Américaine
38, ave Hoche
75008 PARIS
Tel: 45.63.28.30
FAX: 42.56.09.75
President: M. Marceau LONG
Director: M. Michel JAOUL
(awards, scholarships, and grants)

**Franco-American Commission
for Educational Exchange**
(Fulbright Scholarships)
9, rue Chardin
75016 PARIS
Tel: 45.20.46.54
Director: M. Roland HUSSON

Language Schools

In the last few years there has been a dramatic increase in the number of language schools in Paris for both French and English. Much of this has been in anticipation of a new, united Europe and all the transpollenation that is expected to follow...with English as the common linguistic denominator. Here is a broad but far from exhaustive selection of schools where French is taught in Paris:

Alliance Française
100, bd Raspail
75006 PARIS
Tel: 45.44.38.28

Berlitz S.A.R.L.
29, rue de la Michodière
75002 Paris
Tel: 47.42.46.54

Langue Executive Service
25, bd de Sébastopol
75001 PARIS
Tel: 42.36.32.32

British Institute
11, rue de Constantine
75007 PARIS
Tel: 45.55.71.99

**Chambre de Commerce et
d'Industrie de Paris-Enseignement**
42, rue du Louvre
75001 PARIS
Tel: 45.08.37.34

Centre d'Echanges Internationaux (C.E.I.)
104, rue de Vaugirard
75006 PARIS
Tel: 45.49.26.25

Centre Linguistique Bouchereau
196, bd Haussman
75008 PARIS
Tel: 42.56.14.96

C.E.R.C.L.E.
202, rue de la Croix Nivert
75015 PARIS
Tel: 45.57.61.93 or 45.57.99.92

Clé International
27, rue de la Glacière
75013 Paris
Tel: 45.87.44.00

Communications Plurielles
5, rue Sainte Anastase
75003 PARIS
Tel: 42.72.32.63 or 42.72.32.22

Cours de Civilisation Française de la Sorbonne
47, rue des Ecoles
75005 PARIS
Tel: 40.46.22.11 ext. 2664 or 2675
Director: Maurice REY

Dialangues
7, rue de Surène
75008 PARIS
Tel: 42.68.18.54

French Language Instruction for Anglophones
34, rue Alphonse Bertillon
75015 PARIS
Tel: 48.28.03.21

Institute Catholique
21, rue Assas
75006 PARIS
Tel: 42.22.63.49

Institut de Langue Française
15, rue Arsène Houssaye
75008 PARIS
Tel: 42.27.14.77

Institut Parisien de Langue et de Civilisation Françaises
87, bd de Grenelle
75015 PARIS
Tel/Fax: 40.56.09.53
Director: James SIMON

Self-Taught French Method

Assimil
(wide selection of books, cassettes, and CDs)
11, rue des Pyramides
75001 PARIS
Tel: 42.60.40.66

Bibliothèque Publique d'Information
Centre Georges-Pompidou
(Language Lab)
75181 PARIS Cedex 04
Tel: 42.78.70.65

Organizations/Clubs

For a complete listing of Paris' many Anglo-American organizations, clubs and alumni associations consulte *Paris-Anglophone,* (Frank Books, 1992).

INSTITUT PARISIEN DE LANGUE ET DE CIVILISATION FRANÇAISES

The Institut Parisien specializes in teaching French to foreigners, welcoming throughout the year students from over 40 different countries. After taking a free placement test, students may enroll in one of the three course options:

GROUP CLASSES

• <u>EXTENSIVE:</u> 4-1/2 or 9 hours per week offered during the academic year. Students may enroll the beginning of each week.
Extensive class options: French for business, French for Tourism and Hostellery (preparation for the Paris Chamber of Commerce Certificate.)

• <u>INTENSIVE:</u> 15 or 25 hours per week offered throughout the year. Maximum 15 students. Students may enroll the beginning of each week.

INDIVIDUAL INSTRUCTION

• Courses "à la carte," individually designed for each student. Instruction ranges from 1 to 45 hours per week.

PRIVATE GROUPS

• Specially tailored programs for schools, universities, and corporations, as well as professional training for French teachers.

The Institut Parisien also offers French Civilization courses on history, art, and literature. Certificates and diplomas can be obtained upon completion of courses. The Institut Parisien is an *Etablissement Libre d'Enseignement Supérieur (Rectorat de Paris, No. 556)* and as such has an agreement for continuing adult education credits. Housing service is available upon request.

Institut Parisien de Langue et Civilisation Françaises
87 Bd. Grenelle, 75015 Paris, Tel/fax: 40.56.09.53

This newly elaborated section of Paris Inside Out *was penned by Sandra Kwock-Silve, Paris art critic and historian originally from Hawaii. Her articles appear regularly in the* Paris Free Voice *and various art publications including* Raw Vision.

Since the late 18th century when the Louvre was first opened to the public, this world-famous museum has ranked high on most visitors' lists of "things to see in Paris." However, for adventurous spirits, classics like the *Musée du Louvre* and the *Musée d'Orsay* should suggest only the beginning of a serious museum sampling. There are nearly one hundred museums to discover in and around Paris. Prestigious private and public collections highlight just about every subject imaginable. There are serious museums devoted to the history of wine, fashion, new technology and the arts from every era, country and culture. Something is sure to capture your interest in Paris' rich museum world, whether it's a glimpse of the future at *La Villette*, or an afternoon stroll through the sculpture garden at *La Musée Rodin.* Visits to the artist's studios will take you to some interesting neighborhoods off the beaten tourist track. And the city's eccentric collection of counterfeits, locks, and spectacles (to name but a few) will keep you exploring.

Major museum exhibitions are an important part of the Paris art scene all year round. The weekly publications *Pariscope* and *Official des Spectacles* have extensive museum and gallery listings of current exhibits. For historical information, the Michelin guide to Paris and the Hachette "*guide bleu*" are considered the best sources available.

Consider going on a museum spree with *La Carte musées et monuments.* This special pass allows unlimited access to over 60 museums and monuments without having to wait in line for tickets. Card prices range from 55 FF for one day to 160 FF for a five day period. Cards can be bought at the tourist office (121, ave Champs Elysées), Métro stations or museums. Some museums are free, or half price on Sundays. Check for interesting student/teacher rates. Teachers are usually free. As a general rule, national museums are open 9h45h-17h00 every day except Tuesday. Municipal museums keep the same hours, but are closed on Monday. Many museums are closed on public holidays, and smaller collections may close during the the month of August.

A list of the major museums is followed by a selection of diverse thematic collection of artists' studios and suggested museum outings for children.

Major Museums

• *Centre Georges Pompidou (Beaubourg):* 19, rue Rambuteau, 75001 PARIS (Métro: Châtelet /Les Halles). Tel: 42.77.12.33. Open weekdays: 12h00-22h00 weekends and holidays: 10h00-20h00 closed Tuesday. Museum entrance fee: 27 FF, 18 FF for those under 25 (proof of age is required); free on Sunday from 10h00-14h00. Contemporary galleries 16 FF.

• *Musée de l'Armée:* Hotel des Invalides, 75007 PARIS (Métro: Latour-Maubourg). Tel: 45.55. 37.70. Open daily from 10h00-17h00. Closed on holidays. Entrance fee: 27 FF, 14 FF.

• *Musée de l'Art Moderne de la ville de Paris:* 11, ave Pres. Wilson, 75116 PARIS (Métro: Ièna). Tel: 47.23.61.67. Open daily from 10h00-17h30 and until 20h30 on Wednesday. Closed Monday. Entrance fee: 28 FF, 14 FF.

• *Musée des Arts Africains et Océaniens:* 293, ave Daumesnil, 75012 PARIS (Métro: Porte Dorée). Tel: 43.43.14.54. Open weekdays from 10h00-12h00 and 13h30-17h30. Weekends from 12h30-18h00. Closed Tuesday. Entrance fee: 24 FF,14 FF. Sunday

14 FF, 8 FF. Aquarium open daily except Tuesday from 10h00-18h00. Under 18 free.

• *Musée des Arts Décoratifs:* 107-109, rue de Rivoli, 75001 PARIS (Métro: Palais Royale). Tel: 42.60.32.14. Open daily from 12h30-18h00. Closed Monday and Tuesday. Entrance fee: 23 FF, 14 FF. Admission to Dubuffet donation 20 FF.

• *Musée des Arts de la Mode:* 109, rue de Rivoli, 75001 PARIS (Métro: Palais Royale). Tel: 42.60.32.14. Open daily from 12h30-18h00. Closed Monday and Tuesday. Temporary exhibitions. Entrance fee: 25 FF, 13 FF.

• *Musée National des Arts et Traditions Populaires:* 6, ave du Mahatma-Gandi, 75116 PARIS (Métro: Sablons). Tel: 40.67.90.00. Open daily from 9h45-17h15. Closed Tuesday. Entrance fee: 14 FF, 9 FF.

• *Musée Carnavalet:* 23, rue de Sévigné, 75005 PARIS (Métro: Saint Paul). Tel: 42.72.21.13. Open daily from 10h00-17h35. Closed Monday and holidays.

• *Musée de Cluny:* 6, place Paul-Painlevé, 75005 PARIS (Métro: Saint-Michel). Tel: 43.25.62.00. Open daily from 9h30-17h15. Closed Tuesday. Entrance fee: 15 FF, 8 FF, under 18 free.

• *Musée Guimet* (Asian Art): 6, Place d'Iéna, 75116 PARIS (Métro: Iéna). Tel: 47.23.61.65. Open daily from 9h45-17h15. Closed Tuesdays and holidays. Entrance fee: 25 FF.

• *Musée de l'Histoire de France:* Hotel de Soubise, 60, rue des

Francs Bourgeois, 75003 PARIS (Métro: Saint-Paul). Tel: 40.27. 62.18. Open daily from 13h45-17h45. Closed Tuesdays and holidays. Entrance fee: 12 FF, 8 FF.

• *Musée National d'Histoire Naturelle:* Jardin des Plantes, 57, rue de Cuivier, 75005 PARIS (Métro: Monge). Open daily from 10h00-17h00. Weekends: 11h00-18h00. Closed Tuesday. Zoo: Tel: 43.36.19.09. Open daily from 9h00-18h00. Entrance fee: 22 FF, 10 FF.

• *Musée de l'Homme:* Palais de Chaillot, Place du Trocadero, 75116 PARIS (Métro: Trocadero). Tel: 45.53.70.60. Open daily from 9h45-17h15. Closed Tuesdays and holidays. Entrance fee: 25 FF, 15 FF.

• *Musée de l'Institut du Monde Arabe:* 23, Quai Saint-Bernard, 75005 PARIS (Métro: Jussieu). Tel: 40.51.38.38. Open daily from 13h00-20h00. Closed on Monday. Entrance fee: 40 FF.

• *Musée de Jeu de Paume:* Gallerie Nationale (Temporary exhibitions-Contemporary art). place de la Concorde, 75001 PARIS (Métro: Concorde). Tel: 47.03.12.50. Open daily from 12h00-19h00; Tuesday until 20h30. Closed Monday.

• *Musée du Louvre:* rue de Rivoli, 75001 PARIS (Métro: Palais-Royal Louvre). Tel: 40.20.51.51. Open every day except Tuesday. Permanent exhibitions: 9h00-18h00. Wednesday until 21h45. Temporary exhibitions 12h00-20h00. Entrance fee: 30 FF, 15 FF.

• *Musée de la Marine:* Palais de Chaillot, Place de Trocadero, 75116 PARIS (Métro: Trocadero). Tel: 45.53.31.70. Open daily from 10h00-18h00. Open holidays. Closed Tuesday. Entrance fee: 22 FF, 10 FF.

• *Musée Marmottan:* 2, rue Louis-Bouilly, 75016 PARIS (Métro: La Muette). Tel: 42.24.07.02. Open daily from 10h00-17h30. Closed Monday. Entrance fee: 25 FF, 10 FF.

• *Musée de la Mode et du Costume:* Palais Galliéra, ave Pierre-1er-de Serbie, 75116 PARIS (Métro: Iéna). Open daily from 10h00-17h40. Closed Monday.

• *Musée de la Monnaie:* 11, Quai de Conti, 75006 PARIS (Métro: Pont-Neuf). Tel: 40.46.55.35. Open daily from 13h00-18h00; Wednesday untill 21h00. Closed Monday. Entrance fee: 15 FF, 10 FF. Free on Sunday.

• *Musée National des Monuments Français:* Palais de Chaillot, place de Trocadero, 75116 PARIS (Métro: Trocadero). Tel: 47.27. 35.74. Open daily from 9h00-18h00. Closed Tuesday.

• *Musée de l'Orangerie des Tuileries:* place de la Concorde, 75001 PARIS (Métro: Concorde). Tel: 42.97. 48.16. Open daily from 9h45-17h15. Closed Tuesday. Entrance fee: 23 FF, 12 FF.

• *Musée D'Orsay:* 62, rue de Lille, 75007 PARIS (Métro: Solferino). Tel: 40.49.48.14. Recorded message: Tel: 45.49.11.11. Program information: 40.49.48.48. Open daily except Monday from 10h00-18h00; Thursday until 21h45;

Sunday 9h00-18h00. Entrance fee: 30 FF, 15 FF; Sunday; 15 FF, under 18 free.

• *Musée du Petit Palais:* ave Winston Churchill, 75008 PARIS (Métro: Champs-Elysées-Clemenceau). Tel: 42.65.12.73. Open daily from 10h00-17h40. Closed Monday and holidays. Entrance fee: 20 FF, 15 FF.

• *Palais de Tokyo (Centre de la Photographie)*: 13, ave du Président Wilson, 75116 PARIS (Métro: Iéna). 47.23.36.53. Open daily from 9h45-17h00. Closed Tuesday. Entrance fee: 25 FF.

• *Musée Picasso:* Hotel Sal, 5, rue Thorigny, 75003 PARIS (Métro: Saint-Paul). Tel: 42.71.25.21. Open daily from 9h15-17h15; Wednesday untill 22h00. Closed Tuesday. Entrance fee: 28 FF.

• *Musée de la Poste:* 34, bd de Vaugirard, 75017 PARIS (Métro: Montparnasse). Tel: 42.79.23.45. Open weekdays and Saturday: 10h00-18h00. Closed Sunday and holidays. Entrance fee: 20 FF, 10 FF.

• *Musée de la Publicité:* 18, rue du Paradis, 75010 PARIS (Métro: Château d'eau). Tel: 42.46.13.09. Open daily from 12h00-18h00. Closed Tuesday. Entrance fee: 18 FF.

• *Musée des Sciences et de l'Industrie:* Parc de la Villette, 30, ave Corentin-Cariou, 75019 PARIS (Métro: Porte de la Villette). Tel: 46.42.13.13. Open daily except Monday from 10h00-18h00. Entrance pass: 35 FF, 25 FF. Cité and Géode: 70 FF.

Museums in Artist's Homes

• *Musée Henri Bouchard:* 25, rue de l'Yvette, 75016 PARIS (Métro: Jasmin). Tel: 46.47.63.46. Open Wednesday and Saturday from 14h00-19h00. Entrance fee: 15 FF, 10 FF. A tour of this official sculptor's studio is given the first Saturday of each month at 15h00. Bouchard lived from 1875-1960. Academic and decorative sculptures and medals are on view in changing exhibits.

• *Musée Bourdelle:* 16, rue Antoine-Bourdelle, 75015 PARIS (Métro: Montparnasse). Open daily from 10h00-17h40. Closed Monday and holidays. Entrance fee: 18 FF, 12 FF. The artist's studio contains a large collection of sketches and sculptures in many styles. Bourdelle lived from 1861-1929. Family portraits, *maquettes* and casts are on view.

• *Fondation Le Corbusier:* 8-10, Square de Docteur Blanche, 75016 PARIS (Métro: Jasmin). Tel: 45.27.50.65. Open during the week from 10h00-12h30 and 13h30-18h00. Closed on weekends. Entrance fee: 5 FF, under 12 free. A fine collection of Le Corbusier's *Esprit Moderne* paintings and sculpture is housed in Villa La Roche, designed by the great architect in 1923. Research library. Theme exhibitions organized each year.

• *Musée Delacroix:* 6, Place de Furstenburg, 75006 PARIS (Métro: Saint-Germain des-Prés). Tel: 43.54.04.87. Open daily from

9h45-12h30; and 14h00-17h15. Closed on Tuesday. Entrance fee: 11 FF, 6 FF. Delacroix's studio and living quarters can be visited to view a collection of prints, drawings and documents. Theme exhibits are organized at times. Charming garden.

• *Fondation Jean Dubuffet:* 137, rue de Sèvres, 75007 PARIS (Métro: Duroc). Tel: 47.34.12.63. Open weekdays from 14h00-18h00. Free Entrance. Changing exhibitions contrast different periods of this prolific artist's work. The charming house once contained Dubuffet's famous Art Brut collection. Research library.

• *Musée National Hébert:* 85, rue du Cherch-Midi, 75006 PARIS (Métro: Vaneau). 42.22.23.82. Open daily except Tuesday from 12h30-18h00; Weekends from 14h00-18h00. Entrance fee: 12 FF, 7 FF. Drawings, watercolors, and paintings of Hébert (1870-1908). Fine decor and furniture. Special exhibitions feature late 18th century art.

• *Musée National Jean-Jacques Henner:* 43, ave de Villiers, 75017 PARIS (Métro: Malsherbes). Tel: 47.63.42.73. Open daily except Monday from 10h00-12h00; and 14h00-17h00. Entrance fee: 13 FF, 8 FF. A large collection of paintings and drawings by Henner (1829-1920). The exotic decor is a perfect setting for works by this celebrated second empire artist.

• *Musée Gustave Moreau:* 14, rue de la Rochefoucauld, 75009 PARIS (Métro: Trinité). Tel: 48.74.38.50.

Open daily except Tuesday from; 10h00-12h45 and 14h00-17h15; Wednesday 11h00-17h15. Entrance fee: 16 FF, 8 FF. Moreau's house and studio contain an extensive collection of paintings and drawings, including *"Salomè"* and *"Les Licornes"*. During the 1890s it was here that the noted symbolist painter taught future greats like Matisse and Roualt.

• *Musée Rodin:* 77, rue de Varenne, 75007 PARIS (Métro: Varenne).Tel: 47.05.01.34. Open daily from 10h00-17h00. Closed Monday. Entrance fee: 20 FF, 10 FF. An important collection that includes some of Rodin's most famous works like *"The Thinker"* and *"The Kiss"*, with works by Camille Claudel. Housed in the stunning 18th century Hotel Byron, this museum is surrounded by a large formal garden.

• *Musée de la Vie Romantique:* Maison Renan-Scheffer, 16, rue Chaptal, 75009 PARIS (Métro: Saint-Georges).
Tel: 48.75.95.38. Open daily from 10h00-17h45. Closed Monday. Entrance fee: 15 FF. The house of Dutch artist Ary Scheffer (1795-1858) is the setting for temporary exhibitions that feature the 19th century Romantic movement. There is a permanent exhibition on the writer George Sand.

• *Musée Zadkine:* 100 bis, rue d'Assas, 75006 PARIS (Métro: Vavin). 43.26.91.90. Open daily from 10h00-17h40. Closed on Monday. Entrance fee: 12 FF, 6,50 FF. Free on Sunday. Works on paper and sculptures by the Russian artist Ossip Zadkine are on permanent exhibition in the house where he lived untill 1967. A lovely sculpture garden.

Museums With Unusual Themes

• *L'Aracine (Musée de l'Art Brut):* Château Guerin, 39, ave de Gaulle, 93330, NEUILLY SUR MARNE, (RER Neuilly-Plaisance). Tel: 43.09.62.73. Open Thursday-Sunday from 14h00-18h00. Important Art Brut collection founded by three marginal artists. Fine temporary exhibitions and an excellent permanent collection with works by major figures such as Wölfi, Van Genk, Lonné and Rattier.

• *Musée de l'Avocat:* 25, rue du Jour, 75001 PARIS (Métro: Louvre).Tel: 47.83.50.03. Open during the week. An appointment must be made to visit the collection of authentic doccuments and works of art. The correspondance between Zola and Dreyfus' lawyer Labori can be seen, as well as a bust of Gerbier known as "the eagle of the bar."

• *Musée Cernuschi:* 7, ave Velasquez, 75008 PARIS (Métro: Villiers).Tel: 45.63.50.75. Open daily except Monday from 10h00-17h45. Entrance fee: 15 FF, 8 FF. Free admission on Sunday, except for temporary exhibit. Henri Cernuschi's private collection was unique at the end of the 19th century. The treasures include neolithique terracottas, ancient bronzes, funerary pieces and fine examples of calligraphy. An impressive collection on the edge of Parc Monceau.

• *Musée de la Chasse et de la Nature:* 60, rue des Archives, 75003 PARIS (Métro: Rambuteau). Tel: 42.72. 86.43. Open daily from 10h00-12h30; and 13h30-17h30. Closed Tuesday and holidays. Entrance fee: 25 FF, 13 FF. Stuffed trophies from around the world; including big game hunts from Africa. Guns and art celebrate the hunt in a beautiful historic house.

• *Musée de Cinéma Henri-Langlois:* Palais de Chaillot, Place du Trocadero, 75116 PARIS (Métro: Trocadéro).Tel: 45.53.74.39. Visits with a guide every hour from 10h00-17h30. Open daily except Tuesday and holidays. Closed between 13h00-14h00. Entrance fee: 20 FF, 12 FF. The history of the Cinema (1895 to present) is illustrated with documents, stage sets, posters and costumes worn by Greta Garbo, John Wayne and others.

• *Musée de la Contrefaçon:* 16, rue de la Faisanderie, 75016 PARIS (Métro: Port Dauphine).Tel: 45.01. 51.11. Open Monday and Wednesday from 14h30-16h00 and Friday from 9h30-12h00. Free admission. The art of forgery is celebrated in all its forms going back to the Romans. Creators have always worried about imitation of original products; you can smell the difference between perfumes, and compare Chanel in Paris with Sanel in Turkey.

• *Musée Dapper:* 50, ave Victor Hugo, 75016 PARIS (Métro: Etoile).Tel: 45.00.01.50. Open daily from 11h00-19h00. Entrance fee: 15 FF, 7,50 FF; Wednesday free. This private house in a bamboo thicket highlights the traditional precolonial arts of Africa. The changing exhibitions on diverse themes such as Pygmie Tapa cloth or Fang masks and sculpture are always superb. The research library can be used by appointment.

• *Musée d'Ennery:* 59, ave Foch, 75116 PARIS (Métro: Porte Dauphine).Tel: 45.53.57.96. Open Thursday and Sunday from 14h00-17h00; closed in August. A private collection of Asian Art that highlights Netsuke and Kogos fom Japan. Chinese dragons and furniture encrusted with mother of pearl create the perfect atmosphere to enjoy this electric collection.

• *Musée de l'Holographie:* Forum des Halles, level 1, Grand Balcon, 75001 PARIS (Métro: Châtelet-Les Halles).Tel: 40.39.96.83. Open daily from 10h00-19h00; Sunday and holidays from 13h00-19h00. Entrance fee: 29 FF, 24 FF. Changing exhibitions of three dimensional works in this new medium by contemporary artists. Lasers and holograms combine technology and art in exhibits that feature new develpments.

• *Musée Kwok-On:* 41, rue des Francs-Bourgeois, 75004 PARIS (Métro: Saint-Paul).Tel: 42.72.99.42. Open during the week from 10h00-17h30. Closed weekends and holidays. Entrance fee: 10 FF, 5 FF. This collection from Hong Kong focuses on all aspects of the theater in Asia with masks, puppets, instruments and costumes from many different countries. There are changing exhibitions and a fine permanent collection, as well as a documentation center.

• *Musée des Lunettes et Lorgnettes:* Pierre Marly, 2, ave Mozart, 75016 PARIS (Métro: La Muette).Tel: 45.27.21.05. Open daily from 10h00-18h00. Closed Sunday, Monday and holidays. Free entrance. An eccentric private collection (housed in a boutique) of several thousand pairs of reading glasses, monocles and binoculars. An opticians paradise; with rare 13th century examples and new trends.

• *Musée de la Parfumerie Fragonard:* 9, rue Scribe, 75009 PARIS (Métro: Opéra). Tel: 47.42.04.56. Open daily from 9h00-17h30. Closed Sunday. Free entrance. This elegant collection tells the story of perfume through the ages. Beautiful glass flacons, vanity cases and a display that explains the process of extracting oils from plants to create a fragrance.

• *Musée de la Serrure:* 1, rue de la Perle, 75003 PARIS (Métro: Chemin-Vert). Tel: 42.77.79.62. Open daily from 14h00-17h00. Closed Sunday and Monday. Entrance fee: 10 FF, 7 FF. Keys and locks through history are featured in this fine Marais house. Ancient bronze keys, gothic locks, and pieces with Dianne de Poitier's emblem are on view. There is a reconstructed locksmith's workshop in the courtyard.

• *Musée du Vin:* 5, Square Charles Dickens, 75016 PARIS (Métro: Passy).Tel: 45.25.63.26. Open daily from 12h00-18h00 and 20h00-23h00 for dinners. Entrance fee: 26 FF, 20 FF. Entrance free for diners in museum restaurant (meals with wine from 100 FF). This museum evokes the process of wine making with wax figures. Documents and objects illustrate the long history of wine in France. A glass of wine is included with the visit. Oenological courses are conducted there.

Museum Visits For Children

Most major museums have workshops, tours, and special art initiation programs for children. These activities include an introduction to the world of robots at La Villette, calligraphy courses at the Institut du Monde Arabe, painting at the Centre Pompidou and art appreciation tours at the Musée d'Art Moderne de la Ville de Paris.

These programs change each season. For complete information contact the individual museums, or the following offices:

• *Affaires Culturelles de la Ville de Paris:* Hotel d'Abret, 31, rue des Francs-Bourgeois, 75004 PARIS (Métro: Saint-Paul). 42.76.67.00. Open 8h45-18h00. Closed Saturday.

• *La Direction des Musées en France:* 34, Quai du Louvre, 75001 PARIS (Métro: Louvre). Tel: 42.60.39.26. Open daily from 9h45-18h30. Closed Tuesday.

Check through this guide's listings for subjects of special interest to your child. Some of the eccentric collections listed under "Unusual Theme Museums" will certainly appeal...the thousands of pairs of eyeglasses and the bronze dragons that guard the museum Cernuschi are a big hit with young children. Classics like the *Musée de l'Homme* or the Aquarium at the *Musée des Arts Africains et Océaniens* will enthrall toddlers as well as adolescents! There are some wonderful museums in artists homes too; everyone loves the *Musée Rodin!*

The following is a list of major museums conceived for children:

• *Halle-Saint-Pierre (Musée Max Fournay):* 2, rue Ronsard, 75018 PARIS (Métro: Anvers).Tel: 42.58.74.12. Open daily except Monday from 10h00-17h30. Entrance fee: 30 FF, 20 FF. School groups: 12 FF; studio workshop: 22 FF. There are two museums; a large collection of naive paintings and sculptures from around the world, and a second space created to initiate younger children to museum viewing. Changing theme exhibits with games and artistic activities.

• *Musée Grévin:* 10, bd Montmartre, 75009 PARIS (Métro: Rue Montmartre). Tel: 47.70. 85.05. Open daily, including holidays from 13h00-19h00. Open during school vacations 10h00-18h00. Entrance fee: 46 FF, 32 FF. This famous wax museum, similar to Mme. Tussaud's in London, traces French history and highlights 20th century figures. There is also a half-hour magic show (Palais des Mirages or Cabinet Fantastique), that runs each day.

• *Musée en Herbe:* Jardin d'Acclimation, (Métro: Sablons).Tel: 40.67.97.66. Open daily from 10h00-18h00. Entrance fee: 13 FF, 11 FF, plus park entrance: 8 FF, 4 FF. This museum was created as a "hands on" experience to introduce children of all ages to museums. Special theme exhibits are animated by games and diverse activities. Past exhibits have in-cluded: "*Uluri; les Aborigènes d'Australie,*" and "*Sur les Paves de Paris.*"

• *Palais de la Découverte:* ave Franklin-Roosevelt, 75008 PARIS (Métro: Franklin Roosevelt). Tel: 43.59.18.21. Open daily from 10h00-18h00. Entrance fee: 20 FF,10 FF; Planetarium: 13 FF, 9 FF. This fine science museum has been overshadowed by the Cité des Sciences at La Villette, but still has a lot to offer in terms of changing exhibits on everything from solar energy to biology. All children love the planetarium.

Galleries

Paris' gallery scene has truly become a moveable feast. In recent years innovative galleries have established mushrooming art districts in both the Marais and the Bastille areas, bringing new life to an art world formerly restricted to distinct neighborhoods on either bank of the Seine

To have a sense of what is going on in the Paris art world today, one should visit the four main gallery districts…and compare art works, trends and the unique atmosphere associated with each area. In 1977 the area around the newly opened Centre Pompidou quickly became a hot-spot for avant-garde galleries promoting the newest trends in the international art world. More recently, during the 80s, contemporary art stormed the Bastille. The city now counts some 200-300 serious galleries showing early modern and contemporary art!

The following list, though far from complete, will give you a good over-view of the four main gallery districts. You will find the Right Bank galleries to be more traditional. This is an area noted for art dealers specialized in old masters and 19th century paintings. There are several galleries of historic interest, such as *Bernheim-Jeune*, which was founded in 1863.

Major post-war art movements from the 50s and 60s were launched in Left Bank galleries. Several scandalous Dubuffet exhibits and many historic Yves Klein events took place in the rue Visconti during the early 60s. The neighborhood is still talking about how he blocked cars and pedestrian traffic for hours with a wall of stacked oil-drums!

Galleries in the Marais (and Les Halles) often highlight major artists and international movements, while many Bastille galleries have continued to feature Paris based trends.

Paris galleries are open Tuesday through Saturday during the afternoon from 14h00-19h00. All galleries close on Sunday and Monday. Double-check morning hours by phone, as they vary greatly and change often.

Look for the *"Association des Galeries"* listing of exhibitions which is distributed for free in most major galleries. You can also check the *Pariscope* and *Officiel des Spectacles* for information on current exhibitions.

Right Bank
(Métro: Miromesnil)

• *Artcurial:* 9, ave Matignon, 75008 PARIS, Tel: 42.99.16.16. A unique commercial center on several levels with a museum-like gallery that features 20th century masters (Magritte, Picasso, and Saura to name but a few), as well as a fine book store, decorative arts department, and jewelry boutique.

• *Marcel Berheim:* 18, ave Matignon 75008 PARIS, Tel: 42.65.22.23. Specializing in late 19th century painting and early 20th century works (Monet, Renoir, Utrillo, Van Dongen). This gallery opened in 1912 and is still going strong.

• *Bernheim-Jeune:* 83, Faubourg Saint-Honoré, 27, ave Matignon, 75008 PARIS, Tel: 42.66.60.31. Another historic gallery responsible for launching the careers of some impressionists; later showing works by Chagall and Matisse.

• *Louis-Carré:* 10, ave de Messine, 75008 PARIS, Tel: 45.62.57.07. This important gallery shows museum-quality works by 20th century greats like Calder, Chaissac, Léger and Geer Van Velde.

• *Mathias Fels:* 138, bd Haussman, 75008 PARIS, Tel: 45.62.21.34. Fine gallery that features works by New Realists Artists from the 60s like Cesar, Rotella, and Spoerri, as well as Kudo, Louis Cane, and Combas.

• *Fanny Guillon-Laffaille:* 4, ave Messine, 75008 PARIS, Tel: 45.63. 52.00. This art dealer is specialized in works by the Ecole de Paris artists of the 50s like Doucet, Estève and Poliakoff, as well as contemporary works by Chasse-pot, Charpentier and Tal-Coat.

• *Lelong:* 12-13, rue de Téhéran, 75008 PARIS, Tel: 45.63.13.19. This gallery was originally part of an international art net-work founded by Aimé Maeght (of the Maeght Foundation in the South of France). Internationally known contemporary artists like Alechinsky, Bacon, Judd, Penck, Serra, Tapiès and Voss show in this superb space.

• *Michele Sadoun:* 108, rue du Faubourg Saint-Honoré, 75008 PARIS, Tel: 42.66.32.72. A small but dynamic gallery that features expressionist painting and Art Brut. Artists of the gallery include Christoforou, Lindström, Picciotto and Zamora.

Left Bank (Métro: Odeon)

• *Claude Bernard:* 7-9, rue des Beaux Arts, 75006 PARIS, Tel: 43.26.97.07. An important figurative gallery that opened during the 60s. Major international names like Balthus, Botero, Tibor Csernus, David Hockney, Lindner and Andrew Wyeth.

• *Isy Brachot:* 35, rue Guénégaud, 75006 PARIS, Tel: 43.54.22.40. This spacious Belgian Gallery is known for its Surrealistic leaning with works by Magritte and Delvaux. Also represents contemporaries; Roland Cat, Gina Pane, and Broodthaers.

• *Caroline Corre:* 14, rue Guénégaud, 75006 PARIS, Tel: 43.54.

57.67. Once based in Montmartre, this lively gallery boasts a large collection of artist's books. Mainly figurative works by artists like Bettencourt, Gilbert Péyre and Facundo Bo.

• *Down-Town:* 33, rue de Seine, 75006 PARIS, Tel: 46.33.82.41. Decorative arts of the 40s and 50s as well as works by Pincemin, Claude Viallat, BP and Takis in this original gallery.

• *Arlette Gimaray:* 12, rue Mazarine 75006 PARIS, Tel: 46.34.71.80. This gallery shows different tendencies in abstraction with artists such as Debré, Degottex, Hartung, Lanskoy and Zao Wou-Ki.

• *Albert Loeb:* 12, rue des Beaux-Arts, 75006 PARIS, Tel: 46.33.06.87. This respected gallery shows figurative works in all mediums by Caballero, Guinan, Lam, Jeanclos and other established artists of today.

• *Adrien Maeght:* 42-46, rue du Bac, 75007 PARIS, Tel: 45.48.45.15. A gallery that has become an institution; showing 20th century masters like Braque, Giacometti, Kandinsky, and Matisse while launching a new generation of artists. Contemporaries include Delprat, Gasiorowski, Kuroda and Labuauvie.

• *Darthea Speyer:* 6, rue Jacques Callot, 75006 PARIS, Tel: 43.54.78.41. An American gallery with an electric selection of high quality works in all media. Some of the artists associated with the gallery are Sam Gilliam, Roseline Granet, Stanly Viswanadhan and Zuka.

• *Stadler:* 51, rue de Seine, 75006 PARIS, Tel: 43.26.91.10. This well-established gallery opened in 1955, promoting non-figurative works by Tapiès, Bluhm, Domoto and the Gutai group. Today major artists include Saura, Arnulf Rainer, Huftier and Rühle.

• *Galerie 10:* 10, rue des Beaux-Arts, 75006 PARIS, Tel: 43.25. 10.72. A fine exhibition program in limited space. This gallery actively launches their discoveries: artists such as Lavocat, Lepoureau, Teffo and Cehes.

Beaubourg/Le Marais (Métro: Hotel de Ville)

• *Beaubourg:* 23, rue du Renard, 75004 PARIS, Tel: 42.71.20.50. and 3, rue Pierre au Lard, 75004 PARIS, Tel: 48.04.34.40. Important gallery promoting contemporary French art, with strong links to the cultural ministry's programs. Major French artists include Arman, Ben, Buren, Garouste, Hains, Klein, Nikki de Saint-Phalle and Villeglé.

• *Farideh Cadot:* 77, rue des Archives, 75003 PARIS, Tel: 42.78.08.36. Avant-garde gallery with many Americain artists. Among the first to open in the Marais. Artists associated with the gallery include Connie Beckley, Joel Fisher, Rousse, Tremblay and David Hodges.

• *Gilbert Brownstone:* 9 and 17, rue Saint-Gilles, 75003 PARIS, Tel: 42.78.43.21. An Americain gallery, highly active in the field of conceptual work. Promotes the works

of Albers, Fontana, Gottfried Honneger, Jesus-Raphael Soto and Raynaud.

• *Jean Fournier:* 44, rue Quincampoix, 75004 PARIS, Tel: 42.77. 32.31. A well-respected gallery that shows abstract works by an international group of artists. Much support surface work by Hantaï and Viallat as well as works by Bishop, Sam Francis, Shirly Jaffé and Joan Mitchell.

• *Galerie de France:* 52, rue de la Verrerie, 75004 PARIS, Tel: 42.74.38.00. A beautiful space on several levels showing works by well known artists like Domela, Degottex, Matta, Soulages and Keiichi Tahara.

• *Baudoin Lebon:* 38, rue Ste. Croix de la Bretonnerie, 75004 PARIS, Tel: 42.72.09.10. A well-established gallery that seriously promotes a wide range of styles in one of the Marais' finest spaces. Artists include Ben, Clareboudt, Frydman, Mapplethorpe, Dubbufet and Bettencourt.

• *Alain Oudin:* 47, rue Quincampoix, 75004 PARIS, Tel: 42.71. 83.65. Lively, active program with installations and performance work as well as painting and sculpture. International artists include Marie Chamant, Thierry Cauwet, Matsutani and Turin.

• *Christian Mollet-Viéville:* 26, rue Beaubourg, 75003 PARIS, Tel: 42.78.72.31. Call or write for an appointment. This well known dealer promotes minimal and conceptual works by artists such as Carl André, Buren and Sol LeWitt.

• *Daniel Templon:* 1, impasse Beaubourg, 75003 PARIS, Tel: 42.72.14.10. Well known gallery specialized in minimal and conceptual art, (Judd, Flavin and Morris), as well as more exuberant works by Alberola, Chia, Fetting, Rauchenberg and Salle.

• *Pierre-Marie Vitoux:* 3, rue d'Ormesson, 75004 PARIS, Tel: 48.04.81.00. A small space with big talents. The gallery represents Hadad, Ben-Ami Koller, Linström, Mazliah and Maurice Rocher.

• *Zabriskie:* 37, rue Quincampoix, 75004 PARIS, Tel: 42.72.35.47. This branch of the famous New York gallery opened in 1977 to feature photography. Photos by Klein, Friedlander and Stieglitz can be seen as well as works in other mediums by Tony Long, Poivret and Shirly Farb.

Bastille
(Métro: Bastille)

• *A.B. Galleries (Formerly Galerie du Génie):* 24, rue Keller 75011 PARIS, Tel: 48.06.90.90. This gallery showcases video work, computer paintings and electronic installations. An international group of artists including major names associated with the fluxus movement as well as Catherine Ikam and Bernard Roig.

• *Gutharc Ballin:* 47, rue de Lappe, 75011 PARIS, Tel: 47.00.32.10. Dynamic gallery. One of the pioneers in this neighborhood. Exhibits range from installations to photography used as documentation. Artists include Pfeiffer, Endo,

Texier and Klemensiewicz.

• *Antoine Candau:* 3, passage Saint-Sébastien, 75011 PARIS, Tel: 43.38.75.51. Formerly in the rue Keller, this gallery has been an active part of the Bastille scene since it opened in 1985. Diverse media with an emphasis on conceptual work and installations. Artists include Golub, Friot, Pelletier and David Brenkus.

• *Durand-Desert:* 28, rue de Lappe, 75011 PARIS, Tel: 48.06.92.23. Recently inaugurated, this fine gallery boasts five levels to showcase monumental sculpture as well as works on paper. Artists include: Beuys, Boltanski, Haacke, Flanagan and Tosani.

• *J.J. Donguy:* 57, rue de la Roquette (in courtyard), 75011 PARIS, Tel: 47.00.10.94. One of the first galleries to open in the Bastille during the early 80s. An active gallery that highlights conceptual work and installations. Artists shown include: Frederic Lormeau, Dupuy and Henry Flynt.

• *Jacqueline Felman:* 8, rue Popincourt, 75011 PARIS, Tel: 47.00. 87.71. This renovated factory space opened in 1985 to promote contemporary figurative work by younger artists. Artists include: Michel Coquery, Buffoli, Hours and Riccardo Licata.

• *Keller:* 15, rue Keller, 75011 PARIS, Tel: 47.00.41.47. A respected gallery specializing in abstract work with an impressive range of international talents. Artists associated with this space include: Delrieu, Jorgensen,

Matsutani, Tsuchiya and Francis Wilson.

• *Lavignes-Bastille:* 27, rue de Charonne, 75011 PARIS, Tel: 47.00.88.18. Spacious, well established gallery that often has simultaneous exhibits that contrast a wide range of styles from neo-expressionism to abstraction. Artists include: Fraser, Grataloup, Rauchbach, Sandorfi and Vostell.

• *Clara Scremini:* 39, rue de Charonne: 75011 PARIS, Tel: 43.55. 65.56. Unique Paris gallery specialized in contemporary glass work. Superb exhibits of international artists such as Sabtarossa, Toots Zynsky, Cummings and Myers.

• *Leif Stähle:* Cour Delpine, 37, rue de Charonne, 75011 PARIS, Tel: 48.07.24.78. Fine gallery opened by important Stockholm art dealer when the Bastille first became an art district. Abstract works by international artists, including Debré, Kallos, Lars Engglunds, Kuhara, Limerat and Susan Weil.

Salons

Modern art history begins with the rejection of the impressionists by the official French academic *salon.* Significant *salon* events are many during the late 19th century. The *Salon des Refusés* rocked the Paris art world, and some years later the famous Fauve scandal heralded a new era of modern painting at the *Salon d'Automne* in 1905.

It is curious to remember that the *Salon d'Automne,* (considered the most traditional *salon* today), was originally created as a rather violent reaction against the prevailing academic criteria of the time. In 1903, artists Rodin, Jourdain, Renoir and Cézanne founded a new *salon* that was to serve as an alternative exhibition space for a new generation of artists whose experimental work was not deemed acceptable by the official *salons.*

At the end of the 20th century, art history repeats itself with the emergence of off-shoots from established *salons.* Artistic quarrels seem to be a lively part of the *salon* tradition, and today there are at least 35 *salons* in and around Paris. A current example of this principle is the highly successful *salon* MAC 2000, which began as a splinter group from the *Salon de la Jeune Peinture.*

The launching of young artists is an important part of of the *salon* tradition. Painters and sculptors from other countries envy the opportunities French *salons* offer to Paris-based artists. Today the *salon* tradition continues to interest a large audience of art lovers. Each *salon* is highly publicized by posters about town and on a giant billboard in front of the Grand Palais. The following list includes the most important of the French *salons* held in the Grand Palais. Application requirements and fees vary. Individual *salons* should be contacted for further information.

• *Grand Palais:* 2, ave Winston Churchill, 75008 PARIS (Métro: Champs Elysées-Clémenceau). Tel: 42.89.23.13. This immense, domed exhibition hall was built at the same time as the Petit Palais for the Universal exhibition of 1900. There are several large exhibition spaces to receive major retrospectives and temporary theme exhibits. The Grand Palais is also "home" for most Paris *salons*. Exhibitions are open daily excepting Tuesday, from 10h00-20h00; Wednesday until 22h00. Entrance fees vary.

• *Salon d'Automne:* Porte H, Grand Palais, 2, ave Winston Churchill, 75008 PARIS, 43.59.46.07. (15h00 -18h00). A historic *salon* which maintains the great *salon* tradition. Annually, each November.

• *Salon des Artistes Décorateurs:* Porte H, Grand Palais, 2, ave Winston Churchill, 75008 PARIS, Tel: 49.59.11.10. Every aspect of interieur design. A professional *salon* that involves manufacturers/ artists/designers and decorators. Once every two years during autumn.

• *Salon Comparaisons:* Grand Palais. President: Bernard Mougins, 5, rue du Général de Maud'huy, 75014, PARIS, Tel: 43.39.45.06. International *salon* featuring diverse trends. Once every two years in June.

• *Salon Figurations Critiques:* Grand Palais. President: Mme Dors-Rapin, 1, rue Louis-Gaubert, 78140 VELIZY-BAS. A *salon* that promotes figurative work. Held during September.

• *Salon de la Jeune Peinture:* Grand Palais. President: Katerine Louineau, 143, bd Jean-Jaurès, 92110 CLICHY, Tel: 47.31.66.37. A post-war *salon* founded in 1949 that supports painted works by emerging talents. Annual. February.

• *Salon des Independants:* Porte H, Grand Palais. Tel: 42.25.86.39. Historic *salon* founded in 1884. Exhuberant but often very crowded. Highly ecclectic selection. Annual. Held during winter (February or March).

• *Salon de la Jeune Sculpture:* Porte d'Austerlitz, 75013 PARIS, Tel: 43.04.68.86. Association de la Jeune Sculpture, 10, Square de Port-Royale. 75013 PARIS. A bi-annual *salon* that takes place during the spring and fall to promote contemporary sculpture of all *tendances.*

• *Salon de Mai:* Grand Palais. Secretary: Jacqueline Selz, 8, ave Victorien Sardou, 75016 PARIS, Tel: 42.88.44.01. A *salon* that highlights artists of repute as well as emerging talents. Annual. Held in May.

• *Salon Grands et Jeunes d'Aujourd'hui:* Grand Palais. President: Marylène Dénoval, 12 bis, rue de l'Etoile, 75017 PARIS, Tel: 43.80. 38.75. A well-respected *salon* with a

rigorous selection policy that provides a fine overview of contemporary trends. Annual. October.
• *Salon MAC 2000:* Grand Palais. President: Concha Benedito, 28, rue du Sergent Godefroy, 93100 MONTREUIL, Tel: 48.59.19.30. A unique *salon* that features a series of one person shows for confirmed artists. Careful selection and high quality work. Annual. Held in November/December.
• *Salon de Montrouge:* Centre Culturel et Artistique de Montrouge. Tel: 46.56.52.52. President: Nicole Ginoux-Bessec, 32, rue Gabriel Péri, 92120 MONTROUGE. The most important of the *salons* outside of Paris; well known for launching artists. Fine quality of work. Annual. During Autumn.

Off the Beaten Track: Art Factories

The *Bateau Lavoir* in Montmartre and *La Ruche* on the edge of the 15th *arrondissement,* in which the Cuban painter Alvarez-Rios currently resides, are two classic artist studio complexes that housed a number of modern masters early in the century. Since that nostalgic period, Paris' real estate has soared and an artists studio in Paris has gone from being a high-priced commodity to a nearly extinct species. Increasingly, contemporary artists of the 90s are gathering in reconverted factories and warehouses to produce their art.

Most of these large abandoned spaces are to be found in the grimmer parts of the city, or the nearby suburbs. Social security sources suggest there may be more than 40,000 (declared) professional artists living in the Paris region. This staggering figure would account for the growing edge to an already competitive art scene, and the increasing sense of alarm over the scarcity of studio space. In recent years, artists' squats have called media attention to these pressing problems of space.

The following is a list of art factories that may be visited by the general public. There are exhibition programs and open studio visits. It is best to call for an appointment.

• *Quai de la Gare:* 91, Quai de la Gare, 75013 PARIS, Tel: 45.85. 91.91. A former refrigerator warehouse situated between the train tracks and the Seine. Over 250 artists work in diverse mediums in private studios. Lively open studio events several times a year.
• *La Base:* 6 bis, rue Vergiaud, LEVALLOIS, (Métro: Louise-Michel), Tel: 47.58.48.58. A reconverted factory with a fine exhibition space and an artists-in-residence program. An art center with an international scope, showcasing works produced on the spot by major talents.

• *Hôpital Ephémère:* 2, rue Carpeaux, 75018 PARIS (Métro: Lamarck-Caulaincourt), Tel: 46.27.82.82. The former Bretonneau Children's Hospital in Montmartre has been transformed into studios, exhibition halls, photo labs and theaters. Space for 40 artists. Ongoing exhibition program.

• *Art Factory at Asnières:* 93, bd Voltaire, ASNIERES, (Métro: Asnières), Tel: 46.27.82.82. Newest space funded (in part) by the Ministry of Culture. Studios and exhibition space.

Bookstores

Paris is a sheer delight in its proliferation of small bookshops. Additionally, Paris wouldn't be Paris without its rows of *bouquinistes* (book stalls) most of which line the Left Bank *(rive* or *quai)* of the Seine. These are independently-owned, mainly by individuals who have a passion for used or rare books. In recent years the quality of the offering has dwindled to include tacky postcards and cheap prints, but fortunately the integrity of the traditional buying, selling and browsing on nice days along the Seine has remained in tact.

The book as object plays a sacred role in Parisian life. In general, the quality of book production is higher in France than in North America, with serious covers reserved for quality literature. The most prestigious literary publishing houses in France include the classic Gallimard, le Seuil, Grasset, Calmann-Levy, etc. but there are scores of excellent publishers of literary, political, social and pure science books. Despite contemporary economic pressures, much effort is made in France to protect the life of the small bookshop and the small publisher. The retail prices of books are regulated so that large outlets, department stores and supermarket chains cannot simply slash prices. The most you'll ever find a new book marked down is 5%. The FNAC (see department stores) has one of the most exhaustive collections of French and foreign language books in Paris, and is particularly well-stocked with travel books.

As English-speakers and readers you'll probably be more directly interested in sources of English books in Paris. Fortunately, there are a lot of resources at hand. If you're not already aware you should be—Paris has an illustrious and important tradition of English and American expatriate writers, poets and artists, as well as editors and publishers who have made fabulous contributions in Paris with their work. Although this tradition may not be the source of your inspiration for coming to live and/or study in Paris, it certainly does generate much of the aura and myth about Paris that attracts tourists and long term visitors each year. And if this glorious past is what drew you to Paris, you might be disappointed to find a changed Paris. For in-depth discussion of Paris' expatriate literary and artistic history see: Ernest Hemingway's *A Moveable Feast*, Noel Fitch Riley's *Sylvia Beach and the Lost Generation*, and *Literary Cafés*, Brian Morton's *Americans in Paris*, Maurice Girodias' *The Frog Prince*, Hugh Ford's *Published in Paris*, and Dougald McMillan's *transition*, among others. Christopher Sawyer-Lauçànno's study and John Calder's intimate history of postwar expatriate literary Paris are forthcoming.from Grove Press and Simon & Schuster, respectively.

There are a few things to remember regarding books. First, in most cases, new ones are a lot more expensive than what you are probably used to. The price in francs is not a simple conversion from dollars or pounds; each bookstore has its own conversion mark-up rate to compensate for shipping and customs charges. So, for those special copies of books dear to your heart you might want to carry or have them shipped to you from home. There are, of course, libraries (see Libraries).

Professors, students, writers or researchers will not be able to anticipate in advance all of their reading needs. Additionally, the English language bookshops in Paris contribute to the vitality of the literary scene. There are several excellent bookshops in the suburbs as well that you might want to check out, such as Footnote in Fontainebleue and *Folie d'encre* in Montreuil. You'll probably want to renew your contact with your language and culture by frequenting some of the following shops on a regular basis:

Abbey Bookshop: 29, rue Parcheminerie 75005 PARIS, Tel: 46.33.16.24. Fax: 46.33.03.33.
This Canadian-owned, small but well-organized and pleasant shop in the Latin Quarter has carved an important place for itself in the English-language literary scene in Paris in the last few years. One of its real advantages is the shop's ability to

procure titles from North America in record time. Owner Brian Spence offers his clients plenty of service, including an up-to-date ROM bibliographic search and efficient mail order capacity. Strong in fiction, poetry, and the humanities. On occasion the Abbey also has readings, usually concentrating on Canadian writers.

Albion: 13, rue Charles V, 75004 PARIS. Métro: St. Paul. Tel: 42.72.50.71. Closed Sunday and Monday morning. Classical and contemporary Anglo-American literature, some history and science.

American University of Paris Bookstore: located in the basement of the American Church, 65, Quai d'Orsay, 75007 PARIS, Tel: 45.55.91.73. (Ask for bookstore) principally serves the university community. Under the management of Bill Gadsby, the bookstore has expanded its operations to function as a vital and effective source of academic and trade titles. New titles from the U.S. or U.K. can be ordered at competitive prices and with efficiency. Although a university bookshop, it's open to walk-ins.

Attica: 23, rue Jean de Beavais, 75005 PARIS, Tel: 43.34.62.03 and 64, rue de la Folie Méri-court, 75011. Métro: Ober-kampf. Tel: 48.06.17.00. Closed Sunday and Monday morning. Attica is an old stand by for English books in Paris. More British-oriented than American, Attica in its new location is a densely packed space for new fiction, poetry, journals and guides. The store also caters to French students looking for English titles for their university English courses, thus a lot of classics and 19th century fiction. Students get a small discount upon request. The second location specializes in practical books and language methods.

Brentano's: 37, ave de l'Opéra, 75002 PARIS. Métro: Pyramides. Tel: 42.61.52.50. Fax: 42.61.07.61. Open daily 10-19h. Closed Sunday. Anglo-American literature, art books, magazines and newspapers. Brentano's rides on a long and illustrious reputation. Today it greatly serves the French anglophile market and business and tourist crowds interested in English paperbacks and best-sellers. Although less connected to the indigenous anglophone population than some of the other literary bookshops, Brentano's is the only English bookshop in the neighborhood of the Opéra. The back entrance area hosts a large selection of

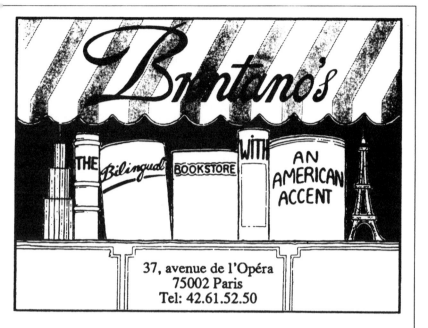

Brentano's

THE Bilingual BOOKSTORE WITH AN AMERICAN ACCENT

37, avenue de l'Opéra
75002 Paris
Tel: 42.61.52.50

We are a large (but not too !) English - language bookstore, joined by a long corridor filled with art books, travel books, and gift items to a "traditional" French bookstore and international press department.

Intercultural Issues
Bilingualism
Law and Management
Children's Books and Videos
Art and Photography

"L'Art de vivre" in France
(cooking, history, wine, literature, ...)

CUSTOMER SERVICE • MAKING YOU FEEL WELCOME
IS OUR SPECIALITY !

English-language periodicals. Other areas of speciality include American hobbies, arts and crafts, sports, and an impressively complete selection of children's books. Brentano's also hosts signatures for prominent authors in Paris and services important events including Bloom, Expolangues, and diverse charities fairs. Brentano's offers an efficient international magazine subscription and mail order book service.

Cannibal Pierce Australian Bookshop: 7, rue Samson 93200 SAINT DENIS, Tel: 48.09.94.59. Irregular hours and by appointment. This is Paris's only Australian bookshop and gallery. Although it's a bit out of the way, it's worth the trip. The collection is eclectic and stimu-lating. There are regularly sched-uled readings, openings, and performances in the store led by resident Australian poets June and Ken.

Galignani: 224, rue de Rivoli, 75001 PARIS, Métro: Tuileries. Tel: 42.60.76.07 Call for hours. Closed Sunday. Books, guide-books, maps, newspapers, and magazines. This bookshop is actually the oldest English book-store on the continent. It had for many years enjoyed a fine reputation as a supporter of the anglophone literati. Its selection of fiction, travel and art books is extensive.

Nouveau Quartier Latin (NQL): 78, bd St. Michel, 75005 PARIS, Métro: Luxem-bourg. Tel: 43.26.42.70. Closed Sunday. Only new titles. Here's a store that you can call to find out if they have what you need. Well-organized and highly modern, NQL specializes in Anglo-American literature and guide books and also distributes to its network of bookshops through France.

Shakespeare & Company: 37, rue de la Bûcherie, 75005 PARIS, Métro: St. Michel. No telephone. Open daily from noon until midnight. George Whitman's Shakespeare & Company is by far the single most celebrated bookshop on the continent. Much of this reputation comes from Sylvia Beach's original Shakespeare & Company which was located nearby on the rue de l'Odéon in the Twenties and Thirties. It was there that James Joyce's *Ulysses*, published by Beach in 1922, first saw the light of day. Ernest Hemingway, Gertrude Stein and a whole stable of luminous literati congregated there. Beach's store was shut by the Germans at the beginning of the

Occupation. George Whitman, the self-acclaimed illegitimate grandson of Walt Whitman (his father was also Walt, but a writer of science books in Salem, Massachusetts) resurrected the name in the spirit of the original enterprise, tagging on "the Rag and Bone Shop of the Heart." Everything you hear about Shakespeare & Co. is true. It's unruly, chaotically organized, overrun at times by weirdos and dubious writers, but the bookshop is a living legend and a wealthy storehouse of fabulous first editions and signed copies of novels and volumes of poetry whose authors came through Paris and gave a reading or book party under the supervision of poetic and iconoclastic George. He is often offering tumblers of iced tea on chipped plates of Irish stew to visiting writers, wanderers and the mildly down and out. The store has thousands of used books and a spotty selection of new titles. It's impossible to predict what you'll find. The prices are high for the new stuff, but can be excellent for used and obscure hardcovers. George will buy your used books and pay you cash if you bring identification. In the warm months, the sidewalk in front of the store—exquisitely set in the Latin Quarter oppo-site Notre Dame—becomes a favorite hang-out for visitors, backpackers and local riffraff, a scene which will give you a good whiff of the state of contemporary Bohemia. And if you are writing poetry or fiction ask George to be slotted into the Monday night reading series—a good way to test your voice. The shop sells its own mag called *Paris Magazine*, which is now preparing its fourth issue in twenty two years as well as *Fire Readings,* an anthology of new writing from benefit readings in Paris, London, Boston, and New York following the 1990 fire that destroyed much of the shop and nearly 5000 rare books. The bookstore is fully operational as the first floor library was rebuilt.

Tea and Tattered Pages: 24, rue Mayet, 75006 PARIS Tel: 40.65.94.35. Fax: 39.50.33.76. This cozy and friendly spot owned and run by former Californian beachcomber Christy Chavane de Dalmassy, near Métro Duroc specializes in used and inexpensive paperbacks. The selection has grown rapidly over the last two years—over 10000 books. The prices warrant a visit—so do the brownies.

Village Voice: 6, rue Princesse, 75006 PARIS, Métro: Mabillon. Tel: 46.33.36.47. Fax: 46.33. 27.48. Closed Sunday. Monday open from 2-8, Tuesday-Saturday 11-8. Founded in 1983 by French owner Odile Hellier, the Village Voice (no connection to the newspaper) has evolved into one of the most significant literary English bookshops in Europe. Tucked into a small street just off the Boulevard Saint Germain, the store hosts a lively reading series that has included some of the most important American, Canadian, British and French authors writing today, including Don Delillo, William Kennedy, Raymond Carver, Alison Lurie, Mavis Gallant, and Louise Erdrich. These readings are free and often conclude with wine and discussion. Odile, assisted by her nephew Jan, diligently attempts to stock a rich collection of the newest literary titles from both the U.S.and the U.K. in her bright and pleasant store. Additionally, the collection is vast in modern and contemporary fiction, poetry and translations as well as works in the social and political sciences, philosophy, the environment and women's studies. The store also has a wide variety of literary journals and intelligent magazines—*The Village Voice, Times Literary Supplement, New Yorker, Harper's, Paris Review, Frank, Granta*, etc. Ask to get on the mailing list. Offers 5% discount to students.

W.H. Smith: 248, rue de Rivoli, 75001 PARIS. Métro: Concorde. Tel: 42.60.37.97. Closed Sunday. Part of the major British bookstore chain. Anglo-American literature, cookbooks, guidebooks, maps, magazines and newspapers. This large, well-stocked and busy store offers a broad selection of contemporary titles and gift books as well as a vast display of English-language publications. Well situated at the Pl. de la Concorde. The upstairs tearoom no longer exists. The staff is very helpful and highly know-ledgeable about the selection of books available. Hosts books signings and special events.

Unesco (Librarie de l'): 9, place de Fontenoy, 75007 PARIS. Métro: Ségur. Tel: 45.68.10.00. Closed Saturday and Sunday. Newspapers and UNESCO publications (Education and Science).

Virgin Megastore
52, ave des Champs-Elysées
75008 PARIS
Tel: 40.74.06.48
Large, but not very litterary.

French Bookstores

As for French literary bookshops, there are scores of excellent ones, with a high concentration in the fifth and sixth *arrondissements*. A few well-known ones include *La Hune*, 170, bd St. Michel, and *Le Divan* at 37, rue Bonaparte, near the Place St. Germain-des-Prés in the 6th *arrondissement*, and Flammarion at the Pompidou Center. The *l'Oeil de la Lettre* group of literary bookstores are first class, one of which is Librarie Compagnie on the rue des Ecoles next to the Sorbonne.

The FNAC, the largest retail cooperative of electronic, stereo and photographic equipment with plans for European expansion to Berlin and Madrid, also has the most extensive collection of books and records in France. Its three-story international bookstore in the Latin Quarter opened its doors in late 1991 under the direction and vision of manager Mme Isabelle Surin. The store is well-stocked in its offerings of international publications on the first floor and foreign language trade editions upstairs. Its literary collections are less complete but growing as its series of literary readings and cultural *rencontres* also takes form. Looking for something special in the English section, ask for Mme Pons.

FNAC Internationale
71, bd St. Germain
75005 PARIS
Tel. 44.41.31.50

FNAC Forum Halles
1, rue Pierre Lescot
75001 PARIS
Tel: 40.41.40.00

FNAC Montparnasse
136, rue de Rennes
75006 PARIS
Tel: 49.54.30.00

FNAC Etoile
26, ave des Ternes
75017 PARIS
Tel: 44.09.18.00

For guides, maps, and travel titles, Espace Hachette Evasion is particularly well-equipped.

Espace Hachette Evasion
77, Bd St. Germain
75006 PARIS
Tel: 46.34.89.51

An especially useful address for students is the Parisian institution, Gibert Jeune and Gibert Joseph, a three-store operation that specializes in academic and university texts and school supplies, and buys back used books on the fourth floor. Bring your student I.D.

Gilbert Jeune
26 bd St. Michel
75006 PARIS
Tel: 46.34.21.41

As for specialized bookshops these may come in handy:

Cinema
Librarie de la Fontaine
13, rue Médicis
75016 PARIS
Tel: 46.33.35.41

La Chambre Claire
14, rue St. Sulpice
75006 PARIS
Tel: 46.34.04.31

Photography/Theater
Association Liko
161, rue Rennes
75006 PARIS
Tel: 45.48.69.49

Women
Femmes Savantes
73bis, ave Niel
75017 PARIS
Tel: 47.63.05.82

Librairie des Femmes
74, rue Seine
75006 PARIS
Tel: 43.29.50.75

Science Fiction/Bande Dessinée (Comic Books)
Cosmos 2000
17, rue Arc de Triomphe
75017 PARIS
Tel: 43.80.30.74

Music
La Librairie Musical de Paris
68bis, rue Réaumur
75003 PARIS
Tel: 42.72.30.72

Politics
Librairie des Sciences Politiques
30, rue St. Guillaume
75007 PARIS
Tel: 45.48.36.02

Third World
Librairie Harmattan
16, rue des Ecoles
75005 PARIS
Tel: 43.26.04.52

Cuisine
Librairie Gourmande
4, rue Dante
75005 PARIS
Tel: 43.54.37.27

Government Publications
La Librairie de la Documentation Française
29/31, Quai Voltaire
75007 PARIS
Tel: 40.15.70.00

Spanish/Latin American
Ediciones Hispano-Americanas
26, rue Monsieur Le Prince
75006 PARIS
Tel: 43.26.03.79

Librairie Espagnole
72, rue de Seine
75006 PARIS
Tel: 43.54.56.26

Russian
Librairie du Globe
2, rue de Buci
75006 PARIS
Tel: 43.26.54.99

Les Editeurs Réunis
11, rue Montagne Ste Geneviève
75005 PARIS
Tel: 43.54.74.46

Librarie Russe
9, rue Eperon
75006 PARIS
Tel: 43.26.10.60

Arabic
Al Manar Librairie
220, rue St. Jacques
75005 PARIS
Tel: 43.29.40.22

German
Calligrammes Librairie
8, rue Collégiale
75005 PARIS
Tel: 43.36.85.07

Marissal Bucher
42, rue Rambuteau
75003 PARIS
Tel: 42.74.37.47

Indian
Adi Shakti Tapovan
9, rue Gutenberg
75015 PARIS
Tel: 45.77.90.59

Italian
Librairie Italiennes
Tour de Babel
10, rue du Roi de Sicile
75004 PARIS
Tel: 42.77.32.40

Librairie Italienne
54, rue de Bourgogne
75007 PARIS
Tel: 47.05.03.99

African
Présence Africaine
25bis, rue des Ecoles
75005 PARIS
Tel: 43.54.15.88

Japanese
Tokyo Do
8, rue Ste. Anne
75001 PARIS
Tel: 42.61.08.71

Espace Japon
9, rue de la Fontaine au Roi
75011 PARIS
Tel: 47.00.77.47

Polish
Librairie Polonaise
123, bd St. Germain
75006 PARIS
Tel: 40.51.08.82

Portuguese
Librairie Portugaise
Michel Chandeigne
10, rue Tournefort
75005 PARIS
Tel: 43.36.34.37

You may find, in dealing with the libraries in Paris, the same sort of inconvenience as you did in other areas of daily life, such as shopping. The inconvenience in this case stems from a certain degree of inaccessibility and inherent lethargy which takes a little time to adjust to. If you are coming from a small university where you had your own desk at which you could camp out until early morning hours, you may find the adjustment difficult. You may have to keep a more civilized schedule when it comes to your treks to the library. The libraries frequently have quite limited hours. One exception is the *Bibliothèque Publique d'Information* at the Pompidou Center which is open until 22h.

Limited hours are not the only handicap in getting research done or a term paper finished, for most libraries do not allow you to borrow books. So be prepared to take good notes. Laptop computers can be helpful here. These libraries only offer *consultation sur place* (books don't leave the library). You may or may not find working photocopy machines. The one machine in the Sorbonne library requires one franc per copy!

Some libraries require that you register and obtain a card to enter and consult books. Be prepared to have to wait in a line when you go. You'll need some identification, such as your passport and proof of address and a couple of photographs. Another thing to be aware of is that in many libraries you are not free to browse through the stacks. Instead, you must go to the *salle de catalogues* and fill out a description of what you are looking for *(fichier)*. An employee, in one of those omnipresent blue smocks that sets workers apart from white collar employees, will look for the book and send it to the *centre de distribution*, where you collect it.

The library at the Sorbonne is a fascinating place to visit but a frustrating place to use. It can take up to twenty minutes to obtain each book, depending on which *guichet* your book is filed under. Of course, don't expect to do much research around lunchtime. In addition, special permission must be obtained from the "president" of the *salle* for access to the reference section. There are a number of excellent libraries though in Paris with extensive collections and priceless resources and archives.

Here's are the major libraries:

• **American Library in Paris:** 10, rue du Général-Camou, 75007 PARIS, Tel: 45.51.46.82. The largest collection of English language books in Paris. Open Tuesday-Saturday from 10h-19h. Membership allows you to check out books, but is required for admittance. Annual membership fees are as follows: 500 FF for the individual rate, 400 FF for students, and 700 FF for a family card. You need to bring a recent photo, student identification, proof of residency in Paris (such as telephone bill) and another piece of identification. If you do not want to be a member, you may spend the day in the library for 30 FF but you cannot check out books. AUP students are automatically members. This library owns over 80,000 volumes and over 700 periodicals and journals.

• **American University of Paris Library:** 9, rue de Monttessuy, 75007 PARIS, tel. 45.51.44.31. This library is physically connected to the American Library in Paris. It is open more hours than any other library in France—seven days a week for a total of eighty hours per week. It has over 50,000 titles and adds close to 3000 titles every year. Reserved for members of The American Library and AUP students (but they cannot check things out).

• **Benjamin Franklin Documentation Center:** 2, rue St.-Florentin, 75001 PARIS, Tel: 42.96.33.10. 9,000 volumes in English. Housed in the U.S.Consulate building, Tallyrand, at place de la Concorde.

Open 13h-18h Monday-Friday. Extensive documentation on the USA. Open to university students. Bring your passport.

• **Bibliothèques et Discothèques de la Ville de Paris:** 31, rue des Francs Bourgeois, 75004 PARIS, Tel: 42.76.66.25. This is the main branch of the City of Paris' 55 municipal public libraries.

• **Bibliothèque de France:** Place de Valhubert, 75013 PARIS, Tel: 44.06.01.00 (information). One of the great building projects of the decade, this is to be the largest library in France. Currently under construction with projected opening in 1995. Will be open to both researchers and the public.

• **Bibliothèque Nationale:** 58, rue de Richelieu, 75002 PARIS, Tel: 47.03.81.26. Known as the BN, this library houses one of the world's most important and complete collections of books, periodicals, manuscripts and archives. Dark, dense and serious, the BN is accessible to graduate students and researchers with letters of accreditation.

• **Bibliothèque Publique d'Information:** Centre Georges Pompidou, 19, rue Beaubourg, 75004 PARIS, Tel: 42.77.12.33. Minitel: 3615 BPI. Open Monday, Wednesday, Thursday and Friday from noon to 10h. Saturday, Sunday, and public holidays from 10h to 22h. Closed Tuesday. *Consultation sur place.* Free access to books. No inscription required.

• **Bibliothèque Sainte Geneviève:** 10, place du Panthéon, 75005

PARIS, Tel: 43.29.61.00. Open Monday-Saturday from 10h-13h. Personal library card is required, which you can obtain Monday-Friday before 17h30 and on Saturday between 14h-17h30. Bring a photo and identification, no charge. *Consultation sur place.* Distribution center.

• **British Council Library**: 9-11, rue de Constantine, 75007 PARIS, Tel: 49.55.73.00. Open daily 11h-6h. Saturday from 10h30-16h. Membership costs 230 FF a year (with passport and photo) and allows you to check out books. Otherwise you may use the library at 25 FF a day. Mainly books from or about Britain.

• **English Language Library for the Blind**: 35, rue Lemercier, 75017 PARIS, Tel: 42.93.47.57.

• **Mairie du 5eme**: 21, place du Panthéon, 75005 PARIS, Tel: 43.26.85.05. Feminist library.

• **Université de la Sorbonne**: 13, rue Santeuil, 75005 PARIS, Tel: 43.31.53.94. Open Monday from 13h-19h; Tuesday-Friday from 9h30-19h; Saturday from 10h-17h30. Membership is required unless you are enrolled at Paris III. Cost is 75 FF. Distribution service, which always closes one hour before the library does. You are allowed to borrow two books for 15 days.

Other Libraries

• **Agence Culturelle de Paris**: 12, rue François Miron, 75004 PARIS, Tel: 42.71.84.93.

• **Bibliothèque Internationale de Musique Contemporaine**: 52, rue Hôtel de Ville, 75004 PARIS, Tel: 42.78.67.08.

• **Bibliothèque Service Métier d'Art**: 107, rue de Rivoli, 75001 PARIS, Tel: 42.61.46.36.

• **Bibliothèque de Géographie**: 191, rue St. Jacques, 75005 PARIS, Tel: 43.29.42.04.

• **Bibliothèque de l'Opéra**: place Charles Garnier, 75009 PARIS, Tel: 47.42.07.02.

• **Bibliothèque de l'Union des Arts Décoratifs**: 109, rue de Rivoli, 75001 PARIS, Tel: 42.60.32.14. Open Tuesday-Saturday, 10h-17h30; Monday 13h45-17h30. Closed Sunday. No registration is needed. More than 100,000 works, from the origins to contemporary art.

• **Bibliothèque des Arts**: 3, place de l'Odéon, 75006 PARIS, Tel: 46.33.18.18.

• **Bibliothèque Musicale Gustave Mahler**: 11bis, rue Vézelay, 75008 PARIS, Tel: 42.56.20.17.

• **Bibliothèque Polonaise**: 6, Quai Orléans, 75004 PARIS, Tel: 43.54.35.61.

• **Bibliothèque Roumaine Pierre Sergesco Marya Kasterska**: 39, rue Lhommond, 75005 PARIS, Tel: 43.37.82.74.

• **Bibliothèque Russe Tourgenev**: 11, rue Valence, 75005 PARIS, Tel: 45.35.58.51.

• **Bibliothèque Ukrainienne Simon Petlura**: 6, rue Palestine, 75019 PARIS, Tel: 42.02.29.56.

• **Centre Information Documentation Israël Proche Orient**: 134, rue Fbg. St. Honoré, 75008 PARIS, Tel: 43.59.75.40.

- **Centre Protestant d'Etudes et de Documentation**: 46, rue de Vaugirard, 75006 PARIS, Tel: 46.33.77.24.
- **Institut de France, Bibliothèque Thiers:** 27, place St. Georges, 75009 PARIS, Tel: 48.78.14.33.
- **Institut des Hautes Etudes Cinématographiques**: 9, ave Albert de Mun, 75016 PARIS, Tel: 47.27.06.32.
- **Institut des Hautes Etudes de l'Amérique Latine**: 28, rue St. Guillaume, 75007 PARIS, Tel: 45.48.00.98.
- **La Joie Par Les Livres**: 8, rue St. Bon, 75004 PARIS, Tel: 48.87.61.95.
- **Métrolire**: 6, place Nation, 75012 PARIS, Tel: 43.43.32.17.
- **Service Information Documentation Juifs-Chrétiens**: 73, rue Notre Dame des Champs, 75006 PARIS. Open Monday to Friday from 14h30-18h.
- **Société Asiatique de Paris**: 3, rue Mazarine, 75006 PARIS, Tel: 46.33.28.32.
- **Université Paris I, Bibliothèque Centre Pierre Mendès-France**: 90, rue Tolbiac, 75013 PARIS, Tel: 40.77.18.14.
- **Ville de Paris**: 2, rue Guadeloupe, 75018 PARIS, Tel: 46.07.38.25.

Record Libraries

About 26 Parisian libraries specialize in lending records, cassettes, or CDs. Contact the *Direction des Affaires Culturelles* at the *Mairie de Paris* to find out the *discothèques* in your district. Tel: 42.74.22.02. They publish a booklet entitled *Bibliothèques Discothèques de La Ville de Paris* specifying which libraries have this option. Some *discothèques* require that you present the needle from you turntable for inspection before they lend you records.

Film/Cinema

One of the new and improved additions to Paris Inside Out *is the Cinema/Film section. Film critic Lisa Nesselson, who moved to Paris from Chicago in 1978, provided the following comments on Paris' celluloid scene. Her film reviews appear regularly in* Variety, Paris Boulevard, *and the* Paris Free Voice. *Lisa reminds her readers that not only has she never owned a television set, in 1991 she screened 344 feature films.*

As the devout make pilgrimages to Mecca or Jerusalem, so should the true believer in cinema come to Paris. For although movies may be made in Hollywood, only in France are they worshipped. The French themselves are surprised to hear it but, in terms of sheer variety and accessibility to the movies of many lands, Paris is the viewing capital of the world.

As the commemorative plaque at 14 Boulevard des Capucines indicates, history's first public projection of motion pictures for paying customers (courtesy of France's own Lumière brothers) took place in the *Salon Indien* of the Grand Café on December 28, 1895. So, as the world gears up for the centenary of motion pictures, Paris, with its film archives, *ciné* clubs, repertory cinemas and fabulous concentration of commercial movie houses, is the perfect place to catch up on nine and a half decades of the 7th art.

Say, why do they call it that, anyway? Glad you asked. It was in Paris, in 1911, that the Italian critic Ricciotto Canudo declared the Cinema to be "the 7th art," following architecture, music, painting, sculpture, poetry and dance. (Every so often someone has the temerity to suggest that television/video might be the "8th art" but such people are usually found—bound with celluloid and gagged with cathode ray tubes—at the bottom of the Seine.)

Paris, with 331 commercial screens for a population of roughly two million (Manhattan, by comparison, has only 139 screens) sports some of the best-equipped theaters on the planet. French audiences still respect the notion that a public theater is not a private living room—i.e. extraneous comments and play-by-play accounts ("He's got a gun!—He's going to shoot her!—Look, he shot her!") are practically unheard of. Reverence toward projected celluloid is particularly acute at the *Cinémathèque Française*, the hallowed yet happening film archive where generations of film buffs (including the gents known collectively as the French New Wave) have studied Saint Cinema in the dark. Your chances of coming across a film crew or even bumping into a major director or actor while walking down the street, riding the Métro or standing in line for a movie are excellent. And, although refreshments are served at many theaters, you'll never find gum stuck to the floor.

That's the good news. The bad news is: Movies aren't cheap. The average admission price is close to 40 FF, or nearly $8 U.S.or £4.25 at the current exchange rate. But the CNC, the government body that regulates all film production and exhibition in France, wants everybody to be able to afford to go to the movies at least once a week. So, since 1980, ticket prices on Mondays have been 30% cheaper for one and all.

With official documentation, there are discounts (*tarif réduit*) for the unemployed, military personnel, senior citizens, families with three or more children and students. A valid student I.D. card (local or international) is worth its weight in gold since hundreds of theaters offer a 30% reduction to students at daytime shows and some (including the Action cinemas, the Forum Horizon and the Saint-Germain-des-Prés) extend the privilege to every show, seven days a week. There are other alternatives to paying full price, which will be discussed further along.

Films change on Wednesdays, which is when the weekly entertainment guides hit the newsstands. (These are a better bet than the daily papers for complete addresses and show times). *L'Officiel des Spectacles* is neatly organized and costs only 2 FF. Some folks prefer *Pariscope* (3 FF) which offers listings by "category" (Westerns, Comedies, etc.) as well as by neighborhood. If you read French, you might want to spring for *7 à Paris* at 7 FF, a more comprehensive city maga-zine. (The title is a pun on the aforementioned 7 arts and, spoken aloud, *"c'est à Paris"* means "What's happening in Paris").

When you're scanning the weekly listings or spontaneously ducking into a theater, pay special attention to whether a given film is being presented in "V.O." or "V.F." V.O. (for *version originale*) means the film will be shown with its dialogue intact (be it English, Danish or Pig-Latin) accompanied by French subtitles. V.F. (for *version française)* indicates that the film has been dubbed into French. Most of the theaters in the Latin Quarter and along the Champs-Elysées specialize in V.O. prints. The Montparnasse area deals in both dubbed and subtitled fare. The theaters of the Grands Boulevards and Montmartre are almost all purveyors of V.F. films. If, as is increasingly the case, a French-speaking director (Jean-Jacques Annaud) has made an English-language film (*The Name of the Rose, The Lover*), you may come across the designation V.A. (*version anglaise*). This is important in that, as one English speaking Parisian remarked, "It's a real drag paying to see Woody Allen in French."

As for titles, it's not difficult to deduce that *9 Semaines et Demies* is *9 1/2 Weeks* but if you don't know your directors and actors, it might be hard to guess that *Voyage au bout de l'enfer* (Journey to the End of Hell) is actually *The Deer Hunter*, *Aux portes de l'enfer* (At the Gates of Hell) is *Angel Heart* and *Personne n'est parfait* (Nobody's Perfect) is *Torch Song Trilogy*.

Most cinemas list two show times for each presentation. The first, known as the *séance*, consists of anywhere from 10 to 40 minutes of coming attractions and commercials. Theoretically, the house lights are to be only partially dimmed, leaving patrons the option of reading Proust, conjugating irregular verbs or otherwise ignoring the ads. However, if you hail from a country where it would probably not occur to the telephone company to use topless women in its advertising campaigns, you may want to direct your attention to the screen, where you're also likely to see a buck naked hunk romping in the surf on behalf of a popular brand of men's underwear. Condom ads tend to be clever.

Sometimes sex references turn up in the most unlikely places. A few years ago one of the major French banks used an instrumental version of Lou Reed's "Walk on the Wild Side" to accompany its commercials. One wonders if the bank's officers had any idea when selecting a melody to convey fiscal responsibility that the song's lyrics refer to unbridled male hustlers and at least one transsexual administering oral sex from coast to coast.

On weekend nights or during the first few days of a film's run you should arrive for the *séance* to be assured of a good seat. (Some theaters, including the Max Linder and the Kinopanorama will sell you a ticket for a specific show up to a week in advance). Otherwise, if the movie's not a runaway hit, you can generally safely plan to arrive just before the second time listed, for the *film* itself.

The ubiquitous usherette or *ouvreuse*, (so named because the base of the seats in legitimate theaters had to be unlocked—*ouvrir* being the French verb "to open"—and the usherette, who had the key, was loathe to do so unless assured of a tip) has, in recent years given way to salaried personnel. In the heyday of regular movie-going, working for tips at one of the bigger theaters was considered such a plum position that jobs were jealously guarded and "sold" for elevated sums. The ushers at the major theater chains (Pathé, Gaumont, UCG) no longer expect a tip, but those at art houses and a few first-run cinemas still rely entirely on your generosity. A minimum *pourboire* of 2 francs per person is polite. Although some multiplexes have installed vending machines or built concession stands, in many theaters the usherettes walk the aisles before the show carrying wicker trays stocked with ice cream bars and candy. Take the precaution of opening any potentially noisy wrappers before the feature starts—patrons have been seen coming to blows over one too many crinkling of cellophane.

Ticket prices range from 35 to 50 francs, with student (*réduction étudiant*) and senior citizen discounts running roughly 10 francs cheaper. Interestingly enough, you can expect to pay the same amount of money for an art house revival of *Citizen Kane* as you would for the very latest Hollywood fare. (After all, the reasoning goes, art is art, whatever its vintage). Stanley Kubrick's *A Clockwork Orange,* made in 1971 and last shown in theaters in the mid-80s, was one of the top box-office performers of early 1992.

Although American films are often released at roughly the same time in the North America and in France, there is sometimes a gap of several months. (Sometimes six to twelve months.) Some films, however, come out in Paris *before* they are released in North American theaters. Examples include *Highlander II*, Clint Eastwood's *Bird* and *White Hunter, Black Heart,* Jim Jarmusch's *Night on Earth* and Woody Allen's *Shadows and Fog.*

Although Parisians can be relied upon to smoke everywhere else, smoking is not permitted in cinemas. Depending on your tolerance for tobacco fumes, this in itself could be a major incentive to spend time at the movies.

Discounts

If you're planning to do a lot of mainstream film-going, you may want to invest in the magnetic debit cards offered by Pathé (10 admissions for 300 FF) and UGC (116 FF for four individual admissions or 174 FF for six admissions for a maximum of two people at a time) which also entitle bearers to priority entry. (UGC does not offer reductions to students.)

At 22-28 FF, noon shows also represent terrific savings and no lines. Bargain matinees are offered at the Forum Horizon, Forum Orient Express and Gaumont Les Halles (in the 1st *arrondissement*), the Ciné Beaubourg (in the 3rd), the Epée de Bois and the Reflet Medicis Logos, (in the 5th) the

Saint-Germain-des-Prés, Racine, and Luxembourg (in the 6th) and the George V (in the 8th).

For just 20 FF, the Action Rive Gauche (5 rue des Ecoles in the 5th) shows a different classic film weekly at noon, excluding Sundays and holidays.

The somewhat scruffy but very well programmed Ciné Beaubourg Les Halles (next door to the Pompidou Center) charges only 22 FF until 1 pm.

The Pathé Hautefeuille, which sports four screens, charges only 28 FF until 6:30, including weekends.

Certain independent theaters reward repeat customers with one free ticket for a specific number of paid admissions. Ask for a free *carte de fidélité* at the Action cinemas (the Ecoles and Rive Gauche in the 5th, the Christine in the 6th and Mac-Mahon in the 17th) and enjoy a free movie after five paid visits.

Other practitioners of the buy-five-get-one-free policy are: Studio Galande (5th), Republic Cinemas (11th), the Denfert and the Entrepot (14th) and the Grand Pavois (15th). The Balzac, in the 8th, antes up one free seat after *six* paid admissions.

Other individual theaters give quantity discounts. The Latina two-plex (the only movie theater in the 4th *arrondisse-ment*) specializes in films from Latin America and sells cards good for 6 admissions for an unbeatably low 100 FF. The Utopia (in the 5th) offers 10 admissions for 240 FF. The quaint and historic Studio 28 is the only V.O. outpost in the 18th and offers a five-admission card that's valid for two months for 120 FF.

Some discount systems take a little prior thought but are well worth the effort for the would-be frequent filmgoer.

As part of the general "movies are good for you" attitude, many companies make discount vouchers available to their employees. *Ticket Spectacle 30* (for "30 % off" the regular ticket price) extends this same privilege to ordinary folks who are willing to go a little bit out of their way. For 280 FF you receive a *carnet* (booklet) of 10 vouchers good toward the reduced rate admission at nine Paris cinemas (including the Bretagne, the George V and the Forum Horizon) totaling 49 screens. The vouchers, which can save you up to 13 FF per film, are valid seven days a week, for a one year period. The *Ticket Spectacle 30* booklet is sold directly to the public at one location:

Cinéma Le Village: 3 rue de Chézy, Neuilly-sur-Seine, 92200. Tel: 47.22.83.05.

You can tap into the excellent art house programming at the three *"Ecran"* theaters in the nearby suburb of Saint-Denis for only 22 FF per show (including weekends) if you pick up a copy of "Campus" (a freebie newspaper that come out every two weeks) and show it to the box office cashier. (Copies—which include a complete schedule of Ecran films and show times—are always available at the Gibert Joseph bookstore at 26-30 bd Saint-Michel 75006).

Archives (Non-Commercial & Miscellaneous Film)

• **Cinémathèque Française:** *Palais de Chaillot,* Place de Trocadéro (Avenue Albert de Mun and Avenue du Président Wilson, in the 16th) Métro: Trocadéro. *Palais de Tokyo*, 13 Avenue du Président Wilson, 75016 Métro: Iéna. Tickets 22 FF for members, 15 FF. Recorded program: 47.04.24.24

The *Cinémathèque Française* has remodeled its theater in the left-hand wing of the Palais de Chaillot (projected re-opening: May 1992) and has cut back its programming to just two films a day at its theater in the Palais de Tokyo down the block. Still, those two films may be the best ones showing on any given day in Paris.

The now legendary *Cinémathèque* was founded in 1936 by film fanatics George Franju and Henri Langlois when they were barely out of their teens. Langlois (1914-1977), who believed that every film was a potential masterpiece and collected accordingly, is largely responsible for the grudging acknowledgment that the movies can be art as well as entertainment. Don't be daunted by the pasty-faced regulars affectionately known as "the rats of the *Cinémathèque*." Although generations of film lovers have come to the *Cinémathèque* to see what could not be seen elsewhere, you needn't be a walking encyclopedia of film trivia to feel comfortable on the premises. Past retrospectives have been devoted to Russ Meyer, Frank Capra and Clint Eastwood as well as lesser known and downright obscure "film folk." Programs are listed in the weekly guides or may be picked up at the theater.

• **Musée du Cinéma-Henri Langlois:** Palais de Chaillot (45.53.74.39) Métro: Trocadéro. Admission: 22 FF. 3You know how you can see your favorite movies over and over and appreciate them a little more each time? Well, the same principle is at work in the fabulous museum that Langlois designed to display a portion of the *Cinémathèque*'s peerless collection of *cinemabilia*. Original cameras, costumes, post-ers, set designs and props from all over the world serve to illustrate Langlois' brilliantly eclectic vision of the evolution of moving images. Guided tours only (in French) at 10h, 11h, 14h, 15h, 16h, lasting approximately 90 minutes. Closed Tuesday.

• **Salle Garance**: Centre Pompidou (42.78.37.29) Métro: Rambuteau or Hotel de Ville. Tickets: 22 FF. The Salle Garance (entrance to the rear of the main floor of the Pompidou Center) is a no-frills theater that hosts excellent comprehensive retrospectives at reasonable prices. Pick up a program at Beaubourg's infor-mation desk or check the weekly entertainment guides. Garance is also the site, each March, of the *Cinéma du Réel* festival of ethnographic films.

• **Vidéothèque de Paris**: 2 Grande Galerie: porte Saint-Eustache—Forum des Halles. (40.26.34.30) Métro: Châtelet-Les Halles. Tickets 22 FF (per day). Memberships available. Opened in 1988 as a public-access archive of film and video documents concerning Paris, the Vidéothèque, located under-ground, offers individual video consoles for research (a state of the art robot can select any of the 4000 films on tap in under a minute). Despite its name, the *Vidéothèque* projects as many as seven feature films daily (always preceded by an appropriate newsreel or film trailer) in its impeccable (if sterile) screen-ing rooms. Chunks of programming are loosely organized around themes (children, music, public transportation). One of the advantages here is that titles are repeated on different days and at different times in the course of a retrospective, which gives you more than one chance to catch a given film. Pay 22 FF and stay all day or become a member and reserve a video console via Minitel.

Outstanding, Unusual, & Historic Movie Theaters

For technical excellence and sheer hipness, the Max Linder Panorama (24 Boulevard Poissonnière in the 9th) is the grooviest theater in town. With its jet-black walls, 700 seats (each named for a film personality or movie title) on three levels, enormous slightly curved screen and ultra sharp optics and sound system, it may be said that one would be an utter dolt to see a given film elsewhere if it's playing at the Max Linder. (What's more, their first show of the day and the Saturday night midnight show cost only 30 FF).

Other satisfyingly large screens include that at the Kinopanorama (60, avenue de La Motte-Piquet in the 15th), all six screens but especially the THX *salle* at the Forum Horizon (underground at 7, place de la Rotonde in the Nouveau Forum des Halles shopping mall in the 1st) and the main auditorium of the spiffy, pleasantly retro Escurial Panorama (11 Boulevard du Port-Royal in the 13th). As a general rule, any screen listed as *grande salle, salle prestige*, or *Gaumont Rama* should deliver a large viewing area, comfortable seating and high standards for projection and sound.

If you're in the mood for a cheap martial arts double feature first thing in the morning, head to the Trianon in the 18th, where the doors open at 10h30. This registered landmark was built in 1902 and has been showing movies since 1939. For the princely sum of 18 FF, enter the faded glory of the Trianon's semi-spacious lobby, proceed up the once-elegant staircase to the foyer with its bar and Versailles-style windows, pause to examine the grime-coated cherubim on the ceiling and enter the nicer-than-you'd-think auditorium through one of the port-holed doors flanked by topless ladies made of plaster. Then settle into a wood and leatherette seat to watch "Fists of Fury" and "Bionic Ninja." Trianon: 80, Boulevard Rochechouart, 75018. Tel: 46.06.63.66.

In October 1988 over a dozen people were seriously injured when five religious fanatics firebombed the Saint-Michel movie theater because it dared to show Martin Scorsese's *The Last Temptation of Christ*. Declaring that no attack on a filmmaker's freedom of expression would be tolerated, the government vowed to help rebuild the theater. It took a while, but the all-new Espace Saint-Michel opened in October of 1991 sporting two screens and a pleasant restaurant/exhibit space. Espace Saint-Michel, 7 Place Saint-Michel, 75005. Tel: 44.07.20.49.

The new Café Ciné in the Passage du Nord Ouest in the 9th (13 Fbg Montmartre, Tel:

47.70.81.47), opened in late 1991 and may or may not catch on. The Café Ciné functions as both a movie theater (in the afternoon) and a café. This was a common configuration in several European countries both before and during WWII. Bring your monocle and a dose of world weary disdain.

Studio 28: 10 rue Tholozé in the 9th (Tel: 46.06.36.07) Métro: Abesses or Blanche. 30 FF/reduced 25 FF 120 FF (5 entries, valid 2 months). If a recent film got yanked before you had a chance to see it, keep your eye on the listings for one of the most charming movie houses in Paris, if not the world. Founded in its namesake year of 1928, the marvelous cinema Jean Cocteau dubbed "a masterpiece among theaters, the theater of masterpiece" was trashed by hooligans when Salvador Dali and Luis Bunuel's *L'Age d'Or* premièred there in 1930. The Studio programs a different film (in V.O.) every two days. In honor of Studio 28's 60th anniversary, veteran art director Alexandre Trauner redecorated the slim lobby of this family-run enterprise, which displays molded footprints of film celebrities. The kitschy duncecap lamps in the auditorium and the homey little bar and courtyard are just a few of the reasons to visit Studio 28. Closed on Mondays and most of August.

As its name suggests, the Latina (20 rue du Temple in the 4th) shows films mostly from Spanish-speaking countries. *Images d'Ailleurs* (21 rue de La Clef in the 5th) specializes in movies by black and third world filmmakers. The Utopia (9 rue Champollion in the 5th) often programs outstanding Iranian films. The Europa Pantheon (13 rue Victor-Cousin in the 5th) is dedicated to showing fare from the nations that make up the new united Europe. The Cosmos (76 rue de Rennes in the 6th) is devoted to films past and present from what used to be called the USSR. The greatest concentration of movies for kids can be found at the Saint-Lambert (6 rue Péclet in the 15th), an adorable neighborhood theater that charges just 26 FF for children under 15.

Every Christmas season, The Grand Rex—the city's biggest theater at 2,800 seats—presents a kitschy show involving dancing fountains and colored lights. (For reasons unknown, programming jets of water to bob and spurt to music is something of a French art form.) The only true "atmospheric" movie palace left in operation (the star-sprinkled cieling with projected clouds is meant to approximate an exotic evening under the open sky), the Rex sometimes shows features in *Grand Large*, meaning that a colossal retractable screen takes up most of the extremely comfortable main floor, forcing patrons to scurry into the balcony for a momentous view. The only drawback to the Grand Rex is that foreign films are almost always dubbed into French.

Rex (only the "Grand Rex" is of interest—the other 7 Rex theaters are run-of-the-mill), 1 bd Poissonière in the 3rd.)

If your lifestyle calls for regular exposure to *The Rocky Horror Picture Show,* the 92-seat Studio Galande (42 rue Galande in the 5th) keeps the tradition alive on Thursday through Sunday nights.

And if you've never seen Marcel Carné's masterpiece *Les Enfants du Paradis* (Children of Paradise), it plays regularly at the magnificent 19th century Ranelagh, the only movie house in the 16th apart from the *Cinémathèque.*

The Action cinema chain celebrates its 25th anniversary in 1992. Founders Jean-Marie Rodon and Jean-Max Causse display almost flawless programming taste, strike fresh prints of film classics and survive in a tough field by having the good sense to honor student I.D. cards 7 days a week. They also offer a discount to people under twenty who don't happen to be attending school.

Film Festivals & Special Events

There is a film festival going on in one or more French towns or hamlets nearly every weekend of the year. The "International Festival of Films and Horses" (held in October in the Ardeche region because, as the director once said, "The people around here like movies and they like horses") even hosts a competitive "screenplay-writing marathon" during which pre-selected writers work around the clock for three days and three nights to turn out scripts that are eligible for production money.

The celebrated Cannes International Film Festival held its 45th edition from May 7-18, 1992. Unless you have friends to put you up and some legitimate connection to the film industry, a trip to the Fest could be both costly and frustrating.

That said, a certain number of tickets *are* sold to the general public (or given away by generous souls) for the so-called "parallel sections," (Directors' Fortnight, Critics' Week, A Certain Regard, Perspectives in French Cinema) whose line-ups can prove more interesting than the films in the Official Competition. Throughout the Festival, the cultural center called "Studio 13," (roughly a 20 minute walk uphill from the Palais des Festivals), welcomes the general public to meet fest filmmakers and view their work for very reasonable fees. The *Fédération Française des Ciné-Clubs* organizes two "cultural expeditions" to Cannes and secures accreditation for participants. (For details: F.F.C.C., 5, passage Magrou 34500 Béziers. Tél: 67.31 27 35)

In recent years, the *Videothèque de Paris* and the *Cinémathèque Française* have shown many of the parallel section films immediately following the Festival. Since the *Vidéothèque* has a "pay once and stay all day" policy, for just 22 FF, the devoted film fan can recreate the Festival-goer's diet of four pics a day and still sleep in his or her own bed.

The annual *Fête du Cinéma* (slated for June 25 in 1992) is a cross between trench warfare and the proverbial free lunch. Every theater in town participates and it works like this:

customer pays full admission price at the first movie he or she attends that day. For each subsequent film, customer pays only one symbolic franc. Wear comfortable shoes, pack sandwiches and mineral water, plan your itinerary with stopwatch in hand and you may be able to fit in five current releases for the price of one.

In late February, City Hall runs a grand week-long event called *"18 heures/18 francs."* What this means is that the show that begins closest to 6 p.m.(18h on the 24-hour clock) costs only 18 FF.

The annual International Women's Film Festival, held each Spring in the nearby suburb of Créteil, is completely geared to the general public and assembles outstanding female film talent from all over the world. *Films de Femmes,* Maison des Arts, Place Salvador Allende, 94000 Créteil Tel: 49 80 38 98

The annual French-American Film Workshop (9th edition slated for June 30 through July 5, 1992) in Avignon is a model of everything a manageable, unpretentious mini-festival should be. Under the sharp eye and pungent cigar of octogenarian American legend Sam Fuller, the *Rencontres Cinématographiques Franco-Américaines* is dedicated to the independent spirit in filmmaking on both sides of the Atlantic. Varied intelligent programming and lively bilingual panel discussions make this casual event an outstanding way for film buffs to meet and talk with film-makers (past guests include Louis Malle, John Sayles, Agnes Varda, Nicholas Roeg and Theresa Russell) producers and distributors. Avignon is a quick four-hour train trip from Paris on the TGV. For information contact: Jerome Rudes, The French-American Film Work-shop, 10 Montée de la Tour, 30400 Villeneuve-les-Avignon. Tel: 90.25.93.23. Fax: 90.25. 23.24.

Reading Matter

For those who read French, there are dozens of monthly magazines devoted to the cinema, with *Studio, Première, Positif* and *Cahiers du Cinéma* being the best known. *Cinéphage* is an entertaining newcomer. *ActuaCiné*, given away free in theaters, provides a non-critical overview of upcoming releases. The American edition of *Première* magazine is readily available at the more cosmo-politan news kiosks.

The André Malraux public library maintains a good cinema reference collection and sub-scribes to all of the major film periodicals. Bibliothèque André Malraux, 78 Boulevard Raspail, 75006. Tel: 45 44 53 85. Open 14h-19h Tues-Fri and 10h-12h/14h-17h on Saturday.

For serious film research, the library of the *Cinémathèque Française* is open to the public on weekday afternoons. Its reading room high atop the Palais de Chaillot affords an excellent view of the Trocadero gardens and the Eiffel Tower.

It is true that more and more Parisians are becoming fitness conscious, but the fact remains that recreational sports do not yet play a very important role in daily Parisian life. The closest you'll see in Paris to the jogging phenomenon in New York's Central Park or along Boston's Charles River is in Luxembourg Gardens. The air quality in Paris is not ideal for running, although the Bois de Vincennes and Bois de Boulogne are vast, lush, relatively pollution-free and well-marked for runners.

In France, you're either *"sportif"* or *"non-sportif."* So make up your mind. *Non-sportifs* outnumber the *sportifs* and most smoke cigarettes. The *sportifs* tend to be very *sportif* and often belong to clubs, where they regularly swim, ride, work out or play tennis or squash. Other *sportifs* only "spectate" *le foot* (football/soccer) matches and horse racing, read *l'Equipe*, and hang around the special cafés marked PMU on the awning. Several sports events in France are of great importance. The *Tour de France* international bicycling race; Paris-Dakar international car rally; the French Open tennis matches at Roland Garros; the Paris Marathon for runners; and Europe Cup soccer matches are a few highlights.

University Sports

Team sports at French universities are organized by clubs and student organizations. They tend to be only moderately organized and modestly equipped. There are no large scholarships to entice middle linebackers to the Sorbonne. They can be serious, but rarely obsessed, other than insisting that all participants have proper enrollment cards, health certificates, and insurance forms. If you show up at a university sports complex in your gym clothes but have forgotten your active Student ID or membership, a guardian at the door will most likely not let you in. Always carry identification with you.

A few years back the starting five for the basketball team for the Sorbonne included two short Americans, a scrappy Mexican, a Japanese forward who owned no white socks, and a lanky French student who was more or less flat-footed. So playing organized sports for a French university team can be fun and recreational, but it won't be ruthlessly competitive. University exchange programs have a variety of facilities available to them. AUP, for example, has an arrangement with the gym and swimming pool at Mabillon-St. Germain-des-Près. Others organize games and matches with French university teams and sports clubs. For pickup basketball games go to the courts in the Champ de Mars on Sunday mornings or the American Church on Saturdays. For up-to-date sports information, including upcoming sporting events, call *Allô-Sports* (Tel: 42.76.54.54)—a recorded phone line operating from 10h30-17h Monday-Thursday and 10h30-16h30 on Friday. In the last few years the French have become more interested in playing American baseball and football. The Japanese have organized a complete league of baseball players in Paris and play in the Bois de Vincennes. Canal Plus regularly broadcasts Monday Night Football. Tennis has become more and more available, although is still mostly limited to clubs and is rather expensive and class oriented.

Here's a listing of sports contacts in the Paris area:

Baseball
Baseball Club de France
Tel: 42.50.50.01

**Association Club
de Baseball & Softball**
3, allée de la Tour d'Auvergne
91150 ETAMPES
Tel: 60.80.14.17
President: M. Jérôme LEBRUN

Basketball
Espace Vit'Halles
48, rue Rambuteau
75003 PARIS
Tel: 42.77.21.71
(Saturday mornings at 11 am at nearby gym)

Marché St. Germain
75006 PARIS
Tel: 43.29.90.97

Bir Hakeim
3, rue Doct. Finlay
75015 PARIS
Tel: 40.59.99.72

American Church
65, Quai d'Orsay
75007 PARIS
Tel: 47.05.07.99

Bowling
Bowling Club de Paris
Jardin d'Acclimatation
Bois de Boulogne
75116 PARIS
Tel: 40.67.94.00

Paris Université Club (PUC)
31, ave Georges Bernanos
75005 PARIS
Tel: 43.26.97.09

Bowling Mouffetard
73, rue Mouffetard
75005 PARIS
Tel: 43.31.09.35
(everyday 10h-2h, Fri. and Sat. until 4h)

Bowling de Montparnasse
25, rue Commandant-Mouchotte
75014 PARIS
Tel: 43.21.61.32
(Mon-Fri, 10h-2h. Saturday and Sunday until 4h)

Boxing
Fédération Française
de Boxe de l'Ile de France
Tel: 47.42.82.27

Cycling
Bicyclub de France
8, place de la Porte de Champerret
75017 PARIS
Tel: 47.66.55.92

Fencing
Ligue d'Escrime
de l'Académie de Paris
Tel: 47.66.93.63

Football
Fédération Française
de Football Américain
37, rue Lafayette
75009 PARIS
Tel: 42.41.51.02

Golf
American Golf
14, rue du Regard
75006 PARIS
Tel: 45.49.12.52

Horseback Riding
Bayard UCPA Centre Equestre
Bois de Vincennes
75012 PARIS
Tel: 43.65.46.87

Centre Hippique du Touring Club
Rte. Muettte à Neuilly
75016 PARIS
Tel: 45.01.20.88

Ice Skating
Patinoire des Buttes Chaumont
30, rue Edouard-Pailleron
75019 PARIS
Tel: 42.39.86.10

Fédération Française
des Sports de Glace
Tel: 40.26.51.38

Roller Skating
La Main Jaune
rue Caporal Peugeot
75017 PARIS
Tel: 47.63.26.47

Rugby
Fédération Française de Rugby
Tel: 43.42.51.51

American Rugby Company
171, rue St. Martin
75003 PARIS
Tel: 40.27.86.00

Comité de l'Ile
de France de Rugby
Information on amateur
clubs and organizations
Tel: 42.46.68.66

Soccer
Information
Tel: 47.20.65.40

Stade Olympique de Paris
90, rue Jeanne d'Arc
75013 PARIS

Squash
Stadium Squash Club
66, ave d'Ivry
75013 PARIS
Tel: 45.85.39.06
(every day 14h-2h)

Squash Quartier Latin
17, rue Pontoise
75005 PARIS
Tel: 43.54.82.45

Squash Puc Pontoise
19, rue de Pontoise
75005 PARIS
Tel: 43.54.82.45

Squash Rennes Raspail
149, rue de Rennes
75006 PARIS
Tel: 45.44.24.35

Sporting Club Loisir
24, rue Richard-Lenoir
75011 PARIS
Tel: 43.67.13.98

S w i m m i n g
(Here are a few of the best pools)
Piscine de Pontoise
19, rue de Pontoise
75005 PARIS
Tel: 43.25.52.58

Piscine Deligny
25, Quai Anatole France
75007 PARIS
Tel: 45.51.72.15
(Situated on a barge on the Seine)

Piscine Buttes-aux-Cailles
5, place Paul-Verlaine
75013 PARIS
Tel: 45.89.60.05
(Art-deco pool built in 1910)

Aquaboulevard
4, rue Louis Armand
75015 PARIS
Tel: 40.60.10.00

V o l l e y b a l l
Marché St. Germain
6, rue Clement
75006 PARIS
Tel: 43.29.90.97 or 46.34.10.64

H e a l t h   C l u b s
Over the last several years, there has been a dramatic upsurge of interest in health clubs and fitness centers. Garden Gym is well-adapted for younger people, with seven locations around Paris, while Gymnase Club, with its 15 locations, is the largest and thus a bit more impersonal. A series of discounts are available to students and others. Currently, Gymnase Club offers a 12 month membership to AUP Students at 1400 FF. There are several other alternatives. Most university programs, organizations, and companies have been offered special discounts for their members, employees, or students. Here are some numbers for inquiries.

Garden Gym Beaugrenelle
208, rue de Vaugirard
75015 PARIS
Tel: 47.83.99.45
Métro: Volontières
Open Mon-Fri 7h30-9h30,
Sat 9h-14h.

Garden Gym Quartier Latin
19, rue Pontoise
75005 PARIS
Tel: 43.25.31.99

Garden Gym Elysées
65, ave des Champs-Elysées
75008 PARIS
Tel: 42.25.87.20
Métro: Franklin D. Roosevelt
Open Mon-Fri 9h-22h,
Sat. 10h-17h.

Gymnase Club Denfert Rochereau
10, rue Victoire
75009 PARIS
Tel: 48.74.58.49

Gymnase Club Denfert Rochereau
28, ave du Général Leclerc
Les Portiques d'Orléans
75014 PARIS
Tel: 45.42.50.57

Gymnase Club Nation
16, rue des Colonnes du Trône
75012 PARIS
Tel: 43.45.93.12

Parks

Paris has fabulous parks for strolling, sunning and passive recreation. The idea of the park in France differs from its North American equivalent in that Parisian green spaces are aesthetically planned, surveyed, and regulated. Lawns are for looking at, not walking on or sporting picnics. A uniforned guard with a whistle will let you know if you step out of line and use the public space for ball playing or frisbee. Sports are for the *bois*, not the parks. Parks are for strolls, for reflection, reading, lovers' rendezvous, concerts.... Paris parks usually close at dusk and are locked. The following are the some of the major parks in Paris:

• **Bois de Boulogne:** 16e, Métro: Porte de Neuilly, Porte Dauphine or Les Sablons.

This park has existed as a green wooded space for centuries, and once stood just inside the fortified boundary of Paris. Now it has been transformed into 2000 acres of varied terrain which includes a rose garden, a museum, two world-famous race courses, a small zoo, a polo ground, a "Shakespeare Garden" where all the plants mentioned in the bard's plays can be found and the plays are staged in the summer, two lakes, broad avenues for riding and paths for biking. You can even stay here in the campground. The *Jardin d'Acclimatation* has a little zoo, a playground, and a restaurant where you can share your table with the goats and chickens on Wednesdays. Nearby is the *Musée des Arts et Traditions Populaires.* There are boats for hire in the Lac Inférieur, and the Parc de Bagatelle is nearby with its castle, flower garden, and pick-up softball games. At night the park changes character though. Crime and vandalism are not unheard of, and a most interesting variety of outdoor prostitutes and a hybrid of Brazilian transvestites flourish. Recently, the police have begun an unprecedented crack-down on the prostitution in this park and have closed down access to motor vehicles at night, due to the increased number of AIDS cases.

• **Bois de Vincennes**: 12e, Métro: Porte de Charenton or Château de Vincennes.

Noted for its Parc de Floral, *hippodrome* and stables, this park has two lakes with rowboats for hire, biking and jogging paths, a medieval castle, playing fields, three fine restaurants. and Paris' largest zoo. There is also an annual ecological fair called *La Marjolaine.*

• **Jardin des Plantes**: 5e, Métro: Jussieu or Gare d'Austerlitz.

This lovely parc houses a formal garden, a botanical greenhouse, the Natural History Museum, a hidden gazebo and a *ménagerie* (zoo).

• **Jardin du Luxembourg**: 5e, Métro: Luxembourg. Located at the edge of the Latin Quarter along the bd St. Michel.

This garden/park captures the contrasts of modern Paris, with its joggers, wooden toy sailboats, wrought iron park chairs, *Guignol* (matinee puppet shows), pony rides, tennis courts and *pelouse* (lawn) specially designated for infants. The gardens are formal in the classical French style, with long open vistas and a popular central fountain. On the north side, the Château du Luxembourg, built by Marie de Medicis in 1615 (and which served as German headquarters during the Occupation) now houses the French Senate and a museum of art.

• **Palais Royal**: 1er, Métro: Palais-Royale.

In the classic but now out-of-print and difficult-to-find *Nairn's Paris,* Ian Nairn describes the "luminous melancholy" of the elegant home and gardens of the Duc d'Orléans as "surely among the greyest joys in the world."

• **Parc des Buttes-Chaumont**: 19e, Métro: Buttes Chaumont.

Lesser known to tourists and visitors, but absolutely charming, with two restaurants, exotic trees, and deep ravines.

• **Parc Monceau**: bd de Courcelles, 8e, Métro Monceau. `

One of the loveliest spots in Paris, set amidst exemplary bourgeois apartments. You'll find artificial waterfalls and ponds, glades and romantic statuary in this park. Nearby

(63, rue de Monceau) is the Musée Nissim de Camondo, a completely preserved 18th-century mansion.

• **Parc Montsouris**: 14e, Métro: Cité Universitaire.

Elegant formal park with unusual temple-like structure, located near the Cité Universitaire, the residential campus for international students in Paris. This *cité* is the closest one will find in Paris to the American style university campus, organized according to national "houses," such as the Fondation des Etats-Unis, Casa de Cuba, Sweden House, etc.

• **Jardin des Tuileries**: 1er, Métro: Tuileries.

Contains over 20 original Rodin sculptures.

Arts & Entertainment

You don't have to be in Paris very long to notice that the French pay much more attention to the sensual side of life than to the practical side. This is not good news only for the late night *bon vivant* who likes to wander home through the empty streets at dawn after a night of major-league clubbing. The daylight hours, too, are often packed with possibilities for tasting a bit of what the Parisians call *"la qualité de la vie."* It would take a very dull mind and a seriously withered heart to be bored in this city.

The great battle in Paris over the last two centuries, in art and in life, has been between the avant-garde and classical: the Impressionists shocking the academics in the 1800s, the Dada and Surrealist movements shocking the bourgeoisie in the 1920s and 30s, the writers of the *nouveau roman* shocking the reader in the 1950s and 60s. The avant-garde and the classical act like tides that ebb and flow, one temporarily conquering the other. The waves caused by their inevitable clashes tend to keep things bubbling, and interesting for the casual observer and leisurely partaker of all kinds of entertainment, French or foreign. Though much has changed over the decades, Paris remains a place where the new and strange are not only tolerated, but welcomed and even proudly displayed. When it comes to the performing arts, this is still in evidence, just as it is in fashion —which in Paris has become a performing art of its own.

Music Scene

Choices run from the upper-crust, tuxedo and *escargot* atmosphere of the old *Opéra Garnier* to the merely crusty, like the head-bashing rock club *Le Gibus* near République. There's a lot in-between—like jazz, for instance. Paris is one of the world's most jazz-appreciative cities, and France actually has a state-funded National Jazz Orchestra. Even in the years before World War II, black American musicians found the Parisians a better audience than anything in the US, and the trend continues today. The city sponsors a *Festival de Jazz* each fall (usually in October) but year round you can watch and listen to some of the best American and international acts at intimate cellar clubs like *New Morning*, the two *Petit Journal* clubs at Saint Michel and Montparnasse, the *Petit Opportun* at Châtelet and a number of others scattered across the city.

Experimental, electronic, and avant-garde composition in music and sound occurs year round at the underground attachment to the Pompidou Center, IRCAM, which attracts musicians, composers, and researchers each year from around the world.

Parisians are serious jazz afficionados. Most clubs are small, crowded, smoky and fairly expensive. There is usually a cover, and the price of drinks can seriously unbalance the average checking account. But people don't come to these places to drink, they come for the music, which begins at about 22h, lasts long and loud through multiple sets and ends about 4h on weekends. Lots of people stay for the duration. When the band breaks, it's time for a Gauloise and loud conversation, in the honorable Paris tradition. And unlike most American establishments, no obnoxious waiter will force drinks on you and give you the bum's rush if you don't consume enough.

Rock

For Paris rock, the choice is between the *salle* where you pay to sit and the club where you pay to dance. There's live music in either spot, but the livelier nights tend to be in the clubs. The big venues for live bands start at the new, massive Palais Omnisport de Bercy, one of the city's few buildings that has to have its walls mowed, to the belle-epoquish, more human-scale *Zénith*, *La Cigale*, *Olympia* or *Elysée-Montmartre*. In general, Paris is not one of the essential stops on every band's concert tour, mostly because of the lack of big-profit-generating stadiums, so the selection for live bands is less than you'd see in some smaller North American cities. But the big acts make it through town at one point or another.

Palais Omnisports de Paris Bercy
8, bd Bercy
75012 PARIS
Tel: 43.42.01.23
for reservations, call 43.46.12.21
Minitel: 36.15 BERCY

La Cigale
120, bd Rochechouart
75018 PARIS
Tel: 42.23.15.15

Théâtre de l'Olympia
2ter, rue Caumartin
75009 PARIS
Tel:47.42.25.49

Elysée-Montmartre
72, bd Rochechouart
75018 PARIS
Tel: 42.52.25.15

Le Rex
44, rue Poissonière
75002 PARIS
Tel: 40.28.08.55

C l u b s

The club scene is much livelier and more varied, the beat for fashion zombies, celebs and apprentice celebs, and people who just like to get out and move it round. There are the "classic" joints that have been on the scene for years, like *Le Palace* (almost a Paris institution) and *Les Bains*, where people-watching is at least as important as dancing. And then there are the African clubs, like *Le Tango*, *Mambo Club* and *Keur Samba*, for some serious shaking and a taste of the exotic.

And, of course, there are the high-tech discos like *La Scala*, lots of glass, aluminum, lasers and decibels in the auditory-damage range. The bouncers in these places tend to be numerous and over-trained in rapid intervention, which is fine if your primary concern is protecting your designer clothes from some drunken *zonard*, but bad news if you're not on best behavior. As a rule, North American clubs and discos tend to be a lot rowdier than the Paris version. Public drunkeness or other overt signs of altered behavior are in *très mauvais goût* (very bad taste) here.

Not to be missed on the music and dance scene is the tiny rue de Lappe near the Bastille, home of *Le Balajo*, one of this area's several ex-tango ballrooms that date from the nineteenth century. The atmosphere on certain nights is surreal in its mix: forty-ish prostitutes dancing with African immigrants, French sailors on leave and on the prowl, the young and hip *branché* (connected or plugged-in—the now dated French word for "in") crowd moving to live and recorded music, sometimes retro, sometimes rock. It's an experience. Note: Not that long ago, the very *branché* used the invented language *verl'en* (the syllabic reversal of *l'envers*, meaning "backwards," thus *chébran* for *branché*) to communicate their hipness. This, for the time being, has dropped out of mode, and is considered rather *ringuard.*

As a general rule, the club scene in Paris gets started late, rarely before 23h, and doesn't get rolling until the tiny hours, sometimes, depending on the club, around 3h or 4h. The hard core spill out at dawn.

La Locomotive
90, bd Clichy
75018 PARIS
Tel: 42.23.55.00

Les Bains Douches
7, rue Bourg l'Abbé
75003 PARIS
Tel: 48.87.01.80

Le Tango
115, rue Jules Lamant et Fils
93330 NEUILLY SUR MARNE
Tel: 43.08.20.49

Keur Samba
79, rue de la Boétie
75008 PARIS
Tel: 43.59.03.10

Opera & Classical

Paris now has two operas, the ornate *Opéra-Palais Garnier* which could easily pass for a wedding cake if it were not so large, and the new state-of-the-art *Opéra de la Bastille*, which looks more like a postmodern ocean liner, only bigger. The Bastille Opera now specializes in mega-productions of the repertory and modern classics, while the old Opera features ballet and other forms of dance. Each is well worth the visit, although not always the steep ticket prices. The *Palais Garnier*, finished in the late 1800s, is a marvel of extreme architectural romanticism—lots of gold paint, red velvet and swarming cherubim. The Bastille accepts casual dress and offers modern interpretations of both classics and new operas. Guided tours are offered. Inexpensive tickets are available; you'll be too far away from the stage to get really involved but close enough to admire the Chagall fresco ceilings.

The *Châtelet* hosts mainly visiting operas and dance companies as does the venerable *Opéra Comique.* Many modern works are performed in the suburban theaters or *Maisons de cultures*, which are reachable by Metro or RER and often perform American works of John Cage, Philip Glass or John Adams.

Other spots for an inspiring dose of Bach or Beethoven are the *Salle Pleyel* and *Salle Gaveau* in the 8th, the *Théâtre des Champs-Elysées* and the *Théâtre Musical de Paris/Châtelet.* Over in the 16th, Radio France, the national radio network, offers concerts at very reasonable prices in their spacious and comfortable auditorium. Certain churches around the city make good use of their excellent acoustics and sponsor concerts throughout the year, especially in the summer. during the annual Festival Estival. And for the very latest in contemporary compositions, there is the famous *Ensemble Intercontemporain* led by Pierre Boulez, based in their underground studios next to the Centre Pompidou.

One particularly nice way to spend an evening of classical musical and dinner is at:

Opus Café
Café de la Musique
et des Arts Lyriques
167, Quai de Valmy
75010 PARIS
Tel: 40.38.09.57

Theater & Dance
If you like theater, you're in the right city. There are about a hundred and fifty theaters in and around Paris within Métro distance, and some two hundred shows a night in the high part of the season. France's rich theatrical tradition, like England's and Italy's, goes back to the late Middle Ages. Today the quantity is not always matched by the quality, but there's a lot to savor no matter what your taste.

At the top of the list is the *Comédie Française*, the famous *"Maison de Molière,"* founded more than three centuries ago by Louis XIV. Here some of the best actors in Europe perform the ancient and contemporary classics. Productions and costumes are lavish, and the audiences are extremely knowledgeable, especially when one of the French national treasures like Racine or Molière is on stage. Little old ladies in the front rows have been known to shout out the words in the rare event of an actor forgetting his line. The theater itself, called the Salle Richelieu after the Cardinal who was Louis' top cop for culture, is worth the price of entry, if only to witness firsthand its luxurious architecture. The *Comédie Française* offers one of the best ticket deals in town: fifteen minutes before curtain, you can get upper balcony seats for next to nothing.

There are other large and luxurious, state funded theaters in Paris. The Odéon is also administered by the *Comédie Française* but features more contemporary work, especially in its smaller theater, Le Petit Odéon. At Trocadéro is the Théâtre National de Chaillot housed within the massive marble interiors of the Palais du Trocadéro, and across town in the 20th is the new Théâtre National de la Colline, while the city-run Théâtre de la Ville is situated next to the Seine at Châtelet. All three program high-quality work (at least technically). There are dozens of good, middle-size theaters that offer a wide variety of styles and periods, like the Athenée-Louis Jouvet near Opéra, and the Théâtre de la Bastille that presents avant-garde work by younger writers and directors. To these are added the good theaters in the close suburbs that ring the city, like Saint Denis, Aubervilliers, Gennevilliers and Bobigny.

There are also many small theaters where the quality varies widely. The genre of café-theater, usually very small cellar performance spaces that are a lot like jazz clubs, can be fun, but the quality is sometimes as low as their subterranean setting.

The price of theater tickets also varies greatly. The genre of boulevard theater, similar to Broadway in New York or the West End in London is very expensive and snobbish, for the over-forty crowd. The good state-run theaters have subsidized ticket prices, and good seats are available for 100 to 150 FF, sometimes less. Smaller theaters have smaller prices. Student discounts are often available.

Major Theaters in Paris

Amandiers de Paris (Nanterre)
Tel: 43.66.42.17
Athénée Louis Jouvet
Tel: 47.42.67.27
La Bastille
Tel: 43.57.42.14
Comédie Française
Tel: 42.96.10.24
Comédie de Paris
Tel: 42.81.29.36
Huchette
Tel: 43.26.38.99
Espace Cardin
Tel: 42.66.17.30
Le Gymnase
Tel: 42.46.79.79
Lucernaire Forum
Tel: 45.44.57.34
Madeleine
Tel: 42.65.07.09
Marigny
Tel: 42.56.04.41

Mathurins
Tel: 42.65.90.00
Montparnasse
Tel: 43.22.77.74
Palais des Glaces
Tel: 42.02.27.17
Palais Royal
Tel: 42.97.59.81
Paris Villette
Tel: 42.02.02.68
Theatre National de L'Odéon
Tel: 43.25.70.32
St. Georges
Tel: 48.78.63.47
Théâtre des Champs-Elysées
Tel: 47.20.36.37
Théâtre Grévin
Tel: 42.46.84.47
Théâtre de l'Est Parisien
Tel: 43.64.80.80
Théâtre de la Main d'Or
Tel: 48.05.67.89
Théâtre National de Chaillot
Tel: 45.05.14.50
Théâtre National de la Colline
Tel: 43.66.03.00
Théâtre de Paris
Tel: 48.74.10.75
Théâtre de la Ville au
Théâtre de la Bastille
Tel: 42.74.22.77

Theaters for English-speakers
Théâtre Marie Stuart
4, rue Marie Stuart
75003 PARIS
Tel: 45.08.17.80
Director: Robert CORDIER
(An institution in contemporary anglo-franco productions in Paris)

ACT (English Theatre Company)
20, rue du Ct. René Mouchotte
75014 PARIS
Tel: 43.21.48.02

Theater Essaion
6, rue Pierre au Lard
75004 PARIS
Tel: 42.78.46.42

Voices (Assoc. of English & American Actors)
13, rue Chambéry
75015 PARIS
Tel: 45.31.65.48

Sweeney Irish Pub
18, rue Laplace
75005 PARIS
Tel: 46.33.28.12
(Houses a series of well-produced one act plays in its *cave*)

Dance

The French dance scene is a very healthy one these days, and there's lots of activity in Paris and the close suburbs. The *Théâtre de la Ville* programs the big, internationally known dance companies throughout the year. The Opéra features the work of the *Ballet de l'Opéra de Paris*, as well as another in-house group, *Groupe de Recherche Choréographique*, formerly headed by Rudolph Nureyev, that is more experimental in nature. Both do very high-quality work. Elsewhere, on a less exalted level, there is some very interesting dance work shown at the

Théâtre de la Bastille, usually during the beginning of the year, as well as at the *Ménagerie de Verre* and the *Café de la Danse*, both in the Bastille neighborhood. The Centre Georges Pompidou programs some interesting avant-garde companies from France and abroad. The numerous smaller dance companies based in and around Paris perform at various locations, sometimes in theaters, often in dance studios scattered across the city.

Of a far more rustic nature is the city's annual summer program called Paris Villages. In some neighborhoods, mostly the ones on the eastern side of the city, a bandstand is set up in one of the squares, party lights are strung up, and a retro band complete with accordion and female vocalist plays the old French favorites while everybody from the baker to your *concierge* comes out for a drink and a dance. It's lots of fun, very *vieux Paris*. Not to be missed under any circumstances are the local Bastille Day dances held at every fire station (called *Sapeurs-Pompiers*) the night of July 13th. Here you can dance the night away to live music that is usually so bad, it's an experience in itself. Everyone in the neighborhood comes out for these, from infants to the elderly. The wine flows, there are games and prizes, neighbors who steadfastly refuse to speak to each other during the rest of the year are suddenly great friends, while the firemen gallantly dance with every available woman or young girl. You will probably learn more about the French character in one evening like this than in a year's worth of observation and study. And you can work off your *gueule de bois* the next day by watching the Bastille Day parade on the Champs-Elysées.

Here's one English language dance studio in Paris:

Dance Studio
252 rue de Faubourg
(sixth floor, studio 617)
75008 PARIS
Tel: (studio) 45.63.32.90
(home) 47.64.96.73
(Dance classes offered: Etienette, Morgan, Classic, Jazz and Stretching.)

Eating in France is a ritual and a religion. No city in the world has a greater density of eating establishments per square meter than Paris. Nothing of importance happens in France where food, somehow, is not included. Amidst the French adoration of quality-filled form exists another important but unwritten rule: ANYTHING YOU DO AT THE TABLE THAT ENHANCES YOUR ENJOYMENT OF A MEAL IS PERMISSIBLE.

For advice and information on everything food-related in Paris, Patricia Wells' *The Food Lover's Guide to Paris* is an excellent resource. It has information on shopping for food, restaurants and cafés, as well as comprehensive restaurant recommendations, including hours of operation, restaurants open on weekends, restaurants open after 23h, restaurants open in August, and restaurants with sidewalk tables or outdoor terraces, as well as cross-listings by price, regional specialties, and location. Her book is a must for frequent restaurant-goers and food lovers.

Café Culture

Cafés are places where people go to be among friends and acquaintances. They are meeting places, solariums (the French are notorious sun-worshipers) or shelters from bad weather, places to sit, talk, dream, make friends, make out or eat. They are also handy for their telephones and *toilettes*. Café and bar-sitting are an integral part of daily French life. Knowing a little about how cafés function will save you from a lot of surprises. First of all, the large, well-situated cafés on the Champs-Elysées, on the Boulevard Saint Germain at Saint Germain-des-Prés, at Montparnasse, along all the major boulevards, and in the Latin Quarter are expensive. But remember, you are not paying for your cup of coffee or glass of beer as much as for your right to sit in a pretty spot for as long as you like and talk, read, watch, or daydream. If you're spending 12 FF for an *express* or 20 FF for a *demi* (half a pint of draught beer), think of it as rent for the time and space. You should know that the prices of drinks in cafés depend on whether you're standing at the *zinc* (counter bar) or sitting, and then, of course, where you're sitting. Drinks are less expensive if you are served at the bar. The outside terrace is always the most expensive. And then don't forget that the prices of drinks go up after 20h. Also, you can order some drinks at the bar which you cannot order sitting down. A glass of draught of lemon soda (*limonade*), the cheapest drink available and very refreshing on warm days, can only be ordered when you're standing at the bar. Otherwise you get the more expensive and overly sweetened bottled lemon soda. No matter where you're sitting or when, the tip is always included. Although not required or even really expected, it is customary to leave the copper-colored coins *(feraille)* in your change as a little extra tip. At the counter, you'll be presented with a little plastic dish for payment, which is then flipped over to signify that the barman has collected from you. At the tables, the *serveur* leaves a slip of paper from the cash register indicating what you owe. Usually, you pay at the end of your stay, but sometimes the *serveur* (not to be called *garçon*, even though old guidebooks will still indicate so) will come around to collect as he goes off duty. When you've paid he'll crumple or rip slightly the paper indicating that you've paid. *Chacun son style!*

Cafés are open very early for coffee and croissants. One of the more delightful and simple practices is to ask for a *tartine*—a buttered stick of *baguette*—to dunk in your coffee. *Très Parisien.*

The most common beverage in a café is obviously *un café* (coffee), and the nuances need enumeration and explanation: When you just want to sit and talk, read, write or pass away the time and you don't want to spend much, order *un café.*

---

café noir, un café(express)—classic strong coffee served in a
tiny cup

café noir double—twice the dose of an *express*

café au lait—*express* with steamed milk

petit crème—*express* with steamed milk

grand crème—larger version of the *petit crème*

café allongé—*express* with extra hot water, also called
un café long or *un café américain*

café serré—extra strong *express* with half the normal
amount of water

Note: Very weak coffee is humorously labelled *jus de chaussettes*
(sock juice).

In the daily cycle of most cafés, there are three periods of peak activity: at breakfast time (before 9h30); at lunch (between 12h00 and 14h00); and before dinner at the *heure de l'apéritif (apéro)* (cocktail hour) from about 17h30 to 19h30. It is not unusual to see two different sets of regulars at different times of day, one at breakfast and lunch and the other at the *apéritif* hour. Between the peak periods customers come for a rest from their work, to meet other people or simply to sit alone with their thoughts.

The choice of beverages in a Parisian café is superb. The French make popular drinks by mixing syrups with either Vittel mineral water or milk. Thus, you can order a *Vittel menthe* (or *menthe à l'eau*) or *Vittel grenadine*, or a *lait fraise* or *lait grenadine*. As for beer, you can order *un demi* (8 ounces), *un sérieux* (pint), or *une formidable* (liter). Or a *panaché* (a mixture of draught beer and draught lemon soda), a popular drink in the summer and one that foreigners acquire a taste for after four or five tries. A final twist on the *panaché* is called a *pinochet*, which is a *panaché* with grenadine. Other popular drinks include:

un thé citron	tea with lemon
un thé nature	plain tea
un thé au lait	tea with milk
un chocolat froid	chocolate milk
un chocolat chaud	hot chocolate
un citron pressé	fresh-squeezed lemon juice (comes with water and sugar)
une orange pressée	fresh orange juice (comes with water and sugar)
un jus de fruits	fruit juice

Many cafés will specialize in a certain brand of beer on tap *(en pression)*, usually marked clearly on the café's awning.

un demi, un demi pression	a quarter liter of draft beer
un demi Munich	a quarter liter of German beer
une bière	a beer in a bottle

Wine: You should not judge French wine by what is served in most cafés other than the Nouveau Beaujolais when it comes out each fall. Cheap café wine is seldom very good. Cafés normally serve wines in two sizes of glass, *un ballon* (large) and *un petit* (small). For a more complete discussion see the section on Wine. Other popular wine drinks include:

un blanc sec (petit or ballon)	dry white wine
un kir	white wine and *crème de cassis*
un kir clair	white wine with just a touch of cassis
un kir royal	a kir with champagne instead of white wine

There are a variety of *apéritifs* served in cafés, usually served over ice with a twist of lemon. These drinks are mixed with water and sometimes *sirop de menthe (un perroquet)*. A Martini in France is not the dry thing with the olive; it's a brand of vermouth ordered by itself as an *apéritif*. Ice is provided only with certain cocktails, whiskey, Pernod, Pastis, or Ricard, that glorious Mediterranean anise *apéritif* that pours out rich and yellow and goes cloudy when mixed with water. Great on a hot afternoon on a café terrace with Lawrence Durrell's *Justine* in hand. If you prefer bottled water there's Perrier or Badoit on the sparkling side *(avec les boules)*, and Vittel and Vichy on the flat side *(plat)*. The only mixed drink served correctly in most cafés seems to be a *gin-tonique*. Other drinks include:

un grog	hot rum with lemon, water and sugar
un cognac	brandy from Cognac
un armagnac	brandy from Armagnac
un calvados, (un calva)	apple brandy from Normandy
une poire Williams	pear brandy

A word on café-restaurants: if the tables are set with cloths, they are reserved for those wishing to dine and should not be taken if you only plan to have a drink, snack or even a small salad.

Café Services

Toilets and telephones are always found in cafés—usually downstairs in the *sous-sol*, S/S, or somewhere at the back. If you want to use the rest room of a café without consuming anything, you have the law on your side. But getting away with it can sometimes be another matter. Be somewhat discreet. In chic cafés there might be a toilet attendant that has a plate out for a franc tip. Some toilets require a franc coin, but most don't. Although they are becoming rarer, the old Turkish toilets (hole in the porcelain floor with spots for your feet) are still common. They are a bit hard to get used to but a highly Parisian experience. Just get ready to jump out of the way before you pull the flusher if you want to avoid flooding your feet. Toilet paper is usually available, but not always, and very often a stiff, crinkly kind that is not very comfortable or practical. The telephones in cafés usually take one franc coins for local calls, but some cafés, mostly the smaller or older ones, still have booths with regular phones and the barman has to activate the line for you. You have to ask for a line out for each call *(Est-ce que je peux avoir la ligne, s'il vous plaît?)*. You pay afterwards at the bar, where there is a counter, usually one or two francs per unit. Occasionally, you'll still find the old phones that require a token *(un jeton)* from the bar. These have become almost extinct and are a bit quirky to use. A lot of cafés and restaurants now use a new telephone service, *téléphone bleue,* which costs 1,50 FF or 2 FF per local call.

Restaurants

There is no reason for not eating well in Paris. However, learning how to eat very well, with good value, maximum ambiance (atmosphere) and exciting variety is an art. It has become increasingly easy to pay a lot for *pas grand chose.* And, in Paris these days it's not certain that you'll be impressed by the service offered at inexpensive and moderate priced eateries. Thus, the need to chose well.

Restaurants are run by a *patron* or *patronne* who on the whole regards his/her position more as one of host than business person. As in all human interactions in France, a smile and a polite *bonsoir monsieur/ madame,* lots of *s'il vous plaît* and *merci bien* during service as well as an *au revoir monsieur/ madame, merci* upon leaving will serve you well in getting friendly service and recognition when you return. The quick meal is not really understood so don't get too impatient if service is too slow for you to catch your 21h30 movie. Next time, eat earlier or see a late film. It's hard to rush service in Parisian restaurants. And waitresses and waiters don't work for tips. 15% is always included. *Service compris* means that 15% is built into the prices. *Service non compris* means the 15% will be automatically added to the bill. Don't tip on top of the tip, other than a few coins you leave in the dish as a token of your pleasure.

First, a word about the strictness of eating hours. As of about 11h30 or noon most restaurants have their tables set for the onrush of lunchers. In Paris, 13h is the start of the lunch rush hour. Generally, you must be seated for lunch no later than 14h if you want to eat anything greater than a sand-wich or a *salade composée* (mixed salad), 14h30 at the extreme if you're lucky. In the provinces, lunch is served between 12h30-13h. At 14h you could beg and plead and offer your first born child and still be refused a hot meal. Between 15h-18h it's pretty much impossible to have a sit-down meal. An early dinner would be at 19h; a normal time

to dine would be between 20h-21h. But later than 21h30 is getting dangerous again (21h in the provinces). At 23h it's too late, except in pizzerias, *couss-cousseries,* some brasseries and bistros, and some American style restaurants in Paris. There are exceptions of course as noted in Patricia Well's book. And as the New Yorkization of Paris deepens in the Nineties several 24-hour establishments have cropped up.

The typical French meal—from simple to elaborate—is graceful and balanced: an opening course, a main dish, cheese, a dessert and coffee. And of course, wine. Most people ask for a pitcher of tap water *(un carafe d'eau, s.v.p.)* with their meal. This is highly expected. No real need to order a bottle of mineral water unless you prefer it; Paris city water is perfectly fine. Don't expect ice cubes though—very little ice is consumed in France. It's hard, if not impossible, to purchase cubes by the bag. The French are not in the habit of drinking their beverages at extreme temperatures. When something is very cold or very hot, the French will tell you, the flavor is less prominent. And flavor is more important, *n'est-ce pas?* They're right. Flavor and quality come before superficial exterior appearances. French people are often disappointed by American-style supermarket fruits and vegetables; the huge, colorful, waxed objects are visually pleasing but the intensity of flavor is often *fade* (bland). So, to get back to the point, don't expect ice with your water. Paris' culinary diversity and the keen attention Parisians give to food should contribute to the richness of your experience. There are about 30 guidebooks on Paris in which eating establishments are featured. Here are a few operating principles when selecting a restaurant, followed by a few of *Paris Inside Out's* favorites.

• In general, don't plan on eating in a large café on a major boulevard. You'll pay a lot of money for quickly prepared, average food and rapid, not particularly careful service. Here, slapped together salads at high prices is standard fare. If you're caught between hours and you're famished, use the café for a quick *croque-monsieur* (a ham sandwich with grilled cheese on top) or an *œuf dur* (hard-boiled egg with salt) at the counter. Otherwise, cafés are for coffee, drinks, passing time, meeting people, etc.

• Distinguish yourself from the unknowing tourist. Running shoes, guide books, cameras, and loud voices are give-aways. Attempting to re-compose a fixed menu is not only revealing, it's a taboo. As for ketchup, learn to settle for mustard.

• Read the menu posted outside before entering. It's uncool in Paris to be seated and then change your mind.

• Be prepared in advance to be squeezed into tight tables and booths. Paris restaurants can be densely packed, but privacy is respected. Don't get too annoyed if in a half-empty restaurant your preference for a larger table is refused. If you're a party of two you will not be given a table for four. Non-smoking sections are all but nonexistent although more and more Parisians are beginning to realize that some people don't like smoke.

• *Steack tartare* is raw, but delicious. *Carpaccio*, thinly sliced, cured beef, is also raw. Very uncool to order these, be repulsed, and then send these back.

• If the food (or service) is absolutely horrible, don't eat it—and leave. Have an iron stomach and head for the door. If you eat half, forget it; they'll be no recourse, no refund, no apologies, no free meal your next time back.

• Avoid the Champs-Elysées area unless someone else is paying. And even then suggest somewhere else.

Le Menu

The lunch or dinner composed daily by the owner or chef of a restaurant is called *le menu* (don't get confused between the words *menu* and *carte*; the French *carte* is the English menu, and menu is a complete and prescribed meal, often the best bargain and the most promptly served). In simple restaurants there is often just one *menu;* otherwise there are often two or three packages to choose from, each a bit more complex or complete and expensive than the former. You can still find little restaurants with *menus* under 50 FF but these are getting rare. Some couscous restaurants or Chinese or Vietnamese restaurants have menus at 40 FF. These are getting rarer and are always in the less chichi neighborhoods, but a number still linger in the Latin Quarter.

The hot dish of the day is called *le plat du jour* and may very well consist of roast veal and a heap of braised Brussels sprouts, or a thin steak and some French fries, or salted pork with lentils.

In a restaurant, if you try to order something *à la carte* that breaks the rhythm or balance of the meal, you may find that the agreeableness of the service is reduced. This will be true if you try to order two appetizers (called *entrées,* because they are your entry into the meal)—or want to share a dessert or compose anything else that is original, personal or outside of the way that things are usually done. So beware.

When ordering red meat, remember that the French *cuisson* (cooking degrees)—*saignant* (rare), *à point,* (medium rare), and *bien cuit* (medium well)—tend to run rarer than you're used to. The French medium is the North American medium-rare on the rare side. So either compensate accordingly or let the chips fly and you may find that you've been really eating meat overcooked for years. In some restaurants frequented by tourists, waiters exasperated at sent-back steaks automatically compensate for Anglo-saxon preferences. If there truly is a problem with your food, don't eat it. If you eat some of it it may be difficult to get the waiter not to charge you. The art of public relations has not really made it yet into the average French eatery. A waiter or maitre'd may end up arguing with you that your *magret de canard* is fine when you contend that it's inedible. Stay cool and polite, but hold your ground and don't eat half before complaining. Many small restaurants do have ketchup, but they're certainly not obliged to provide it. The French use mustard in a rather expansive way. And the French mustard is so flavorful you should try a dab or two if you're not in the habit. Note: the cheaper Dijon mustard that comes in jars that can be used as glasses when the mustard has been finished tends to be wickedly strong.

Good Value
Chartier
7, rue du Faubourg Montmartre
75009 PARIS
Tel: 47.70.86.29
This is a late 19th century gem that, despite its abundant tourist crowd, has preserved its authenticity. Extremely casual, inexpensive and lively. You're often seated with strangers, share baskets of bread and conversation. A large menu of typical, everyday French home-style dishes. Notice the little wooden drawers in the walls; these were for the linen napkins of the "regular" customers. Waiters, often feisty and entertaining, tally up the bill from memory on the paper tablecloths. Get there before 21h. Crowded but worth doing from time to time.

Le Drouot
103, rue Richelieu
75002 PARIS
Tel: 42.96.68.23
Owned by same people as Chartier. Same concept although a bit less picturesque—but also less tourists. Good idea for lunch.

Le Commerce
51, rue du Commerce
75015 PARIS
Tel: 45.75.03.27
Another restaurant in the Chartier family. Open every day.

Le Polidor
41, rue Monsieur le Prince
75006 PARIS,
Tel: 43.26.95.34
Very reasonable prices, *cuisine traditionnelle, "vieux Paris"* ambiance.

Le Petit St. Benoît
4, rue St Benoît
75006 PARIS
Tel: 42.60.27.93.
Also very *vieux Paris. Cuisine traditionnelle (hachis parmentier, cassoulet,* etc.). Sartre and Simone de Beauvoir were customers; Marguerite Duras dines here occasionally.

Julien
16, rue du Faubourg St. Denis
75010 PARIS
Tel: 47.70.12.06
Pleasant, fashionable, an in-spot in a tacky part of town. Plan on spending a bit more. Ornate decor. Don't miss the *profiterolles* for dessert.

Roger la Grenouille

26, rue des Grands Augustins
75006 PARIS
Tel: 43.26.10.55
Great spot for fun-loving bawdiness with style, excellent French provincial cooking, served up with popular casualness. *Coq au vin* and *canard à l'orange* stand out. So do the not-so-timid waitresses. Good house wine. Order the designed-to-be-embarrassing *dessert spècial* for those highly Puritanical friends.

Le Gamin de Paris

51, rue Vieille du Temple
75004 PARIS
Tel: 42.78.97.24
This Marais restaurant has captured fine food, soulful atmosphere, and a sinful chocolate mud pie. Ask for Sammie, the manager; he knows how to lay on that special extra touch. Closed Fridays.

Le Trumilou

84, quai de l'Hotel de Ville
75004 PARIS
Tel: 42.77.63.98
Situated on the quai near Hotel de Ville, this unassuming *resto* serves highly reliable and tasty traditional dishes at fair prices. The duck with prunes is always wonderful.

Le Procope

13, rue de l'Ancienne Comédie
75006 PARIS
Tel: 43.26.99.20
Believed to be the oldest reatusant in Paris. A popular meeting-place for both politicians and intellectuals during the French Revolution. Le Procope was recently done up on the occasion of the Bicentennial.

Chez Papa

3, rue St. Benoit
75006 PARIS
Tel: 42. 86.99.63
Traditional French cuisine served in a cosy, chatty atmosphere.

American Food

One obviously doesn't come to Paris to eat burgers and hot dogs. However, for those nostalgic moments when you're *croque-monsieured* to death, and tripe doesn't fit the bill, you'll be reassured to know that there are over 30 Anglo/American/Tex-Mex/etc. style restaurants now in Paris. The number keeps growing as North American entrepreneurs and their local clones keep opening up new ones. Without much difficulty you can find ribs to root beer, chile to cookies, although a few cultural culinary icons such as bagels, and the bottomless cup of coffee are still rare. A few stand-by American joints include: Joe Allen, Cactus Charly, Café Pacifico, Chicago Pizza Pie Factory, Harry's New York Bar, Marshall's, Mother Earth's, Rio Grande, Sam Kearny's, Hollywood Canteen, and The Studio. Although the cuisine here is pretty much authentic, these places tend to fill up with a certain type of trend-seeking French clientele that emulates the look of "the American way of life." They also tend to be on the expensive side and haven't quite captured the spirit of the huge American portion.

For commercial peanut butter, crumpets, corn meal, or brownie mix, try the General Store at 82 rue de Grenelle, 75007, and Marks and Spencer, 6-8 rue des Mathurins, 75009, across from the Galeries Lafayette. For complete listings of Anglo-leaning eateries consult Paris-Anglophone or FUSAC. Here a few reliable anglo culinary leads:

Susan's Place
51, rue des Ecoles
75005 PARIS
Tel: 43.54.23.22
Tex-Mex cuisine, excellent carrot cake.

Chez Marianne
2, rue des Hospitalières St. Gervais
75004 PARIS
Tel: 42.72.18.86
Great pickles, corn beef, cheese cake. Friendly atmosphere in the midst of the Jewish sector on rue des Rosiers in the Marais. Ask for André, the spirit of the street.

Hard Rock Café
14, bd Montmartre
75009 PARIS
Tel: 42.46.10.00

Hayne's
3, rue Clauzel
75009 PARIS
Tel: 48.78.40.63
Original soul food—since the 50s.

Mother Earth's
66, rue des Lombards
Tel: 42.36.35.58
Jazz on weekends.

Slice Pizza
62, rue Monsieur le Prince
Tel: 43.54.18.18
New York style pizza by the slice; home delivery.

Randy and Jay's
14, rue Thouin
PARIS
43.26.37.09
Barbecued ribs and chicken. As good as you find in Paris.

Spizza 30'
43.44.91.11
Free delivery of American style pizza. Based on the Domino theory.

Natural's
15, rue Grenier-Saint-Lazare
75003 PARIS
Tel: 48.87.09.49
Macrobiotic take-away.

Cactus Charly
68, rue Ponthieu
75008 PARIS
Tel: 45.62.01.77

International Cuisine
Paris is an international crossroads for cuisines from all corners of the world, Kurdish to Korean. One could almost trace the colonial history of France in the restaurants of its capital, from North Africa to Vietnam to the Caribbean (antilles) to black Africa to the Middle East.

For the purchase of exotic and esoteric foods and goods from the Third World and politically correct collectives try one of Bertrand Tellier's: Artisan du Monde, 20, rue du Rochechouart, 75009 PARIS, Tel: 48.78.55.54.

Lebanese

Currently, one of the best international cuisines in Paris comes from Lebanon. With the political upheaval and economic instability in Lebanon, there has been a veritable exodus of Lebanese wealth from Beirut and subsequent investment in Paris. Lebanese business people have preferred to invest substantially in Paris knowing at least their capital is protected against run-away inflation and the risk of violence and terror. Lebanese restaurants in Paris tend to be both elegant and casual at the same time and the quality, quantity and prices are all rather favorable.

Marrouche
32, bd St. Michel
75006 PARIS
Tel: 46.33.22.11

Chinese

Paris has hundreds of Chinese restaurants, a number of which can be a good deal for days when your wallet is thin. Many, especially in the Latin Quarter, can be extremely reasonable if you order the *menu*. On the whole, the best and most authentic Chinese food in Paris is concentrated in Paris' two Chinatowns: the 13th *arrondissement* between the Place d'Italie and Porte de Choisy, and Belleville, in the northeast part of the city, formerly dominated by North Africans, or Maghrebins. Many Chinese restaurants in the city, ironically, are run by Vietnamese. The result is a mixed bag of Vietnamese, Chinese and Thai influences, overpowered by the tastes and demands of the French palate. Go to the 13th or Belleville for the real thing. There are too many to list.

Japanese

The Japanese have recently been investing heavily in France, from 18th century *châteaux* to Paris real estate, especially in the area around l'Opéra, which has become a kind of "Japanese quarter" with many Japanese restaurants and luxury boutiques. Lots of new restaurants around the Opéra as well as in the St. Germain area.

Spanish

If you're looking for Spanish food here are a few suggestions:

L'Auberge Espagnole
1, rue Mouffetard
75005 PARIS
Tel: 43.25.31.96
Closed Monday noon. Service until 12:00 AM.

Burro Blanco
79, rue Cardinal Lemoine
75005 PARIS
Tel: 43.25.72.53
Dinner only, served until 1:00 AM.

Casa Pepe
5, rue Mouffetard
75005 PARIS
Tel: 43.54.97.33.
Dinner only.

Don Quixote
10, rue Rochambeau
75009 PARIS
Tel: 48.78.01.80. Closed Sunday. Service until 11:30 PM.

Roberto
8, rue des Tournelles
75004 PARIS
Tel: 42.77.48.37.
Closed Sunday noon.

Greek

The Latin Quarter is noted for its Greek restaurants complete with extravagant window displays of brochettes of seafood, stuffed eggplant and suckling pig. Also complete with aggressively affable male hosts beckoning the tourists. Most of these places serve reasonably priced, sometimes good food. Fun to do once in a while.

North African

There are hundreds of North African restaurants specializing in couscous. The Bebert chain is good but a bit more expensive than others. Here's one unusual find:

Le Méditerranée/Couscous Flash
14, rue Robert Giraudineau
94300 VINCENNES
Tel: 43.74.80.56
Although located on the edge of Paris in Vincennes, this is one of the only couscous restaurants that also offers home delivery service. Copious, stylish and not too expensive, owned and managed by Asdin, a charismatic marathon runner from Djerba, Tunisia.

Vegetarian

The choice for vegetarians in Paris is slim, but new restaurants seem to appear every week as health consciousness becomes more à la mode.

Banani (Indian Restaurant)
148, rue de la Croix Nivert
75015 PARIS
Tel: 48.28.73.92
Closed Sunday. Service until 11:00 PM. Indian food, wide variety of curries.

Bol en Bois
35, rue Pascal
75013 PARIS
Tel: 47.07.27.24
Closed Sunday. Service until 10:00
PM. Natural and macrobiotic specialties, with adjacent bookstore
and *épicerie.*

Naturesto
66, ave des Champs-Elysées,
Galerie Point Show
75008 PARIS
Tel: 45.56.49.01
Closed Sunday. Service until 5:00
PM. Specialty: fresh fruit and vegetable juices.

Rayons de Santé
8, place Charles-Dublin
75018 PARIS
Tel: 42.59.64.81
Closed Friday evening and
Saturday.

Country Life
6, rue Daunou
75002 PARIS
Tel: 42.97.48.51

Resto U

Students can also take advantage
of the French university-run
student restaurants called Resto-
U, managed by the CROUS
(Centre Régional Oeuvres Univer-
sitaires Scolaires de Paris). Tel:
40.51.37.13. These are crowded
and noisy but the food is
plentiful and really cheap. You'll
need to purchase tickets, available in the lobby of each of these
establishments.

Assas, 92 rue d'Assas, 75006,
Métro Notre-Dame-des-Champs
C.H.U. Bichat, 16 rue Henri
Huchard, 75018, Métro Porte
de Saint Ouen
Bullier, 39 ave Georges
Bernanos, 75005, Métro Port-
Royal
Censier, 31 rue Geoffroy Saint
Hilaire, 75005 Métro Censier-
Daubenton
Châtelet, 10 rue Jean Calvin,
75005, Métro Censier-
Daubenton
Citeaux, 45 bd Diderot, 75012,
Métro Gare de Lyon
Clignancourt, rue Francis de
Croisset, 75018, Métro Porte de
Clignancourt
Cuvier-Jussieu, 8bis rue Cuvier,
75005, Métro Jussieu
Dareau, 13-17 rue Dareau,
75014, Métro Saint Jacques
Dauphine, ave de Pologne,
75016, Métro Porte Dauphine
Grand Palais, cours de la Reine,
75008 Métro Champs-Elysées
I.U.T., 143 ave de Versailles,
75016 Métro Chardon Lagache
Mabillon, 3 rue Mabillon,
75006, Métro Mabillon
Mazet, 5 rue Mazet, 75006,
Métro Odéon
C.H.U. Necker, 156 rue de
Vaugirard, 75015, Métro
Pasteur
C.H.U. Pitié, 105 bd de
l'Hôpital

Fast Food

Fast food, which is anything but truly fast, has unfortunately overrun the Paris cityscape in the last five years, especially McDonalds but also Burger King, along with their French competition, Quick, which has recently bought-out Free Time and has 27 locations in Paris and has impressive franchises along the high-rent Champs-Elysées. French business people, office workers, students and kids flock to these meccas of American hamburger prestige, and at lunchtime it's often nearly impossible to get into one of these places, especially on Wednesdays, when there is no school, and school children line up for their "Happy Meal." The McDonalds in the Latin Quarter is a fine example of market-researched kitsch. The walls are lined with façades of fake bookshelves of fake leather editions of the classics of French literature —this being the traditional student quarter of the city, a hundred meters from the front door of the Sorbonne. McDonalds has flourished wildly in Paris and even has cornered a share of real prestige, after a rocky period in the Seventies when the king of burgers pulled out of France due to the shoddy standards of local franchises.

Les sandwiches are commonplace in Paris as more and more Parisians give up the Latin tradition of long meals in favor of the pursuit of more healthful and individual pleasures or simply to save time. Sandwiches usually consist of a third of a baguette with either butter and ham, *pâté, gruyère* (really French emmenthal; the real *gruyère,* which has less holes, comes from Switzerland and is twice the price), camembert, or *rillettes,* a flavorful but fatty paste made from duck, pork or goose— delicious with those crispy and vinegary *cornichons* (pickles). In a café, a sandwich will cost you between 15 FF and 25 FF, depending on where you are. Again, careful about asking for variations. One student once asked for a piece of lettuce on a ham sandwich and was charged double. "*Mais Monsieur, vous avez commandé un sandwich fantaisie,*" he was told. When you see signs for Poilâne bread, take advantage of the occasion. This coarse whole grain bread is both a tradition and delicacy in French culinary life.

When the weather is fine, or at least not too gray and sad *(triste)* as Paris can often be, you can always buy some bread, cheese, *charcuterie* (deli goods), etc. and sit in one of the parks (see Parks)—but not on the grass, as the *"pelouse est interdite"* (the grass is off-limits) since it is part of the landscaping. Or you may want to sit down by the Seine. In the fifth *arrondissement*, it's very pleasant to duck into the Arènes de Lutèce, an uncovered Roman amphitheatre that is hidden behind a row of apartment houses on the rue Monge just below the Place Monge. In the seventh *arrondissement*, the Champs de Mars, the open space below the Eiffel Tower, is lovely. Other options —the Luxembourg Gardens, the Bois de Vincennes, the Bois de Boulogne, the elegant Parc Monceau, or wherever there is a likely-looking bench.

You will see people in restaurants, cafés, and even McDonalds, paying for their food with coupons called *tickets restaurants*. These are like money —usually 35 FF each—that employers offer their personnel at half price as an additional benefit. They're cumulative. Establishments that accept them have stickers on their windows.

Weight

At first you may think you've come to a country where being overweight is against the law; where fatness is a mortal sin. You may wonder how it is that in a country with such a passion for food, everyone seems underfed. You may find yourself perplexed to see so many vices being committed with impunity. You may ask yourself how, with so much sugar being consumed, the population can be so uniformly *mince* (thin). It is true that much of what one associates with classical French food is the rich sauce, the buttery and sweet bakery delights. But these do not constitute the average diet— they are special treats. Quality is important, and as in every aspect of French life, so is moderation.

A second reason for the relatively petite waistlines of the French comes from the fact that Parisians are obliged to be rather active in their daily routines. There is less reliance on cars, more steps to climb, more stops on the shopping circuit, and fewer hours spent mindlessly glued to televisions. The emphasis on form also contributes—meal times are adhered to rather strictly, compared to the haphazard snack times, missed meals and dinners in front of the TV or over work. One must remember also that in France, personal style and the public self is taken seriously. The French don't like going out if they don't look great. The importance of one's physical appearance is thus very important. Lastly, over the past few years a whole new genera-tion of lower calorie prepared dishes with "lite" or *"leger"* on the packaging has appeared in Parisian supermarkets.

Typical Dishes and Special Foods

The following is a sampling of specialties commonly found in France:

Bouillabaisse: a Mediterranean-style fish stew with tomatoes, saffron, mussels, shellfish and the catch of the day. Each version is different than the last one, depending on the whim of the creator. Good ones are becoming hard to find.

Cassoulet: A casserole of white navy beans, shallots and a var-iety of meats such as pork, lamb, sausage, and goose or duck, originating in the southwest region of France. Beans and meat are alternated in a casserole —sometimes topped with bread crumbs—then baked until crusty. Perfect for the winter.

Couscous: Specialty of North Africa originally brought to France by colonialists. A hearty blend of mutton, chicken and a spicy beef sausage (merguez) in a light stock with boiled zucchini, carrots, onions, turnips and chick peas. It is spooned over a fine semolina-like base, called couscous, from which the dish gets its name. A hot, red paste called *harissa* can be stirred into the broth.

Fondue: A Swiss Alps specialty popular in France, especially in the ski regions. There are two types: bourguignon beef—small chunks of beef cooked on long forks in pots of hot oil and accompanied by a variety of sauces; and Savoyard cheese—melted and flavored with kirsch or white wine, lapped up with chunks of stale French bread on long forks.

Farce: Spiced ground meat, usually pork, used for stuffing cabbage *(chou farci)*, green pepper *(poivron vert farci)*, or tomatoes *(tomates farcies)*.

Hachis parmentier: Mashed potatoes and ground meat topped with a bechamel, or white sauce, served in a casserole.

Moussaka: A Greek casserole dish combining slices of egg-plant, tomatoes, and ground lamb, baked with a bechamel topping.

Päella: A Portuguese and Span-ish dish with a rice base, saffron, pimento, chicken, pork and shellfish, cooked in a special two handled metal pan.

Choucroute: Of Alsatian origin, this dish is often served in brasseries as it is a good accompaniment to a strong draft beer. It consists of sauerkraut topped with a variety of sausages, cuts of pork, ham and boiled potatoes.

No insider's guide to French life would be complete without some special commentary on wine and its place in daily life. The following section was prepared by long time residents of Paris and wine lovers and collectors, Petie and Don Kladstrup.

Nearly the first act of King Louis XI, upon subduing the obstreperous Duchy of Burgundy and dragging it back into France, was to confiscate the entire 1477 vintage of Volnay wine. It must have been a good year.

Since then, wine in France has become even more important, and no one can hope to understand or participate in the life and culture of France without knowing something about it. Happily, it is not necessary to be an expert to be an *"amateur"* (lover) of wine because everybody in France seems to drink wine, from the toddler at Grandma's for Sunday lunch to the Grandmas and Grandpas themselves. Almost all dinners include a glass or two, and even many lunches are accompanied by wine. However, as the pace of French life quickens to keep pace with the rest of the world, fewer and fewer working people have either the time or the desire for a two-hour lunch with all the trimmings. Those who do include a glass of wine frequently "baptise the wine" (literally, *baptiser le vin)* by adding some water to it. Heresy, of course, for serious wine-lovers and a mortal sin if the wine is anything but a *vin de table* (table wine).

It is probably the prevalence of wine that made the idea of a weekend bash of drinking parties almost non-existent in France. The difference between young people's attitudes toward drinking in the U.S. and in France was summed up by one U.S. college student who had been raised in France. "In France," he said, "my friends and I used to go out on Saturday night to have a good time and occasionally somebody got drunk. Here in the U.S., everybody seems to go out to get drunk, and occasionally somebody has a good time."

With a legal drinking age of 16, but with enforcement so rare as to be non-existent, it is almost never an issue. Small children run down to the neighborhood grocery store for the dinner wine, bars have no I.D. checks. Of course, the driving age in France is 18, and in the Paris area with public transport of some sort available around the clock, many of the real concerns about drinking and driving are eliminated.

So, like nearly everything else in France, wine has become an art form and an economic force. France produces nearly half of the wine made in Europe, and because of the high-quality—and higher prices—French wine accounts for approximately three-quarters of the money generated by European wine sales.

The French, of course, drink almost exclusively French wine, but the wine-makers do worry about the impact of lowered trade barriers in post-1992 Europe. Those with the most cause for worry are the makers of the medium-range of quality, because in that area, Italy, Spain and Portugal can put up a mighty competition with lower prices. The makers of the famous wines from Bordeaux and Burgundy and Champagne need only worry about having bank accounts that accept all currencies!

Figuring out French wines can seem intimidating, but in reality, it is much easier than trying to decipher the wines of most other countries. That is because the French wines are regionals, that is, named for the region in which they are produced. Almost every other country uses varietal names, so that you have to master the names of grape varieties before you can order. Horrible when you discover that the Pinot Noir (black pinot grape) can make a white wine, and that there is a cabernet sauvignon, a sauvignon blanc, and a cabernet franc grape, and they all make different kinds of wine. Isn't it nice to know that Champagne is just Champagne no matter what grape they make it with? And while Burgundy wines can be either red or white, they stay Burgundy. The same is true for all the wine regions of France—Bordeaux, Alsace, the Loire, Provence, the Rhone Valley. If you know those names, you are already on your way and can make the big connection of brain to palate with tasting and trying the different regions' selections.

Now, while wine does not have to be expensive to be good, it is unfortunately true that most good wines are priced more highly than poor ones. Unfortunately true, as well, is the fact that France makes a lot of bad wine, and if a bottle costs under 20 francs, you are almost assured that it won't be very good. That doesn't mean that it may not be enjoyable in certain circumstances, like an impromptu picnic or for washing down a pizza, just don't serve it at a dinner party or bring it as a gift to one.

Wine seems to absorb and enhance its setting, so get some advice from your local wine merchant or a knowledgeable friend before presenting a host or hostess with an accidental bottle of "plonk." In fact, don't take wine at all, if you don't know your host or hostess very well. Instead, send flowers with a nice note of thanks the morning after the party. If you are the host, don't be afraid to consult wine merchants before buying your dinner-party wine, and as wine is the only acceptable dinner-party drink aside from water in France, be ready to serve some to your guests.

Decide what food you are serving before you select the wine and be prepared to tell your wine merchant the details. Don't be surprised to have him or her ask you how you are preparing the chicken you said you were going to serve. And don't be timid about your budget. If you can only spend 20 or 30 francs, say so, and if you have a merchant who grumbles or complains, take your business elsewhere. There are Nicolas wine stores all over France, and they have a very good, solid selection of wines at all price ranges. In the past, the Nicolas chain was almost as famous for its artistic ads as for its wine, which was considered the best buy in France. That was especially true at Christmas time, when it had a huge "Saint" Nicolas promotion, bringing out of its massive *caves* (cellars) special old wines and offering them for sale in limited quantities for very reasonable prices. Alas, those days have gone the way of the wooden Métro cars, and the mighty chain has been sold and resold, with those famous *caves* going from one buyer and the stores to another. Still, the individual stores have good wines, decent prices and extremely knowledgeable owners/salespeople. And some of the ads are still rather nice. To get a feel for the old ones, stop in at the Nicolas store on the Place de la Madeleine, which is decorated with copies of the classic ads. (Lest you think we exaggerate, those ads were so good there was a museum exhibit of them a couple of years ago.)

A wonderful place to buy wine is the Cave du Château, 17 rue Raymond du Temple, Vincennes (Tel: 43.28.17.50). The owners are an enthusiastic couple who can go into great detail about any wine in their store, and they have lots of good, inexpensive ones. There is nothing fancy about the shop, and they deliver if you are ordering more than a couple of bottles. In fact, most wine stores do the same.

At the other end of the scale is *Vins Rares,* a gorgeous boutique of gorgeous wines. It is run by a charming, English-speaking Swede named Peter Thustrup. His stock of wines includes vintages from the last century as well as more recent classics; it is the place to go if you want a wine from a specific year or a vineyard for a special event. Peter's wines are reasonably priced for what they are, but no 1929 wine comes cheap! *Vins Rares* is located in the Cité Berryer, 25, rue Royale, 75008 PARIS.

A word about vintages. Vintage just means the year it was harvested. Some years are better than others, but any wine with a year attached to its label (and most French wines have that) is a vintage wine. It has nothing to do with quality. Most wine stores hand out vintage charts which rate the years and tell which vintages are ready to drink. The exception to the vintage rule is Champagne. Champagne is dated only in the years the makers consider to be extremely good. Other than that, Champagne can be made from a blend of grapes from more than one year. Vintage Champagne is, of course, more expensive and should be better than others, but because of the blending, the big Champagne houses (Moët—pronounce the "t", Bollinger, Mums, Roederer, Taittinger, Mercier, Lanson) never make bad Champagne. Of course, you may not like all of it, but each house has its own style, so it's just a matter of finding the style you like. And the finding is fun.

Champagne, like all the wine regions, has strict controls on the wine bearing its *appellation* (area name). The wine is made only from grapes grown in that region. They are labeled *Appellation d'Origine Contrôlée* (AOC) or *Appellation Contrôlée* (AC). If a French wine does not have one phrase or the other, it probably does not have much else to recommend it. It may be a blend of any old grapes, including very cheap ones imported from North Africa.

Then there is the system of *crus classée* (classed levels of quality). These are a fairly good guideline to quality, but they haven't been redone in years, so many are out-of-date. However, theoretically at the bottom of the heap are the *vin du pays* (country wines) and the *vin de table* (table wines). At the top are the *premier grand cru classé* (great first growths). There are lots of nice exceptions at the bottom levels as vineyards change hands and ideas, and there are some at the top who need to have their pedigrees re-examined, a cry you will hear from wine lovers, and even some growers, on a regular basis. Most resistant to change are the big vineyards of Bordeaux. These wines in their square-shouldered bottles are some of the big economic powers in France, with large amounts of hectars per vineyard, and major distribution organizations behind them. While may of those unclassed or labeled "fifth growths" when the classifications were done in the 19th century would like to have the whole system reopened, those at the top, are happy. To be fair, most of the *premier crus* have stayed that way, or become even better, but some have slipped disastrously and only nostalgia and hope keeps them in the running.

Wine is subject to fads, which can work in the favor of the discerning and financially-cautious drinker. Currently out-of-fashion are the wines of the Loire Valley, which is very good new for people who like good wines that are inexpensive, because many of the Loire wines are of outstanding quality. For whites from bone-dry to very rich and sweet, look to the wines from Vouvray. Two very good makers are Gaston Huet and Prince Poniatowski. They both also make good sparkling wines at very low prices, generally under 50 francs a bottle. If you can't afford a good Champagne, these are marvelous substitutes, a little more full-bodied and richer, but still light and bubbly to make any event special. Huet and Poniatowski also make sweet wines that can last until your grandchildren are senior citizens. These cost more, but can be a wonderful souvenir of France, especially when drunk with a bit of *foie gras*. For a lovely, cheap red, try the Touraine, made by the Château du Petit-Thouars. This seems to be better-made each vintage.

Myths surround wine, and some of them provide good guidelines—others can be shunted aside. For instance, red wine with red meat, white wine with white meat. That is a good starting point, but lots of chicken dishes are better with red wine, and even some fish is better that way. Just keep trying combinations to see which you like better. Another myth: wine doesn't travel. That is definitely true for badly-made wines, but good wine doesn't mind a trip, they just like to have some time afterward to recover. Of course, no wine likes to sit on a dock in the sun for several hours, so if you want to ship wine, make sure you are dealing with good people who know what they are doing. Don't hesitate to take a bottle or so with you, though, as long as you carry it with you. But remember that the wine that tasted wonderful on a hot summer day in the Cote d'Azur may give little pleasure on a cold, blustery day in a *chambre de bonne* in Paris. Don't blame the wine for that!

When serving wine, get clear glasses, the bigger the better. Don't fill them up; leave plenty room for the aromas to swirl around. Avoid the flat shaped Champagne *coupe* (modeled after either the breast of Helen of Troy or of Madame du Pompadour, depending upon the myth you're listening to), and look for the long, graceful flute, That shows off the bubbles and avoids creating the big head of foam that attacks your nose in the flat glass. You can keep the foam down even more by pouring against the side of the glass instead of directly into the bottom of it. Don't worry too much; sparkling wine makes everything sparkle.

If you want to pursue wine further, look into the courses taught in English at the Cordon Bleu School by James Lawther.

Most of all, taste and enjoy. That is the only true way to learn about wine.

A Selection of Cafés, Bars, Bistros, Brasseries

The following establishments have been listed here for their original style and glorious tradition. Be prepared to pay a premium, though, for the reputation. These places should become part of your working knowledge of Paris, but they probably won't become daily hang-outs. Otherwise, you end up watching tourists watch other tourists. But it is undeniably pleasant just to sit on the terrace and enjoy the moment. Bring out of town visitors or your parents for a look at the grand style they associate with Paris. Some of the best known, celebrated cafés, bistros and brasseries in the great Parisian tradition include the following. For a more complete list of cafés with illustrious literary lore see Noël Riley Fitch's little book: *Literary Cafés of Paris.*

La Coupole
102, bd Montparnasse
75014 PARIS
43.20.14.20

Le Sélect
99, bd Montparnasse
75006 PARIS
42.22.65.27

La Closerie des Lilas
168, bd Montparnasse
75006 PARIS
43.21.95.37

Les Deux Magots
6, place St. Germain-des-Près
75006 PARIS
45.48.55.25

Café de Flore
172, bd St. Germain
75006 PARIS
45.48.55.26

Le Balzar
49, rue des Ecoles
75005 PARIS
43.54.13.67

Wine Bars, Late-Night Cafés & Special Places

Here is a list of great little finds that can make daily life in Paris truly delightful, although the act of finding your own place will be a matter of personal taste:

Au Petit Fer à Cheval
30, rue Vieille-du-Temple
75004 PARIS
A tiny bar with a horse-shoe *(fer à cheval)* shaped bar—there are very few of these remaining.

La Tartine
24, rue de Rivoli
75004 PARIS
One of the oldest, most reasonably priced, and best wine bars in Paris. Also serves great Pain Poilâne sandwiches. The decoration is Deco 20s and seventy years of cigarette smoke has mellowed the interior.

La Palette
43, rue de Seine
(corner of rue Jacques Callot)
75006 PARIS
The room behind the bar has some delightful tile caricatures of Parisians in the Twenties. The meeting place for artists and gallery people.

Le Cochon à l'Oreille
15, rue Montmartre
75001 PARIS
The walls of this café are covered with painted tiles showing the old "Les Halles" market-halls. Early in the morning you can share breakfast (or a last drink if you've been out all night) with the butchers from rue Montmartre.

Le Clown Bar
114, rue Amelot
75011 PARIS
Next to the Cirque d'Hiver, this tiny café has its original painted ceiling depicting clowns and circus entertainers.

Brasserie Lipp
151, bd Saint-Germain
75006 PARIS
Reservations must be made in person. Favorite Friday night spot of literary media star Bernard Pivot and a host of well-known enter-

tainers and politicians. There are a few tables inside to the left where you can order a drink without eating (the enclosed terrace is stuffy and boring). *Fin-de-siècle* decorations. The length of the waiters' aprons denotes superiority.

Brasserie de l'Ile St. Louis
55, Quai Bourbon
75004 PARIS
Stand at the bar and try one of the white Alsatian wines whilst listening to the street musicians on the Pont St. Louis. There is a beautiful old coffee machine at the bar.

Le Petit Gavroche
rue Sainte-Croix-de-la-Bretonnerie
75004 PARIS
On the corner of the bar of this café/restaurant is one of the few remaining examples of the water-holders used in the ritual of absinthe drinking (sale was prohibited in 1915). Water was dripped onto a sugar cube and into the absinthe.

Le Train Bleu
Gare de Lyon
20, bd Diderot
75012 PARIS
Sweep up the curved staircase from the inside of the station and through the revolving door into one of the most astonishing *fin-de-siècle* interiors in Paris. To the left is the bar with its soft leather sofas and an atmosphere of luxury and calm. Whilst most of the travelers below sit in orange plastic chairs drinking over-priced *demis,* you can be sipping a Pimms, wearing a linen suit and sporting a panama hat, dreaming of taking the Blue Train to the Mediterranean. The restaurant, a national historic site, has maintained its elegance amidst sprawling frescos; but the prices are high and the cuisine has slipped.

Le Gutenberg
29, rue Coquillière
75001 PARIS
One of the prettiest cafés in Paris dating from 1913—original lights and mirrors. Try a *café-calva* (coffee and calvados) here on a winter morning.

Twickingham
70, rue des Saints -Pères
75007 PARIS
The young French intellectual *(intello)* watering hole.

Le Balto
rue Mazarine
75006 PARIS
A local *bar-tabac* near the Académie des Beaux Arts. Once a week the *"Fanfare des Beaux-Arts"* (brass band of the Beaux Arts) practices here.

Au General Lafayette
52, rue La Fayette
75009 PARIS
Popular French beer bar trying to look like an English pub. Great selection of beers—greater selection of beer mats, mugs, memorabilia and old Guinness posters.

Good & Sleazy

Académie du Billard
84, rue de Clichy
75009 PARIS
An enormous 19th century billiard hall with a small bar open late where you can watch the intensity of Frenchmen at play.

Polly Magoo
rue St. Jacques
75005 PARIS
Revoltingly sleazy but can you leave Paris without saying you've been there?

Chez George
rue des Canettes
75006 PARIS
Has to be experienced at least once. The only bar in the Latin Quarter with a licence to sell wine to take away *(vente à emporter)*.

Le Baragouin
17, rue Tiquetonne
75002 PARIS
An enormous late-night bar packed with French "rockers". If you can push your way to the back you'll find some serious dart-playing going on.

Café de l'Industrie
16, rue St. Sabin
75011 PARIS
Tel: 47.00.13.53

Le Taxi Jaune
13, rue Chapon
75003 PARIS
Tel: 42.78.92.24
Serves light meals such as salads and Mexican dishes. *Paris Inside Out* readers get a free *apéritif*.

Le Mazet
61, rue St. André des Arts
75006 PARIS
Tel: 46.34.68.81
This rough, rowdy café is the favorite haunt of buskers and late-night musicians.

Special Sites & Events

Fête de l'Humanité: sponsored by the *Parti Communiste* (PC) each September in the northern suburb of La Courneuve, this massive festival features stands from Communist countries around the world. Great music, food and crafts.

Fête de la Musique: *Fête* created in the early 80s by Culture Minister Jack Lang. One Saturday night every June, Paris and its suburbs generously celebrate music of all kinds with neighborhood concerts, balls and free street bands. Not to be missed.

Foire du Trône: Mammoth amusement park every Spring at the Porte Dorée. Try it for kicks.

**Jim Haynes
(Handshake Editions)**
Of the Americans in Paris few are as colorful, free-spirited, and community-minded as Jim Haynes, teacher, publisher, spiritual guru of limitless love and spiritual networking. In the Sixties, with friend Germain Greer, Jim founded *Suck Magazine*, a sexual revolution paper. Every Sunday night in his atelier more than 50 friends, visitors, and new guests take part in (for a nominal fee) a wonderful blue-plate dinner with unlimited wine and beer. Proceeds traditionally have gone to buy food shipments for people in oppressed places. Jim's 14 volume address book tells all, as does his autobiography, *Thanks for Coming* (Faber & Faber). Jim's latest books are his *People to People* guides to Poland and Romania (Zephyr Press, Somer-ville, MA). Reservations for Sunday are made by phone on Saturday afternoon. Jim Haynes Atelier A2, 83 rue de la Tombe Issoire, 75014 PARIS Tel: 43.27.17.67.

Monuments & Excursions

Within an hour of Paris and easily accessible by train there are wonderful side trips to take: Versailles, Fontainebleu, Giverny (seasonal), Chartres, Chantilly. The *Michelin Green Guide for Paris and its environs* is your best bet for full explanations. In Paris, the sights and monuments that eventually must be visited include: the Tour Eiffel, l'Arc de Triomphe, Sacré Cœur, Notre Dame, the Cimetières Montparnasse and Père La-chaise, La Bastille, La Pyramide de Louvre, Les Invalides, La Grande Arche de la Défense, La Villette, the Tuileries Gardens, the Latin Quarter, l'Institut du Monde Arabe, Les Halles, etc. For these consult a tourist guide (see Bibliography). There are organized bus tours but better, cheaper and more fun are the public bus circuits recommended in *Pauper's Paris*. Also, take the public boat on the Seine which makes four stops in Central Paris. The *Bâteaux-Mouches* and host of other Seine boat*s*, despite the hoards of tourists, can be a lovely way to spend a sunny afternoon or enchanting evening. The barge rides up the St. Martin canal between the Bastille and the Villette Boat Basin is also a pleasant way of killing a few hours and seeing another side of Paris.

Bâteaux-Mouches
Pont de l'Alma (Rive Droite)
75008 PARIS
Tel: 42.25.96.10

Batobus
Seine Commuter Boat
Porte Solferino
75007 PARIS
Tel: 45.56.06.35

If your looking for a more unusual outing, try a barge trip or better yet a hot air balloon ride over Burgundy, private chateaux visits, balooning bed and breakfast weekends, and special TGV ballooning packages are available from an American-run outfit:

France Montgolfières
76, rue Balard
75015 PARIS
Tel: 40.60.11.23
Fax: 45.58.60.73
For reservations:
Finch Travel Services
Tel: 43.29.99.02

EuroDisneyland
On April 12, 1992, compulsively on-schedule, EuroDisneyland opened its imported pearly gates in the Marne Valley, 32 kilometers east of Paris, on a land site that is said to be a third the size of the capital. In what was one of the largest press campaigns in the history of the world, this fantasy theme park opened to the buzz of rampant media attention, popular conversation and mild debate. One radical French intellectual titled EuroDisneyland a "cultural Chernobyl," which the press also enjoyed and which Disney Chairman Fitzpatrick dispelled as a disillusioned communist response. Attracted by the wave of new employment—12000—a revved up local economy, and the coming of state of the arts technology couched in inoffensive family entertainment, the French—officials and the public—have shown much enthusiasm and optimism for the park, despite the high entry prices—290 FF for adults/ 150 FF for children per day. The Northern European market of 400 million potential visitors certainly helped EuroDisneyland Resort go public in the USA a year before the opening date. In days, all shares were gobbled up. Believe it or not, these mega-powerful American fantasy brokers even managed to get the RER commuter train to extend its A line directly to the site, and re-do its maps, graphics, poster campaign and information brochures so to instruct EuroDisney visitors.

The SNCF is opening a TGV station on the premises to serve Brits who'll be zooming over by rail through the Eurotunnel in a record three hours. For information call EuroDisney at Tel: 60.01.22.77 or 36.15 on your Minitel. Hotel reservations can be made by calling 49.41.49.41 or writing EuroDisneyland
BP 100
77777 Marne La Vallee Cedex 4.

Pin's

While on the subject of trends and kitch, note that starting in 1991 a fad has swept France: *les Pin's*, pronounced *"lay peens."* These are simply "decorative" pins that you stick on your shirt collar or jacket, or collect and display at home. The design on *pin's* ranges from the logo of your local pizza joint, to Mickey Mouse, the Monoprix, James Dean, Bart Simpson, and just about anything else you can imagine. These little items, which have captured the popular imagination of a country, run from a meager 10 FF in the metro to a whopping 400 FF for well-crafted designer *pin's*. Notice the aberrant spelling; no one can explain why the French use the possessive in place of the plural, other than the marketing explanation—it looks better.

Traveling & Tourism

Paris is a great place to live and work, but you'll even appreciate it more if you leave it once in a while. Paris is a particularly endearing place to return to. But in order to return, you have to leave first, and fortunately, Paris is an excellent point of departure for international as well as domestic travel. The French travel considerably and spend sizeable portions of their savings on travel. As residents or students in Paris you'll undoubtedly want to capitalize on the fine opportunities to visit the diverse regions of France, as well as other European countries. For travel information of all sorts concerning Paris and its environs consult:

Tourist Office of Paris
127, av des Champs-Elysées
75008 PARIS
Tel: 47.23.61.72

Other regions have their own information centers and travel offices in Paris. Regional information on rentals, hotels, sports facilities, *gîtes* (inexpensive, rural farmhouse and vacation rentals), festivals, etc. can be obtained at the following addresses:

Alpes-Dauphine
2, place André-Malraux
75001 PARIS
Tel: 42.96.08.43

Alsace
39, ave des Champs-Elysées
75008 PARIS
Tel: 42.56.15.94

Auvergne
194 bis, rue de Rivoli
75001 PARIS
Tel: 42.61.82.38

Bretagne
17 rue de l'Arrivée
75015 PARIS
Tel: 45.38.73.15

Franche-Comte
2, bd de la Madeleine
75009 PARIS
Tel: 42.66.26.28

Gers et Armagnac
16, bd Hausmann
75009 PARIS
Tel: 47.70.32.63

Hautes Alpes
4 ave de l'Opéra
75002 PARIS
Tel: 42.96.05.08

Ile de la Réunion
90, rue de la Boétie
75008 PARIS
Tel: 40.75.02.79

Limousin
30 rue Caumartin
75009 PARIS
Tel: 40.07.04.67

Lot et Garonne
17-15 passage Choiseul
75002 PARIS
Tel: 42.97.51.43

Lozere
4 rue Hautefeuille
75006 PARIS
Tel: 43.54.26.64

Nord Pas-de-Calais
18, bd Hausmann
75009 PARIS
Tel: 47.70.59.62

Perigord
30, rue Louis-Legrand
75002 PARIS
Tel: 47.42.09.15

Poitou-Charentes
68, rue du Cherche-Midi
75006 PARIS
Tel: 42.22.83.74

Pyrenées
46 rue Berger
75001 PARIS
Tel: 42.33.73.82

Savoie
31 ave de l'Opéra
75001 PARIS
Tel: 42.61.74.73

Tarn
34, ave de Villiers
75017 PARIS
Tel: 47.63.06.26

Additionally, Paris is well connected to numerous locations around the Mediterranean as well as points in Africa. Reasonably priced charter flights are readily available to Corsica,

Greece, Canary Islands, Spain, Turkey, Tunisia, Sicily, and others. Lastly, there has been a veritable proliferation of travel agencies specializing in cut fair tickets to North America, Australia, and Asia. Here is a partial list of travel agencies that offer inexpensive trips, charters, and flights to North American and European destinations:

Access Voyages
6, rue Pierre-Lescot
75001 PARIS
Tel: 42.21.46.94
Fax: 45.08.83.35

Amérique Conseil
10, rue St. Claude
75003 PARIS
Tel: 40.27.81.17
Fax: 40.27.96.88

Any Way
46, rue Lombards
75001 PARIS
Tel: 40.28.00.74

Australie Tours
129, rue Lauriston
75016 PARIS
Tel: 45.53.58.39
Fax: 47.55.95.93

Blue Marble Travel
(organizes bicycle trips)
2, rue Dessoubs
75002 PARIS
Tel: 42.36.02.34
Fax: 42.21.14.77

Cash and Go
54, rue Taitbout
75009 PARIS
Tel: 42.85.38.57
Fax: 42.82.94.24

Carrefour des Etats-Unis
5, Place André Malraux
75001 PARIS
Tel: 42.60.32.51
Minitel: 3615 CDV
Fax: 42.60.35.44

Club Méditerranée
Place de la Bourse
75002 PARIS
Tel: 42.61.85.00
Fax: 40.20.91.44

Forum Voyage, USA
140, rue du Faubourg St. Honoré
75008 PARIS
Tel: 42.89.07.07
Minitel: 3514 FV
Fax: 42.89.26.04

Go Voyages
22, rue de l'Arcade
75008 PARIS
Tel: 45.66.18.18
Minitel: 3615 GO VOYAGES
Fax: 42.66.10.96

Maison des Ameriques
4, rue Chapon
75003 PARIS
Tel: 42.77.50.50

Nouvelles Frontières
87, bd de Grenelle
75015 PARIS
Tel: 42.73.10.64
Minitel: 3615 NF
Fax: 43.06.72.20

Usit Voyages
12, rue Vivienne
75002 PARIS
Tel: 42.96.15.88
Fax 47.03.39.14

Voyageur du Canada
5, Place André Malraux
75001 PARIS
Tel: 40.15.06.60
Fax: 42.60.35.44

World Class Air
90 rue de Richelieu
75002 PARIS
Tel: 42.96.20.55
Fax: 40.15.91.65

Tourist Offices
Here is a list of official European tourist offices in Paris which provide travel information and documentation:

Austria
47, ave de l'Opéra
75002 PARIS
Tel: 47.42.78.57
Minitel: 3615 AUTRI
Fax: 42.66.30.96

Belgium
21, bd des Capucines
75002 PARIS
Tel: 47.42.41.18
Minitel: 3615 BELGIQUE
Fax: 47.42.71.83

Commonwealth of Independent States (C.I.S.)
7, bd des Capucines
75002 PARIS
Tel: 47.42.47.40

Finland
13, rue Auber
75009 PARIS
Tel: 42.66.40.13
Minitel: 3615 FINLAND
Fax: 47.42.87.22

Great Britain
63, rue Pierre Charron
75008 PARIS
Tel: 42.89.04.75
Minitel: 3615 BRITISH
Fax: 42.89.09.59

Greece
3, ave de l'Opéra
75001 PARIS
Tel: 42.60.65.75
Minitel: 3615 GRECE
Fax: 42.60.10.28

Hong Kong
35, ave Georges V
75008 PARIS
Tel: 47.20.39.54

India
8, bd Madeleine
75009 PARIS
Tel: 42.65.83.86

Ireland
33, rue Miromesnil
75008 PARIS
Tel: 47.42.03.36
Minitel: 3615 IRLANDE
Fax: 47.42.01.64

Israel
14, rue de la Paix
75009 PARIS
Tel: 42.61.01.97
Minitel: 3615 ISRAEL
Fax: 49.27.09.46

Italy
23, rue de la Paix
75002 PARIS
Tel: 45.66.66.68
Fax: 42.66.03.96

Japan
4, rue Sainte Anne
75001 PARIS
Tel: 42.96.07.94

Monaco
9, rue de la Paix
75002 PARIS
Tel: 42.96.12.23
Minitel: 3615 MC INFO
Fax: 42.61.31.52

Morocco
161, rue St Honoré
75001 PARIS
Tel: 42.60.63.50
Fax: 40.15.97.34

Netherlands
31-33, ave des Champs-Elysées
75008 PARIS
Tel: 42.25.41.25
Minitel: 3615 HOLLAND
Fax: 42.25.78.85

Norway
88, ave Charles-de-Gaulle
92200 NEUILLY-SUR-SEINE
Tel: 47.45.14.90
Minitel: 3615 OTNOR
Fax: 46.41.07.21

Poland
49, ave de l'Opéra
75002 PARIS
Tel: 47.42.07.42
Minitel: 3615 POLOGNE
Fax: 49.24.94.36

Portugal
7, rue Scribe
75009 PARIS
Tel: 47 42. 55. 57
Minitel: 3615 LE PORTUGAL
Fax: 42.66.06.89

South Africa
98, ave de Villiers
75017 PARIS
Tel: 42.27.40.20
Fax: 42.67.80.15

Spain
43ter, ave Pierre 1er de Serbie
Tel: 47.20.90.54
Minitel: 3615 ESPAGNE
Fax: 47.33.56.38

Sweden
146, ave des Champs-Elysées
75008 PARIS
Minitel: 3615 OTSUE
Fax: 45.63.64.93

Switzerland
11bis rue Scribe
75009 PARIS
Tel: 47.42.45.45
Minitel: 3615 SUISSE
Fax: 47.42.43.88

Tunisia
32, ave de l'Opéra
75002 PARIS
Tel: 47.42.72.67
Minitel: 3615 TUNISINFO
Fax: 47.42.52.68

Turkey
102, ave des Champs-Elysées
75008 PARIS
Tel: 45.62.78.68

Alfa Taxis: 47.30.23.23
Ambulance: 43.78.26.26
Bus Info. (in English): 40.46.42.12
Central Post Office (24 hours):
42.33.71.60
Charles de Gaulle airport:
48.62.22.80
Chronopost: Minitel: 3614 EMS
Customs Information Center:
42.60.35.90
Drug Crisis Center: 45.05.88.88
Enfance et Partage (Hotline for Kids
in Trouble): 05.05.12.34 (free)
Entertainment/Theater Info:
(in English)Tel: 47.20.88.98
European Insurance Commission:
48.24.02.04
Federal Express: 34.53.43.00 or
05.33.33.55 (toll-free call)
Fire: 18
Fax Office, International Service:
40.28.20.00
Gas & electricity information:
43.87.59.99
Highway information center:
48.58.33.33
Information
    Ile de France (Paris region): 12
    provinces: 16.11.12
    international: 19.33
Le Bourget Airport: 48.62.12.12
Locksmith (24 hours): 47.07.99.99
American Express Lost Card:
47.08.31.21
Lost and Found/Objets Trouvés:
45.31.14.80
Lost Animals: 43.80.40.66
Diner's Club Lost Card: 47.62.75.00
Lost Eurocard/Mastercard:
43.23.46.46
Lost Property: 45.31.14.80
Visa Card Lost Card: 42.77.11.90

Marine Radio Information:
05.19.20.21
Minitel Directory: 11
Movie Info: 46.34.00.00
National Railroad Information:
45.82.50.50
News of the Day: 36.36.11.11
Orly Airport: 48.84.32.10
Paris Culture Listing: 47.20.88.96
Police: 17
R.A.T.P. (public transport) Info:
43.46.14.14
Rape Crisis Hotline: 05.05.95.95
Restaurant Information: 43.59.12.12
Search For Hospitalized Persons:
40.27.30.81
SOS HELP English Crisis Hotline:
47.23.80.80
SOS Lawyer: 43.29.33.00
SOS Nurses: 48.87.77.77
SOS Oeil (eye care): 40.92.93.94
SOS Pediatre: 42.93.19.99
SOS Tailor: 40.15.03.14
Stock Market News: 36.69.10.02
Taxis Bleus: 42.02.42.02
Taxis G7: 47.39.33.33
Taxis Radio Etoile: 42.70.41.41
Telegrams in English: 42.33.21.11
Telephone Complaints, Repairs: 13
Telex Office: 42.33.20.12
Tenant's Information: 48.06.82.75
Theater Information: 47.23.61.72
Tourist Office: 47.23.61.72
Train Info: 45.82.50.50
U.P.S.: (01) 48.92.50.00
Wake-up Calls (electronically
programmed): * 55 * plus the time in
4 digits (i.e. 7:30 am = 0730) then #.
Weather Info: 36.69.00.00 (Paris)
36.69.0101 (provinces)
45.56.71.71 (foreign)
Weather Report: 43.69.01.01

Here is a random list of French colloquial expressions and some *argot* (slang), selected on the the basis of what you might hear in daily conversation or in the street. Although these and others are useful to know, be absolutely sure you understand the context and appropriate usage before throwing them around.

aie!	ouch!
argot	slang
avoir la pêche	to be in great form
à bientôt	see you soon
à plus tard	see you later
à table	the meal is served (be seated)
berk	yucky
bêtise	stupidity, foolishness, nonsense
bof!	(a noise used to say "I don't know")
bonne chance	good luck
bonne continuation	keep up the good work
bonne courage	chin up!
bosser	to work
bouffer	to eat (slang)
branché	hip/in
c'est absurde	that's absurd
c'est chouette	it's really great, fab
c'est combien?	how much does it cost?
c'est comme ça	that's just the way it is
c'est dingue	that's crazy
c'est drôle	that's funny, strange
c'est foutu	it's over, it doesn't work, it's broken (for events/people/objects)
c'est galère	it's real tough
c'est géant	it's fantastic
c'est génial	that's great, brilliant
c'est impec	that's impeccable, that's perfect
c'est intéressant	(in business) that's a good deal, opportunity, investment
c'est le bouquet!	that's the last straw!
c'est ma tournée	this one is on me
c'est marrant	that's funny
c'est nul	it's crap
c'est pas evident	it's not easy
c'est pas grave	no big deal, it doesn't matter
c'est pas la peine	it's not worth it
c'est pas mal	it's not bad, rather good (used as a compliment)

c'est pourri	that's rotten
c'est ridicule	it's/that's ridiculous
c'est ringard	it's old fashioned, outdated
c'est super	that's super
chacun son tour	each his turn
con, connard	idiot, clot
connasse	tart, stupid bitch
connerie	rank stupidity
coucou	hi
coup de foudre	to have a rush-on
ça boume	it's hopping (as in a party)
ça chlingue	that stinks
ça cocotte	it smells strongly (perfume)
ça gaze, ça baigne	everything's going great
ça m'arrange pas	it's not conveniant
ça m'estégal	I don't mind one way or the other
ça m'énerve	that unnerves me, annoys me
ça marche	it works, it's okay
ça me gêne	that bothers me
ça me gonfle	that bothers me (literally, that makes my head swell)
ça ne me dit rien	I'm not in the mood, that doesn't ring any bells
ça peut aller	I'm okay (a positive but unenthusiastic response to *ça va?*)
ça suffit	that's enough, cut it out
d'acc (d'accord)	all right, okay
de bouche à oreille	by word of mouth
dégage	get the hell out of here
dégoûtant	disgusting (polite form)
dégueulasse	disgusting (slang version)
elle me fait craquer	she drives me crazy (as in love)
engagé	committed
être dans la merde	to be in the shit
être pompette	to be tipsy
faire un bide	to flop
faire un tabac	to be a roaring success
fais gaffe	watche out, be careful
faucher	to steal
faut pas pousser	there are limits, he's gone too far
ferme ta gueule	shut your face/trap
flipper	to flip out, to freak out
fous le camp, barre-toi, casse-toi	piss off, beat it, get lost (very vulgar)
fous-moi la paix	leave me alone, leave me in peace

franchement	frankly
grosses bises	hug and kisses
grouille-toi	hurry up
gueuler	to shout
il a clamsé	he kicked the bucket
il a pas le moral	he's feeling down
il a perdu les pédales	he's lost control, he's nuts
il a un grain	he has a screw loose
il est accro	he's hooked
il est chiant	he's a pain (vulgar)
il est culotté	he's nervy, cheeky
il est défoncé	he's stoned
il est fauché	he's broke
il est gonflé, il exagère	he's got a hell of a nerve
il est maboule	he's nuts
il est nul	he's hopeless
il faut profiter	to take advantage of something
j'ai d'autres chats à fouetter	I have better things to do
j'en ai assez	I've had enough
j'en ai marre	I'm fed up with (this, it, him/her, everything)
j'en peux plus	I can't go on like this
je craque	I'm giving in to temptation, I can't resist any longer
je m'en fiche, je m'en fous	I don't care a hoot
je n'ai pas envie	I don't want to, I don't feel like it
je suis crevé, KO	I'm dead tired, beat
je suis raide, je suis défoncé	I'm stoned, high
je suis saoûl(e), je suis bourré(e)	I'm drunk
je t'embrasse	I kiss/hug you (for ending friendly phone conversations or letters)
la bagnole, la caisse	the car, wheels
la flotte	water
la nana, la gonzesse	the chick, girl
le bahut	school
le boulot	job, work
le fric	money
le fric, le pognon	bread, money
le gars, le mec, le type	guy, dude
le pinard	wine
le toubib	the doctor
les fringues, les sapes, nippes	duds, clothing
les gosses	children
ma frangine, mon frangin	my sis, sister; my bro, brother

merde	shit
mince, mecredi (replace for *merde)*	darn, shoot
mon cul	my ass
mon paternel	my old man
mon pote	my buddy, pal
ne quittez pas	hang on, don't hang up
ne t'inquiète pas	don't worry
on laisse tomber	let's forget it
on s'apelle/on se téléphone	we'll call each other (call me/I'll call you)
p cul	toilet paper
payer à la romaine	to go Dutch
plouc	country hick
poireauter	to wait (slang)
quel bordel	what a mess!
radin, radine	stingy
râler	to grouse, to complain
roupiller	to sleep
salaud, salope	dirty bastard; son of a bitch; slut, bitch
saloperie	filthiness
se dégonfler	to chicken out, to get cold feet
se pointer	to turn up
si tu veux	it's okay with me
sois pas vache	don't be nasty
ta gueule	shut up (literally, your snout/face-vulgar)
tais-toi, taisez-vous	shut up
tant mieux	so much the better
tant pis	too bad, that's the way it is
truc/machin	thingamajig, whatchamacallit
tu délires	you must be joking
tu parles!	no kidding (sarcastic)
un arnaquer	a con man, a swindler
un bouquin	a book
un canard	a magazine
un flic, les flics	a cop, the cops
un magouilleur	a grafter
un troquet	café, bar
une clope	a butt, cigarette
une manif	a demonstration
une toile	a film
va te faire cuire un oeuf	go jump in a lake!
vachement	tremendously, very, extremely

57 Guide, Gault Millau, Paris (4500 restaurants)

Ardagh, John, *France Today,* Penguin Books, London

Bloom Where You're Planted, The Women of the Church,
  The American Church in Paris (welcome booklet for new residents)

Cityscope Paris, Berlitz (1001 addresses)

Constons, Martine, *Le Guide de Paris,* La Manufacture

Dansel, Michel, *Les Cimetières de Paris,* Denoel

Dictionnaire de Paris, Paris, Larousse, 1964

Dinh, Catherine, *Restaurants Etrangers à Paris,* MA Editions (1000 restaurants)

Guide Consommateur Vert

Guide des Hôtels de Charme de Paris, Rivage

Hillairet, Jacques, *Dictionnaire historique des rues de Paris,* Minuit, 1972

Histoire Secrète du Paris Souterrain, Hachette, (sewers, caves, etc.)

Insight Cityguide's Paris, APA Publications, Singapore

Juvin, Herve, *Paris,* Times Books, London

Kjellberg, Pierre, *Nouveau guide du Marais, Paris,* La Biblio. des Arts, 1986

Le Guide Bleu, Paris, Hachette, Paris

Le Guide des Etudes Supérieures 1992, L'Etudiant, Paris

Le Guide du Routard Paris, Hachette, Paris

Lebey, Claude, *Bistrots Parisiens,* Editions Robert Lafont, Paris

Lémoine, Bertrand, *Les Halles de Paris, Histoire d'un lieu,* Paris, L'Equette, 1980

Leprette, Veronique, *Paris Pressé,* Hermé

Léri, Jean-Marc, *Montmartre, Paris,* Veyrier, 1983

Les Villas d'Artistes à Paris, Les Editions de Paris

Lozareff, *Paris Rendez-Vous,* Guide Hachette (400 addresses for going out)

Martin, Michèle, *Weekends Plaisir aux Environs de Paris,* Editions de Veccehi

McClure, Bert, *Architectural Walks in Paris,* La Découverte/Le Monde

Mengès, Bernard Stéphane, *Dictionnaire des Noms de Rues* (5000 streets)

Paris and Environs, Michelin Green Guides

Paris-Anglophone, Frank Books, Paris

Paris Arts ou Seine, Autrement

Paris City Guide, Price Waterhouse, Paris, 1989

Paris en Bouteille, Flammarion, Paris

Paris en Marché, Autrement

Paris Pas Cher, Flammarion, Paris

Paris sur Seine, Beaudoin, François, Nathan, 1989

Paris Trafic, Editions du May, Paris

Paris Visa, Hachette, Paris

Paris, Guide Arthaud, Paris

Paris-Combines, MA Editions, Paris (3500 inexpensive restaurant addresses)

Simon, François, *Paris Vin,* Editions de Main, Paris

Guide de Paris Mystérieux, Tchou, Paris

Pineau, Carol & Maureen Kelly, *Working in France,* Frank Books

The Economist Business Traveller's Guide to France, Prentice Hall Press, New York

Turner, Miles, *Paupers' Paris,* Pan Books, Ltd., London

Wurman, Richard Saul, *Paris Access,* Access Press

The global newspaper.

**World news.
U.S. news.
Business & finance.
Wall Street stocks.
Sports.
And much more.**

Edited in Paris and printed simultaneously
in Paris, London, Zurich, Hong Kong,
Singapore, The Hague, Marseille,
Frankfurt, New York, Rome and Tokyo.

Herald **INTERNATIONAL** Tribune.

Published With The New York Times and The Washington Post

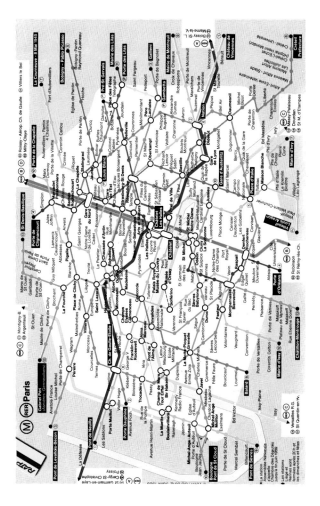